The Initiate's Book of Pathworkings

The Initiate's Book of Pathworkings

A Bridge of Dreams

Dolores Ashcroft-Nowicki
with
Tamara Ashcroft-Nowicki

SAMUEL WEISER, INC.

York Beach, Maine

To Peter Bengston

First published in 1999 by
Samuel Weiser, Inc.
P.O. Box 612
York Beach, ME 03910-0612
www.weiserbooks.com

Library of Congress Cataloging-in-Publication Data

Ashcroft-Nowicki, Dolores.
    The initiate's book of pathworkings : a bridge of dreams /
Dolores Ashcroft-Nowicki, Tamara Ashcroft-Nowicki.
        p.   cm.
    Includes bibliographical references and index.
    ISBN 1-57863-119-X (pbk. : alk. paper)
    1. Astral projection.   I. Ashcroft-Nowicki, Tamara.
    II. Title.
    BF1389.A7A85   1999
    133.9'5—dc21   99–13188
                                                         CIP

VG

Typeset in 11 pt. Sabon
Cover illustration by Chris Hill

Printed in the United States of America

08 07 06 05 04 03 02 01 00 99
10 9 8 7 6 5 4 3 2 1

The paper used in this publication meets all the minimum require-
ments of the American National Standard for Permanence of Paper for Printed Library Materials Z39.48.1984.

Contents

Acknowledgments

Writers never work entirely on their own. They are surrounded by friends, family, and people who encourage them, offer constructive criticism, and supply facts and figures from their own experiences and libraries. I owe a great deal to those students and supervisors who, over the years, have worked these paths and, in many cases, smoothed the kinks out of them. To these must be added the names of Herbie and Jackie Brennan, Anna Branche, John and Elizabeth Fox, Pat and Don Scheu, Lindsey and Rod Flower, Peter Bengtson, and my husband, Michael. They have all been pillars of strength. I would also like to thank my daughter, Tamara, for her support and help in the creation of this book. Her contributions have added tremendously to its potential and it has been a joy to work with her.

—Dolores Ashcroft-Nowicki
Jersey, 1999

Introduction

Since my book, *The Shining Paths,* was published in 1981, there have been many books published about pathworkings, or guided meditations, as some call them. The Servants of the Light School has used these techniques to train students since its inception in the 60s. We have also made available to students and non-students alike, a series of knowledge papers consisting of articles, rituals, and pathworkings to aid their studies and practical work. But it has long been the intention to offer the pathworkings to a wider audience.

With this in mind, I put together a selection of S.O.L. (Servants of the Light) pathworkings used by students over the past twenty-five years, and a few extra written especially for this book. In this effort, I have been greatly helped by my daughter, Tamara. With over a hundred pathworkings in the S.O.L archives, it is time for some to move into the "Outer Court" in order to make way for new material coming into the Adytum.

In this book, you will find magical doorways leading to Egypt, Greece, Celtia, Alexandria, the Tree of Life, Angelic, and Elemental worlds, as well as the Craft and Fairy Faith. Those who follow the old ways will find paths to delight and intrigue them. We have also included some shamanic workings and a few that have no real tradition, but which fit into most of the others somewhere along the line. In the final section, you will find three pathworkings written for the new millennium.

The concept of pathworking is so well-known that it needs little in the way of explanation. But for those entering the astral world for the first time, a little help may not be amiss. It is essential for anyone new to this ancient method of training to remain free from interruption. Most pathworkings run for twenty minutes or so. Those more complicated can take up to an hour. Freedom from noise, a darkened room, and privacy all help the mind to focus on the work at hand. A sudden interruption brings you back to the physical level too quickly for your mind to adjust itself smoothly. This can lead to head-aches, a racing pulse, raised blood pressure, profuse sweating, and disorientation.

Take the phone off the hook or arrange for someone else to answer it. Allow yourself time to relax and be comfort-able. Choose a chair with a firm back and place a small cushion under your feet to raise them from the floor. This takes pressure off the arteries behind the knees, preventing cramping and numbness. Don't lie down or you may fall asleep before you start the pathworking. A second small cush-ion placed on your lap on which you can rest your hands and forearms may also be helpful.

What is a pathworking? It is similar to a virtual reality trip. Pathworkings are perfectly natural and can occur sponta-neously in the form of daydreams. Used as a structured series of visualizations, they hold many possibilities for the student. Some people may find it impossible to visualize scenes in the mind. They may find pathworking difficult in the usual sense, but may find it easier to direct the mind toward "feelings" rather than pictures.

Within the mind of every human being is a cosmos that matches the physical cosmos which surrounds us atom for atom. We can use the "warp" power of the brain and the rich-ness of its data bank to combine the two into an internal Holodeck sequence (to use a *Star Trek* analogy).

With practice and training, these mental workings can be as real as the actual thing. With experience, you can use any-thing—a book, a film, a myth, or an actual event. Ritual is as uplifting when done in the mind as when done in the body. In fact, this is where the rituals of the future will be done. Why build a physical temple when you can have a mental one set up and ready to go at a moment's notice?

A pathworking gives access to the multiverse and contact with great minds of the past. You can walk through the centuries at will to be present at moments that have changed history. All you need are visualization skills to feed your imagination with data. If you have never seen an Egyptian temple, you cannot easily bring it to mind. If you have never stood inside an 11th century castle or climbed steps to a massive wooden door with iron hinges two feet across, it is hard to imagine what it is really like. In such cases, look for pictures to feed your imagination. Read authors with a gift for descriptive prose, and work from their words and images—authors like H. Rider Haggard, Joseph Conrad, Katherine Kurtz, Charles De Lint, Anne Macaffrey, Jules Verne, Gael Baudino, J. H. Brennan, and Alan Richardson. Terry Pratchett's inventive mind offers wonderful mind pictures. Gather data from all around to fill the library of your mind with images.

Observation is the key word. Look around and observe objects, places, and views that can be useful to you in pathworkings. Read books, look at paintings and pictures, subscribe to magazines like *National Geographic* and *Arizona Highways* in the United States, and *English Heritage* in the United Kingdom. All offer wonderful pictures to use as basic imagery. Raid the local library for oversized travel and history books. Learn to project your consciousness into a picture and, in time, you will be able to build astral scenery with a panoramic, three-dimensional viewpoint. Remember the pathworkings of today are the Holodeck programs of the future!!

INVOCATION

TO SEKHMET

O Daughter of Ra
who is lion-headed.
Giver of dreams and visions,
With my voice I call unto thee.
O roamer of deserts,
Mother of souls,
She who thirsts.
Sekhmet Ra,
Whose name is mighty in the temple.
My heart calls out thy name.
O Sekhmet Ra,
Whose enemies tremble before her.
Protector of light and eater of darkness,
My soul calls out to thee.
Thou who art the eye of her father,
Who has placed you above himself.
Beloved of Ptah, Lord of Life.
Sekhmet whose countenance is beautiful.
With all that I am, I call to thee.
For thou art love, and flame, and passion.
Indomitable One.
Bone Setter.
She who is the roar of consciousness
Awaken my soul to the Light of Ra.

—*Tamara Ashcroft-Nowicki*

Egyptian Pathworkings

Thanks to air travel, Egypt is now within the reach of almost everyone as a place to visit. The richness of its ancient culture and the remarkable preservation of its treasures make it one of the easiest traditions to visualize. If a visit is impossible, there are books, videos, and museums that can give you a feeling for the time and place.

All pathworkings can involve you in three ways: purely as spectator, as one of the main characters, or as one of a crowd watching what is taking place. I advise you to try all pathworkings at least once in each of these ways. There is a tendency for the role of spectator to be easier than the others, since, as a spectator, you observe the working as if you were invisible to those around you. While this is the easiest way, it is not always the most satisfying and is used mainly for Point of Focus workings that entail watching the reenactment of historical moments.

If you are taking part as one of a crowd or as a character, go into the working fully. Take time to adjust to the location, time, and season in which you find yourself. Read the working thoroughly and prepare for the sensations that may be expected. Egypt will be hot, but it will be a dry heat. The flies will be a nuisance (but in the context of a pathworking, you can be immune to them).

Clothing will have an effect on your comfort. It may be of wool or cotton; it may be very fine or coarse. Men and women of the noble classes may or may not wear a loincloth beneath a kilt or dress. Lower classes will not bother. Sandals may be worn, but bare feet will be acceptable anywhere. Try to keep the feel of earth, sand, or tiles beneath your feet. Heads of the nobility of both sexes will be close-cut or shaved. Wigs will feel hot and heavy. Often, cones of scented wax are fixed to wigs and this may melt and run down your face and neck. This means that wigs will be sticky and, often, smelly.

You may find yourself flipping into "observer" mode every now and then. This is normal and may be overcome as you gain more experience. Keep looking down at your hands and feet. This means you have to be "in the character" to do it. Spend time feeling and experiencing before beginning the actual working. Like any skill, it requires practice.

When taking on the aspect of an Egyptian god form, study the form beforehand. If it has an animal head, look at pictures of the animal before trying to imagine what it will feel like to become that animal. Begin by feeling the head as a mask over your own face. Once you become used to the idea, take this a step further and reach for the sensation of having an actual hawk, jackal, or lion's head on your shoulders. It is easier than you may think. Whatever experience your character undergoes, strive to make it as real as you can. Your mind is capable of creating every sensation possible for your body to feel.

Try to observe people. Look into their eyes. React to them and they will react to you. The more you react, the more reaction you will get. If you eat or drink, take time to create the taste and the smell of the food and drink offered. If you touch something, create its feel in your hand. It can be done.

Now it is time to take the first step.

Initiation in the Pyramid

As you begin to relax, close your eyes and be aware of a soft, warm darkness. In the distance, a pinpoint of light appears. Move slowly toward it as it grows clearer. It is the hour before dawn. You are warm and relaxed and the last moments of a dream are fading from your mind. Suddenly, you remember that today is the day when you will undergo your final initiation. A wave of excitement, mixed with an apprehension close to fear, sweeps over you. It will not be easy, and you wonder if you will come out of it alive. You know of occasions when candidates have succumbed to fear and lost the control of mind and body essential in such a high initiation.

There is a knock on the door of your room. You rise from the narrow bed, unselfconscious about your nakedness, and open it. A fellow student stands before you. You entered the great Temple of On at age 7 on the same day and have studied and grown up together through the years. Her disciplines are different from yours, for she is a healer and her final initiation will be in the Temple of Ptah, two days' journey down the river from here.

She has brought a gift for you, a talisman made from a seashell. It came from a far-off sea on the other side of the world, a sea so wide that it can be crossed only in dreams. You can remember the day she bought it from a sea captain and you know she has always treasured it. It hangs on a cord made from her own long hair. She places it about your neck. Then, without a word (for today no one may speak to you but the High Priest), she departs.

Closing the door, you cross the room and pour water into a bowl. You wash your hands and face and put on a plain linen robe, tying a white cord about your waist and donning simple leather sandals. You take a few minutes to look around the room, noting things that for ten years you have taken for granted. The square of leather that covers the window opening is rolled up, revealing a room of stark simplicity. Plain white walls, a narrow wooden bed with a linen mattress filled with sweet grasses and herbs, a pillow to match and a coverlet of wool, a wooden chest that is also a table, and a stool. A small clay pot filled with bright yellow flowers, some clay tablets with writing on them. A small statue of Isis and Horus, a gift from your parents on the day you entered the temple, and— something you have loved and treasured since childhood—a wooden hippopotamus with a movable jaw. It was made for you by your elder brother before he went to join the army of Pharaoh. He died defending the Two Lands and you have kept this toy in his memory.

The sound of a gong vibrates through the dormitory area of the temple. It is time to go. You close the door gently, knowing there is a chance you may never open it again. You walk down the corridor, exchanging silent greetings with other students. Instead of following them to the place of eating, however, you go to the main hall. On the way, as you pass through the gardens, you gather some flowers—blue, white, and yellow—binding them with a twist of grass.

The main hall of the temple is big enough to hold several hundred people, and soon it will be filled with those who have come to see you begin the most important journey of your life. Among them will be your parents and sisters. It is the first time since you entered the temple that they have come to the city of On, for it is more than a week's journey from the village. You have seen them only twice since then. Your sisters are almost full grown now and will soon be thinking of marriage. You place the flowers before the statue of Osiris, Isis, and Horus, then stand back, bow, and begin your prayer.

"Great Ones, look upon me, a child of the Two Lands. Today, I go down into the darkness of the Great Pyramid, there to await the blessing of the gods. If it is to be that I will pass into the light and never see Earth again, then I accept that it must be so. If I arise from the sarcophagus as one destined to be your servant forever, then that too I will accept. Be with me in the darkness, help me not to disgrace my parents or my teachers."

You bow and leave the hall, turning into a corridor that leads to a small room where servers are waiting to prepare you. There are four of them and you try not to remember that they symbolize the four sons of Horus who watch over the organs taken from the dead. Those that attend you are of your own sex, for you must be stripped and washed and prepared with as much care as if you were already dead. In fact, at this moment, that is how they see you—dead to your old life. They wash and carefully dry your body, for you must be made as comfortable as possible in order to be able to forget you have a body and move in other worlds without stress.

They oil you, rubbing the fragrant unguent into your body until it is fully absorbed. You are allowed to fill your mouth with water to rinse it, but you are told not to swallow. Your bladder must be as empty as possible for the three days of inaction. A pad of linen filled with fleece is placed between your legs and tied securely into place. After this comes a white loincloth. Then pads of soft linen are bound into place over your elbows, the backs of your knees, shoulders, heels, and buttocks—the points of your body that will press against hard stone, even though a covering of reeds will be placed between you and the actual stone. Over all this goes a robe of fine linen and a plain, pleated apron. A collar of linen sewn with gold thread is placed about your neck and sandals of soft leather are placed on your feet.

Now the priests paint your face with powdered gold mixed with oil to represent the death mask. Your eyes are outlined with black kohl and the ceremonial blue-and-gold striped nemyss is placed on your head. All has been done. The moment has arrived. You lie down on a litter on which is placed a long winding sheet of linen. This is carefully wrapped around you, after your arms have been crossed on your breast. The priests step back, their faces, impassive until now, take on an anxious look that tells of their fears for a friend. To them, you now look like a prepared mummy.

You look at the faces of those who have attended you and smile. Then you slowly close your eyes, wondering if you will ever open them again, see the Sun rise on a summer morning, or watch the geese fly over the marshlands. You feel the bearers lift you on the long poles of the litter and hear the doors being opened. The ceremony is about to begin.

From far away, you hear the trumpets and the gongs and the chants of the temple singers as they precede you into the great hall. Incense fills the air with fragrance and the litter sways with the measured step of the bearers, each of them a friend who will one day take this same road to initiation. The chanting is louder now and, from the rustle and whisper of voices, you know you are entering the great hall. Your family and childhood friends from your village will be present, for your initiation brings great honor to all.

The litter circles the hall so that all may see the form, dressed, masked, and seemingly dead. Then, slowly and with great solemnity, you are borne away through the corridor of pillars and out into the warmth of the courtyard. You picture it all behind your closed eyes. The people of the city line the street leading to the river, the litter sways and the voices of the priestesses chant to the rhythm of their sistrums. Soon you smell the river, hear the rustle of the reeds, and the cry of the water birds. The bearers carefully climb aboard the boat and the litter is lowered onto the bier set into the center of the funeral barge. You hear the call to the oarsmen to cast off.

The boat is rowed out into the center of the river for the short journey to the sacred site of Ah-Heru-Giza. You are shielded by an awning of striped linen, but even so, you feel the gathering heat of the day. It is noon when the boat comes into the landing place and, once more, the bearers take up their burden. From watching others take the same road, you know the road is lined with people all the way to the Great Pyramid. The High Priest has arranged for your family to fol-low you in the procession. To help you through the ordeal, you think about your parents and family and their pride in your spiritual achievements. You know that, whatever may happen, you have given them just cause for that pride.

The procession is slowing down, and you are approaching the place of initiation. The tired bearers are changed for a new set and the sound of the opening of the sealed door grates upon your ears. The guardian appears in the opening and the High Priest leading the procession asks for right of entry.

"I Ptah-Kepher-Hotep, High Priest of Osiris, ask for entry into the Hall of Life on behalf of one who comes for initiation."

"WHAT IS THE NAME OF THE ONE WHO COMES?"

"The dead one has no name, for it has been left behind with all that once was of Earth. When the Osiris rises again, a new name will be given."

Listening to this exchange, you feel a pang of regret at losing your name, for no one will ever call you in that beloved way again. You wonder what your parents are thinking at this moment, then you turn your mind to the ritual. The litter is placed before an altar, set up before the opening of the pyramid, the ceremony begins.

Details of your birth and family are read aloud so all may know who is taking this awesome step. Your teachers speak of your training. Finally, you hear the voice of your friend, the giver of the talisman that now hangs about your neck. She speaks for you, answering the questions of the priests, giving word in your name that you go willingly into the darkness of death in order to rise again in a new form.

"Oh ye Great Ones of the Everlasting Journey, before you comes one who would be among the justified company of Osiris. This one is of the house of Sen-Tep, a free man with land of his own. In the Temple of Atum-Ra, this one has undergone the training required and has been the joy of those who teach the sacred truths. Nothing has been done to reflect against the taking of this step. A good heart and a clean soul has this one."

Now comes the catechism.

"ARE YOU WITHOUT FEAR?"

"I am without fear."

"ARE YOU CLEAN IN YOUR THOUGHTS AND DEEDS?"

"I am clean."

"ARE YOU PREPARED TO TAKE THIS STEP?"

"I am prepared."

"DO YOU GO OF YOUR OWN FREE WILL?"

"Aye, of my own free will I go."

"LET IT BE SO, AND LET ALL HERE KNOW AND UNDERSTAND WHAT IS UNDERTAKEN THIS DAY IN THE NAME OF THE JUSTIFIED OSIRIS."

The entrance is censed with kyphi, and the singers bewail your death with a solemn funeral chant. The litter is lifted and the bearers begin to descend the long sloping path that leads into the heart of the temple. Coldness envelopes your body and you almost cry out as you leave the warmth behind. You hear the labored breathing of the bearers as they reach the lowest point, then the way turns upward and they struggle to bear your weight to the chamber deep within the heart of this ancient temple of silence. So you come at last to the place of testing. You can no longer smell incense, and only faintly hear the chanting of the priestesses at the entrance, and the cold strikes into your heart. The litter halts and the High Priest comes to your side. You hear him speak.

"It is no part of training that you undergo a trial beyond your strength. If you truly feel you cannot take on this task, then open your eyes and rise up. At midnight you will be taken by an underground path to the river and placed upon a boat going to the south. Your family will be told of your death during the trial and thus spared dishonor."

He waits, but you have already made up your mind to go through with the initiation. You make no reply and he withdraws.

You hear the sound of the stone lid of the sarcophagus sliding open, your body is lifted and gently lowered into the interior. There is an increase in the sensation of coldness, then the feel of the reeds beneath you. You hear the words of the High Priest as he blesses you, the faint sound of sandaled feet as the bearers leave the chamber, and the rasp of the heavy lid being lowered into place above you. The darkness is absolute. So is the silence. You lie at the very center of a pyramid that itself is placed at the exact center of the world. You are totally alone.

You begin to breathe deeply and slowly, inducing your body to quiet down and slow its life processes into something close to hibernation. Remember the instructions of your teacher.

"There will be a moment of fear. Allow yourself that one moment, no more. Slow the process of breathing, then concentrate on lowering body temperature so the cold will not numb your thoughts."

You recall his instructions word for word, knowing your life depends upon it. The cold seems less intense now. You are weightless, drifting, spiraling downward into an intensely bright light, then on into a soft, warm darkness full of stars. You feel a sense of excitement. This is where it all begins.

[Pause here so those taking the pathworking can experience the inner self on a level they can handle. These experiences should touch the four elements, and contain a meeting with at least one of the gods. A bell should be rung to alert them to the need to settle down and listen to the narrator again. This period should last at least 10 minutes.]

You can feel yourself drifting upward, as if surfacing after a dive into a warm pool. There is light above you, water on your face, and a dull intermittent buzzing in your ears. Gradually, this becomes a sound that makes sense. A voice, gentle and insistent, is speaking to you, repeating the same words over and over.

"You have come through the ordeal. You are a Risen One. Your new name is Meri-Ab-Ra, Beloved of the Heart of Ra. Rise up, they await your coming forth by day. Come, newly born one, rise up. You are safe and well."

Your eyes, closed for three long days, are gently bathed with warm water. After a while, they flicker open and the darkness is relieved by the soft gleam of oil lamps. The High Priest is rubbing your hands, others are massaging your feet. Water, mixed with a little wine, is held to your lips and you drink in tiny sips. Ripe dates are offered to be chewed slowly. Still dazed, you find you have been lifted from the sarcophagus and now lie on a wooden bed covered with straw. Your body is being gently washed with scented water, as the unavoidable body wastes of three days are removed.

A fresh loincloth is wound about you and a robe of fine linen is eased over your head and girded with a belt of golden links. A collar heavy with gold and precious jewels is placed about your neck, and bracelets slide into place on each arm above the elbow. Sandals with jeweled straps adorn your feet and the ceremonial headdress of an initiate is placed on your head. Finally, the High Priest puts upon your finger the ring that is the sign of your rank as an adept, a priest of Osiris.

The bearers enter, carrying the ceremonial chair in which you will be carried shoulder-high so that all may see and rejoice with you in your triumph. Slowly, for your limbs are stiff and weak after your ordeal, you take your place in the chair. The procession forms around you and you begin your journey back into the world. As the bearers head toward the entrance, you find yourself eagerly awaiting the first sight of the Sun and the blessing of its warmth. At this moment, you feel more alive than at any time in your life.

The bearers pause in the doorway, partly to catch their breath and allow you your first look at the Sun in three days, and partly to give the waiting crowds their first look at the new initiate. The crowd bursts into wild chants of praise and blessing. Flowers, palm leaves, and fragrant herbs are cast before the feet of your bearers. For one fleeting moment, you are taken by surprise. Then your training comes to the fore and you assume the calm serenity of an adept. As you pass through the avenue of people, you see your parents among them, weeping with pride and joy, and you promise yourself that soon you will share a few quiet moments with them.

The stately procession seems to take so long and, throughout it all, you must appear calm and unemotional. By contrast, the boat journey back to On seems almost too quick. On arrival at the temple, there is a lengthy ritual of thanksgiving, with chants, invocations, and praises to the gods for preserving you through the ordeal. Finally, hours later, you are free to escape into the quiet gardens of the temple. Slowly, you walk to where your parents and sisters are waiting.

The reunion is tearful, but full of joy. As the Sun begins to dip and the shadows lengthen, the servants bring wine and food and you sit quietly, sharing each other's company and love. At last, weary beyond belief, you rise to your feet and say goodnight. You make your way back to the small, familiar room you once thought you might never see again and sink into a dreamless sleep.

The Crowning of the Bee King

Prepare yourself for the inner journey, then use any method known to you to pass between the worlds. When you have adjusted to the state of altered consciousness, listen for the voice of the guide.

"Ye who are named as servants of the Mysteries, harken to the voice of the Priestess of Neith, the ancient Goddess of the Delta, Lady of the Reed, Keeper of the Hive, she who giveth sweetness to the mouth of the king. Listen and prepare; send forth the Ka of thy bodies and enter the Unseen Lands that are beyond time and space that you may watch and see the old ways of the Land of Khem."

The voice is silent, but the darkness falls from your eyes. You find yourself traveling in the Body of Light over the Inland Sea toward the Land of Khem and the city-state of Buto.

The old king has passed into Amenti beyond the Sun's setting and now he stands before Osiris that he may be judged. A new king sitteth upon the Reed Throne in the city of Buto. We have come to give the past king honor and to prepare the new king for his crowning. Let us mourn the Justified One who has passed from us, as is the custom. Rend your garments and cast dust upon your head. Go barefoot, wear funeral wreaths upon your head, and wail aloud, for the king has gone forth from the house of his body and it knows him no more.

We stand on the road leading to the place of the tombs of the Pharaohs of Khem. We wait in the hot Sun and wail our grief at his passing. There comes toward us from the city a solemn procession of people, priests, priestesses, chanters, musicians, and palace guards.

Around the body of the one who has left us are members of the court, some weeping, others silent in their grief. Behind them, carried on gilded chairs, are the members of the royal family. First, the new king, uncrowned as yet, bareheaded and quiet, yet with the stamp of kingship already upon his face. The queen and the secondary wives, the younger sons, and the daughters follow. After them, the rest of the court and then the common people, crying out in their grief and respect for the dead ruler.

As the procession reaches us, it parts and surges around on either side. We take our position in front of the sarcophagus and proceed toward the tomb that has been prepared. The cymbals and sistrums and the muted sound of trumpets accompany the dead king on his final journey. Ahead of us, the simple entrance of the rock tomb comes into view, with its double line of ram-headed sphinxes leading to the first steps.

We bend low to enter the tomb and, almost at once, begin to descend a long, narrow flight of steps. On either side are small ledges on which oil lamps have been placed to light the way. There are twenty-eight steps in all. At the bottom, we pass into a corridor tall enough to allow us to stand upright. The walls are painted with brightly colored scenes of the king hunting and going about his normal daily duties as he did during his lifetime. Behind us, the priests and priestesses, the guards, and the royal family follow with the body of the king.

We come to the outer chamber in which those things needful for the ease and comfort of the dead man have been placed.

Along with all this are portions of his treasure. We pass on through successive chambers, each filled with furniture, weapons, chests of clothes, and offerings of food and wine. The innermost chamber holds the great sarcophagus, painted with many scenes of the Duat and the Assessors of the Gods. Its lid lies open and we gather to watch the body of the king laid to rest. The new king and the Queen Mother pile flowers over the body and the lid is placed over it. All is silence.

We leave the tomb in the same order and emerge into the hot sunlight. The procession reforms and wends its way back toward the city. We stay where we are and a cool mist rolls toward us and envelopes us within its dampness. There is a slight saltiness in our nostrils and a buzzing sound, as of many honey bees. Time passes, but without our having any sense of its passing. Then the mist rolls away and we find ourselves within the great chamber in the Temple of Neith. Forty days of mourning have passed and now it is fitting that the new king be crowned. It is here, before the altar of Neith, that the young king has passed the night before his crowning. We are here as priests to prepare him.

He stands before us, having been bathed with water from the Nile and clothed in a single length of white linen. We are to act as witnesses to the robing of the king in order that no substitute may be made between this room and the temple itself. First, the linen is taken away so that we may see that the king is male, the son of the father in truth. Then the robing begins.

First, a loincloth of the finest linen and, just above it, a thin chain of gold links clasped with a bee of amber, gold, and sardonyx. Over this is placed a short ephod, or apron, of soft lambskin embroidered with the sacred emblems of the reed, the hawk, and the bee. In the middle is the eye of Atum-Ra. Now, a finely pleated kilt of white and gold is put on and held with a belt of supple leather covered with thinly beaten gold. This holds the ceremonial apron, richly jeweled. A corselet fashioned like the wings of the goddess Isis, is worn over his breast and, around his neck, a pectoral necklace of golden bees between carved stones of lapis, turquoise, carnelian, and amber. On each arm, at elbow and wrist, goes a wide bracelet of gold. Sandals of supple leather are placed on his feet. The eyes are now painted with kohl, outlined to look like the eye of Ra. His head is shaven, for he, like most nobles wears a wig for ceremonial occasions. Finally, the red crown of Lower Egypt is placed upon his head.

We go forward one by one to place our right hand over his heart and our left upon the phallus in the ancient way. So we make our testimony and pronounce a blessing on him and upon his reign, that this dynasty may prosper. Then the gilded chair is brought and he takes his seat. The men of our sacred company lift it to their shoulders, while the women surround the king and begin a chant of praise to the Goddess Neith.

"Behold a star shall rise, a star of great beauty and wisdom,
and her name shall be called Neith.
Thou art my goddess and my desire, so saith the Earth God,
the son of Tefnut, Lady of the Waters.
Thou art the sweetness of honey and the coolness of water,
so saith the Nile.
Thou art the blessing of the Kingdom of the Reed,
so saith the air that cometh over the desert.
My mouth shall call thy name and I shall praise thee
with many blessings.
Each star shall be as a jewel for thy brow.
In my heart, thou art the star of the evening
and the reflection of my desire.
Thou, and none other, shall have the making of the king,
the filling of the hive, the gathering of the pollen.
The making of the sweet honey.
To thee Neith, Goddess of Khem, are all things possible.
Honor to thee in thy majesty.
Let the land rejoice that thou art among us.
Hear the voice of thy people and make haste to come.
Behold: our souls thirst for thee."

Slowly, we bear the king from the small chamber and pass along the pillared corridors toward the main part of the temple.

The way is lined with people. They cast flowers and sweet herbs before the chair and call blessings upon the head of the new king. Only once does his austere expression slip, as we pass a highly placed noble and his family at the entrance to the great chamber. Among the daughters, a young and slender figure raises her eyes to meet those of the king and a slight smile passes between them.

A cry of triumph greets the entrance of the new ruler and everyone falls back to give room. The chair is taken to the flight of steps that leads to the throne and lowered to the ground. The king ascends and takes his place. The chair is taken and put at the side. We stand at each side of the steps. The High Priest and Priestess of Neith come forward to place in the royal hands the crook of mercy and the flail of justice, we wait to hear the king take his oath before the gods.

He is young to take on so great a task, barely twenty years of age, yet the promise of maturity is there. The anointing and blessing of the king is performed along with songs of praise for his dead father and praises for the new king who will now take his place. Patiently, we stand and wait for the moving climax of the ceremony, for the goddess to give the sign that she accepts this young man as the Bee King of Khem. All is silent and we wait.

We can hear the breathing of those around us and see the sweat gathering on the brow of the king, feel the tension gathering slowly and inexorably. Then we hear a faint sound coming, as if from far away. It is the hum of many bees. It grows louder and louder, until it seems to be all around us. It is not just a single hive of bees, but many thousands. In the silence, we hear the shouting of the populace outside, the doors are flung open and the sunlight streams in. And then we see them—a mighty cloud of tiny symbols of the goddess. They come either to greet and accept the new king or to kill him. He stands and advances to the edge of the steps, giving the crook and the flail to the priests at his side. He takes off the red crown and gives that also to the priests. Then he waits, alone and defenseless.

Into the great hall they come in their tens of thousands, the air is filled with the sound of their wings and the sweet scent of honey and pollen. They circle the hall, filling us with wonder. We stand motionless. In a single mass, they descend upon the king and cover him like a robe. He breathes gently and slowly, trying not to injure or frighten them. They, in turn, make of themselves a living garment of glory for the Bee King. The queens, leaving the hive for only the second time in their lives, link together to form a coronet about his temples. A priestess emerges from our midst to speak for the goddess.

"Behold I shall set my seal upon his brow and upon his lips. Upon his breast and upon his loins shall my seal of royalty be set.

"He shall be the hive master and the honey sweetness of his mercy shall be given to my people. He shall be the giver of life to his chosen queen and she will fill the hive.

"From the earliest days, when the honey bee was brought as a gift from the stars to a newly formed Earth, the Bee King has reigned in Khem.

"This is the way of the honey bee, that it shall work for the good of all within its hive, and shall serve that one who is the symbol of them all. Thus it shall be with all those who shall descend from this dynasty. They shall be the servants of those that come to them, and shall tend to them, healing and teaching and preserving the ancient knowledge.

"You have watched and you have seen. This is the chosen one of Neith. Hear the words of the goddess and rejoice, for She has come among you on this day."

There is a moment of silence. Then the bees begin to take to the air once more. Slowly, they fill the chamber with their gentle song and then they depart into the reed beds and the swamps once more. There is a collective sigh of relief as the doors of the temple close behind them. The goddess has accepted the new king and all bodes well for the new reign.

The king takes back his symbols of royalty and bids the royal guard bring the carrying chair to him. He takes his seat and, to the shouts of his happy people, he is taken from the chamber to greet the crowd waiting outside the temple. Perhaps it is only we who see his head turn as he looks upon the young girl standing by the door. The color rises in her face and she modestly casts her eyes downward. The king smiles at her and this does not go unnoticed by the his mother the queen. This small sign is pleasing to our hearts. The royal line will go on, for Neith has set her seal about the king's head this day.

A mist rolls in, covering the chamber and us. It is cool and damp, almost clammy on our skins, and we shiver a little. When it rolls back again, we find ourselves once more standing behind our physical bodies. The empowerment we have brought back from our journey in the Body of Light will fill our bodies with extra energy for the coming day.

Close your eyes and move forward, allowing the two bodies to meld into one on the physical plane. Feel it close around you, feel the chair, the floor, the air, your clothing. Say your name to yourself silently, affirming that you know your identity. Return in your own time.

The Conception of the Jackal

As always, prepare yourself to go forth into the space between the worlds. There wait for the messenger who will be sent by the gods. That messenger is Thoth, the Lord of Magic and Time. Standing before you, he speaks;

"You who are gathered here, prepare yourselves to know and understand the rite of the gods that brings into the sphere of Earth one of their own kind. For, as it is with humanity, so it is with the gods, though after another fashion. Therefore, build within your mind the images I shall give to you. Then, in the fullness of time, ponder them in your hearts and seek their

inner meaning that it may fill your mind with knowledge and wisdom. Follow me."

He goes before us clad in the splendor of his godhood and brings us to Amenti, the Land of the Setting Sun. We stand in the Hall of Atum Ra, the Lord of the Completed Circle, Slayer of Apep, Father of Time, Child of the Bornless One, Builder of the Primal Mound. The walls are built from the rays of the Sun and the light falls upon us in myriad colors and shades. Here around are gathered the gods of Egypt, mighty in their power and strength.

Atum Ra, himself, a figure of great power, clothed in gold and wearing a crown of flames, is seated on a throne of emerald. On either side of him stand Shu and Tefnut, the first-born of Atum, formed from his own substance within the palm of his hand. Seated around the great hall on thrones of lapis and crystal we see the other gods. Khnum and Bast, Hathor and Tuaret. Horus the Elder, born beyond time, Min and Ptah, Geb and Nuit the Starborn. Seshet and Nektbet, Neith and Sobek, ancient Sokar and laughing Bes. Sekhmet, with her fierce stare, and the gentle smiling Hapi, clothed with the Nile waters. Here is dark-browed Mut, the most ancient of all the gods, who gives birth, not to gods, but to the cosmos itself. Many are the gods of Egypt and here in the halls of Atum Ra, each has a throne of honor. Thoth takes his place among them.

Before Atum Ra stand the four children of Nuit: the bright twins, Osiris and Isis, and their dark counterparts, Set and Nephthys. Around them plays a cosmic fire of many colors, so holy and so great is their destiny. Atum Speaks:

"Nephthys, daughter of my daughter's daughter, I have a task to lay upon you, and also upon you, Osiris of the Golden Face. Hear and listen as I tell of things unknown to you. I speak concerning the birth of a new day of existence, when galaxies and worlds are born anew, when all things are created from the chaos that surrounds the nonbeing that is Mut, the dark-browed one of the Before time.

"Then new gods are born. Even as I, Atum Ra, was born of Mut in the formless Sea of Chaos. It is decreed by Mut that, in turn, that first of all the gods must bring forth unaided those other gods needed to guide the coming life-forms. But in time, the sacred messenger must be born and that one may only be born of two opposite forms of existence.

"The sacred messenger is the forerunner of the one whose destiny it is to go down into the darkness of manifestation and light the way for those that fear physical death. Those messengers exist from age to age and will be the last of all the gods to be withdrawn when this day of existence shall end, when all things are drawn back into chaos. Time and again the Chosen One must cross the Bridge of Ages to become the link with the Sacrificed Ones. Like jewels on a golden thread of love, these two, the half brothers, shall govern the destiny of this world.

"It is my decision that this sacred messenger shall be born of Osiris and Nephthys, the dark and the light together. But this may not be accomplished without the given consent of those involved. How say you?"

Atum Ra pauses and dark-eyed Set steps forward.

"The gentle Nephthys is my sister-wife, given to me to be my love by Nuit the Starborn. Shall I then be barred from her arms and her bed for the sake of a wraith that walks the paths between life and death?"

Now comes the mistress of magic, Isis herself:

"No child have I by my beloved Osiris, and this to me is a great sorrow. Yet in these words of Atum, I see wisdom. My magic shows me the ages that are to come when the world has forgotten the gods and knowledge is bartered for power. In that coming age, such a messenger will be needed. But, I ask the gods to witness that, in return, when the time be right, I, Isis, shall be granted a son by my brother-husband. Khnum, will you spin the body of such a child for me, on your potter's wheel, and will you, Ptah, fill that body with life?"

The gentle ram-headed Khnum inclines his head, saying,

"It shall be so. The word of Khnum is given to thee, Isis."

Ptah raises his staff:

"I give my word to fill the body of such a child with life."

With these promises, Isis is content and steps back. Atum turns his godlike head and the flames forming his crown flare like living gold. He speaks to Osiris and Nephthys:

"You have not yet given consent to my wish. Without this, I cannot call such a one into being. Is this consent given?"

Osiris and his dark sister confer and then Osiris speaks.

"This is the answer we give. We will bend our will to yours, Atum Ra, but it shall be as my sister-wife Isis has asked, that in return, a son shall be born to us."

"It shall be so. The word of Atum Ra is given."

The hall vanishes and we are left in darkness, but in the east, a brightness grows, leaping like a fire. It is the kiln of the potter-god, Khnum. We watch as he carefully selects a piece of black clay and places it upon his wheel. As it spins, Khnum begins to fashion the body of the new god.

He is tall and long of leg, wide-shouldered and narrow-waisted. His face is cleanly cut, with large eyes and a warm and generous mouth. Nephthys appears from the darkness and bends over the form, holding back her long dark hair. She speaks to Khnum and the potter-god makes an adjustment. The goddess nods and smiles and breathes upon the clay figure. Now comes Osiris to look upon the form of his firstborn son. He smiles and speaks to Khnum, who, laughing, takes a lump of gold. He spins another body and places it within the first form, making the form both black and gold, bright and dark, within and without. Then Osiris breathes over the figure and steps back. Khnum places the figure deep in the heart of the kiln, and the scene fades from view.

Hathor comes and parts the darkness and creates within this space a place of beauty—a pool of cool water filled with lotus flowers. Within its depths, fishes glide to and fro. Around the pool grow shade trees laden with fruits. Earth is clothed with green grass and starred with sweet-smelling flowers. Hathor now forms a pathway of lapis and white marble, and a gate to seal the garden from all intrusion.

Nuit brings an armful of stars and makes of them a couch for her children and blesses this sacred space. Then she begins to weave the spell that will be her gift to her new grandchild.

From the farthest point of the universe, she takes the power of the first sound and binds it into the power to hear through all planes of being. From the star of Draconis, she takes the essence of the breath of fire and from this she fashions a power of smell so keen that it can catch the scent of an unfolding flower on the farthest side of Earth. From a comet, she takes swiftness; from a spider, patience; from a dove gentleness; and from the desert, the fierceness, speed, and absence of fear of the jackal. From these things, she forms the astral shape of her grandson. Beneath her hands, there takes shape the smoky form of a young man with the head of a jackal and this she places in a cup of wine.

From the head of Atum Ra, she takes a single hair; from the lips of Ptah, a moment of breath; from Sekhmet, the edge of her sword; from Hathor, a kiss from her lips. These she binds into an amulet of gold, which she places in a loaf of bread. Then she leaves.

Into this place of peace come the brother and sister, dark and light, Osiris and Nephthys. Here within this magical place above and beyond both heaven and Earth, the young jackal-god will be conceived. Nephthys drinks the wine, sharing it with her brother. He breaks the bread and they eat together. In the shade of the trees, they come together in the way that man and woman, god and goddess have always done. The cloak of Nuit is drawn over them, hiding them from our eyes.

In the blackness, a point of light comes swiftly toward us, arriving in an explosion of intense light and heat. Out of the light steps a young man with a jackal's head. On his arm sits an eagle. His voice is deep and vibrant, and soothing.

"I am Anubis, Son of the Light and the Darkness. I am the sacred messenger that walks between the worlds, half brother to the son of the Sun. I am the Opener of the Ways. I am he who serves the Horus of every age. Look for me as the guardian of the Mother, the baptizer into the life that is beyond death."

We see his form change and take on many shapes in many ages to come, but always the light in the eyes is the same. Here, in this son of Osiris and Nephthys, there is the gentle teacher and the fierce guardian. Here, we see intuition and righteous anger brought together. Always, he will be the guardian of the Mother, always he will be the loving half brother, always he will be the one who carries the light. We look and are comforted, for we know that in this being we may place our trust, even unto death. Behind us, a woman's voice begins a chant of great power:

> **"Hail Anubis, Son of the Light and the Dark.**
> **Hail thou greeter of the dawn of Ra.**
> **Guard us through the nights of our lives**
> **And the trials that will test us.**
> **Be thou our sword-bearer and defender.**
> **Guard us against the false speaker of lies**
> **And the sower of injustice.**
> **Be as a cloak about us when we suffer**
> **The coldness of despair and warm us with thy breath.**
> **Thou art the Keeper of the Inner Light,**
> **Anubis, son of the risen king, be with us always.**

Gentle Nephthys, we offer thanks for thy son,
For he is our light in the darkness of death.
Bright Osiris, we rejoice in the fruit of thy seed,
For he will bring us to Thee in the fullness of time.
We rejoice that the darkness of death is now conquered.

Thou Anubis, art the keeper of the keys of the tomb.
Oh wise and loving Atum, whose knowledge did cause
The birth of Anubis to be our guide.
Ever-loving, ever-wise creator of all things
Thou art, now and forever, the giver of life.
Be blessed in Thy wisdom oh ye gods of Egypt;
May your names live forever in Amenti."

We can feel the strength and the gentleness of the newborn god. For a fleeting moment, we see him as he will be down through the ages. The face and the name changes, but always, deep within the form, is the gold and the black, Nephthys and Osiris together in the form of their son. We can be at peace knowing that the Guardian of the Gates of the Duat is with us.

We know also that the strength we feel is for us as well as for the Beloved Half Brother. Here is the gentle bringer of dreams who will guide us over the Bridge of Life into Amenti when it is our time to go. With this in mind, we begin to withdraw. A gray mist rolls over us and we feel ourselves drawn into a slow spiral. There is a feeling of time moving forward slowly and inexorably, until we reach our own place in it. Then the mist is drawn away like a lace curtain and we find ourselves beside our physical bodies. We join with them and begin to feel the weight of the physical plane envelop us. In your own time, allow yourself to awaken slowly.

The Sorrows of Isis

Imagine yourself in a room. It is not over-large, square, with walls of plain brick that have been washed with a mixture of chalk and lime. On this background, there are simple paintings similar to hieroglyphics. There is little furniture, a wooden bed with a solid base. This is covered with a coarse linen mattress stuffed with sweet-smelling grasses and herbs. A roll of the same linen, filled with the same mixture, serves as a pillow. The coverings are made from thick, woven wool. The bed is painted with bright colors. At the bottom of the bed there is a wooden chest or box with a painted lid. Another just like it is set against the wall.

Under the window, that is open to the sky and simply covered with a square of painted linen, there is a table, and before it a stool. Both are carved and painted. On the table are many small jars and wooden boxes and small articles of ivory and copper. Leaning against the wall is a large oval of highly polished bronze.

The small boxes and jars contain oil and sweet-smelling mixtures of animal fats and flower essences. A comb of carved ivory and small pointed sticks for outlining the eyes and eyebrows lie close together. You look in the mirror and see a young, beautiful woman. Your hands and feet are long and elegant, and on your arms are bracelets—two on each arm. A heavy collar of lapis lazuli, gold, and turquoise coils around a slender neck. Matching earrings complete the set. You wear a dress of fine pleated linen and a circlet of gold and lapis lotus flowers on your head. You are Isis, the beautiful queen, loved by her brother-husband and her people alike—Isis, Queen of the Land of Khem.

Picture the great audience chamber, with its rows of pillars, carved and painted. Remember how the people come to place their troubles and requests before you and your husband. Think of the temple of white stone, with its larger-than-life statue of Ra, the great Sun god with his hawk's head. Think of your happiness at this moment and feel it as a light inside you. At this moment, you have everything for which you could wish. You have youth, beauty, a loving husband. You have position and wealth, and, above all, you have wisdom and knowledge far beyond anyone else in the kingdom.

Now go to the door and out into a narrow corridor. At the end of this corridor there is another door that leads into a garden with a small lake full of lotus flowers. When you look down into the water, you can see small fishes swimming about. The sound of laughter fills the air and there, on the grass beyond the lake, you can see your husband, Osiris, playing with a young boy of about eight years. The child is Anubis, your husband's son by your sister, Nephthys. There is no bitterness in your heart about this. The child is beloved by you and he is your special care, for it has been ordained by the gods that Anubis is to be the inheritor of all your wisdom. They are very alike, though Anubis has a darker skin than his father.

They look up as you come toward them, and your husband holds out his arms and draws you close to him. They have been playing with a small lion cub, and now Anubis chases off after it, the two of them running and tumbling over and over in the hot sun. It is quiet in the garden, with only the sound of birds and the insect noises. Now even the sound of the child and the lion cub have disappeared. There is just you and the one you love.

Into your feeling of peace there comes a sudden cold feeling, as if something is about to happen. A feeling of great anxiety overcomes you and you press closer to Osiris, as if seeking comfort. He does not seem to notice and talks of the feast in honor of your brother, Set, that he is giving this evening. The feeling is still there as you walk together back to the palace to bathe and dress for the feast.

Now let the scene change. It is evening and the feast is at its height. The great hall is filled with people. Musicians are playing and there are dancers to entertain the guests. With Osiris, you sit at the head of the table, still filled with the unease of the afternoon. Next to you sits your brother, Set. Tall, like his brother Osiris, but dark as night. His face is cold and proud. As the dancers finish, he stands up and calls for silence. Four men carry into the hall a wooden chest. It is the length and breadth of a man. The workmanship is wonderful, the wood covered with gold leaf worked into designs of winged serpents and other sacred symbols. The lid is covered with a design of lotus flowers worked in lapis lazuli, coral, and ivory. The lock and key are both of gold.

This is a present to Osiris, says Set, a gift to his brother, a peace offering after many years of quarreling. A sarcophagus fit for a great king. Osiris is delighted, but you feel a chill as he goes to inspect the beautiful gift. When opened, the casket reveals a fine linen lining painted with scenes of the gods in the Boat of a Million Years. Osiris leans close to see more clearly. Events happen so quickly that you do not even have time to scream a warning. Set pushes his brother into the chest, snaps the lock, and turns the key. The four men lift the chest, and in the confusion, take it from the hall. All is in confusion.

Some have not seen what has happened. Others try to tell them. Some try to fight Set's men. You know this is the end of the king's rule as you knew it and slip from the hall, back to your room. Tell the woman servant to wake the young prince and get him ready for a journey. Change your court dress for a linen tunic and thick woolen cloak. Gather up a bundle of clothes and jewels and a few other things. You are ready when the servant and Anubis arrive. You have no time to explain to the sleepy child what is happening. With Set in command, only you stand between him and the destruction of all that you and Osiris have done. He will claim you as his queen if you do not escape. Your sorrow for Osiris and your mourning will come later.

At the door is one of Osiris' personal guards, tall and strong and loyal to you. He takes the bundles and the young prince and, with the servant, goes to make ready the small boat that will take you to safety. You pause for a minute to look about you at the place you loved. On the table is a small bracelet, the last gift Osiris gave you. A bracelet of moon flowers carved from carnelian and linked with gold leaves. You pick it up and put it on your wrist. Then the others follow.

You pass like a shadow through the palace. People are running here and there, shouting and fighting. You hide in the shadows as Set himself strides pass. In the flickering light of the torches, you can see he wears the royal uraeus circlet taken from the brow of Osiris. A flame of determination rises within you. You will avenge your husband. His body will be found and given royal burial. He will be avenged and the wrong that has been done to the land set right.

The next corridor leads to the garden, and from there to the river. A boat is waiting and the others are already aboard, waiting for you. You take your place in the prow of the boat and the guard pushes it out into the dark, swiftly running river. The palace is ablaze with lights, and you look back for a last look at the home where you were so happy. Beside you is Anubis, only just beginning to understand. The guard has told him that his father is dead, killed by his own brother. He is trying not to cry, for he has been told that a prince must be brave. He holds a miniature sword in his hand, a gift from his father. With it, he tells you, he will protect you now that the king is dead. He will be your guardian.

The child's love unlocks the tears and you gather him close, telling him he will always be your guardian and, when he is older, he will help you to avenge his father's death. Until then, he must learn all you can teach him of the art of magic and wisdom. You draw him close and rock him to sleep in your arms, but you remain awake waiting for the dawn.

Again, the scene changes. Now you are walking along a dusty road, only you, the servant, now much older, and Anubis. The guard is dead, killed defending you from Set's soldiers. Ten years have passed and Anubis, striding ahead of you, is now full-grown. He is so like his father that your heart aches to see him sometimes. He has kept his promise to you all these years. He has learned all you could teach him and added deep wisdom of his own. Now he is tall and strong and beloved of the gods, who have made him their messenger.

You have heard that, in the city you are approaching, there is a miraculous tree that has grown around the sarcophagus of a holy man. After all these years, you have little hope that it might be the one, but you always pray that it may be so. You have lived like a fugitive, sometimes escaping only just in time from Set's men. The Land of Khem lives in fear. There is treachery, murder, theft, and corruption everywhere.

The little city is hot and dusty and the palace of the king is small and not very clean. It is a vassal state of Egypt, conquered long ago by Osiris. Servants take you to the king, who is very old. He has no son and his wives bear no children. In return for your help in this matter, he will allow you to inspect the holy tree. You stand before him, thinking that, long ago, he would have been bowing before you as the Queen of Egypt. Now, you are merely a woman with a reputation for great healing powers. The name, Isis, is almost forgotten.

The old king is not a good ruler. He is lazy and corrupt and has forgotten to honor the gods. He is one of Set's men and owes allegiance to him. You think it a good thing that his line is coming to an end, and a new and more honorable one will begin. As he speaks the formal words of welcome, you look along the line of royal wives. There are five of them, but one stands out from the rest. You remember her as a child. Her father was once a good friend of Osiris. She has been given to this old man as a gift from Set. Her face is sweet and gentle and reminds you of your sister, Nephthys. She has helped you many times, sending you warning of Set's movements, sending you money and jewels and any news she has gathered about the chest containing the body of the king.

A plan comes into your mind whereby the old king may have his successor, and the future line of this city state can be made safe against Set. You tell him that you and you alone can choose which of his wives will bear the desired son. To this he agrees.

The holy tree stands in the courtyard of the palace. The trunk has grown around a wooden chest. Once it was painted in bright colors and the lid encased in precious stones. Now it is faded and the jewels are gone. But your heart is happy for, as soon as you see it, you know it is the right one. At last, you have found the body of Osiris. But the king must be persuaded to give you the chest and for that you must see that a son is born. It will take time and must be done with great secrecy.

Each night, you take to the king an infusion of herbs. This he drinks and it causes him to sleep heavily. Once he is sleeping, you cause dreams to rise in his mind. It is an ancient art and one of which you are master. He will only remember what you wish him to remember and nothing more. Each night, you weave a pattern of thoughts that will keep him happy, and that will further your plans. The king dreams he is young again, with all his natural vigor at his command.

The young wife you have chosen is summoned to the royal bed, but it is Anubis who takes the kings place. Each night, the old king dreams and each night the young queen receives the royal seed of the line of Osiris. She is taught many things by Anubis and by you, the true Queen of the Land of Khem. She is told of the secret of the chest, and the events that began the long sorrows of the queen. She listens and understands. Her son will rule this small kingdom and make a promise of fealty to the House of Egypt.

When the queen's pregnancy is confirmed, the old king is persuaded to give you the chest, and it is removed from the tree and placed upon an ox cart. Then you and Anubis make your way to the river, where the chest is placed on a boat and taken to an island in the middle of the river. There is a small temple here, and the chest is laid on the temple floor. You kneel beside it, placing your hands upon the lid, as if you would feel the body of the man lying within. All the sorrow of the past years rises up in you and you weep, letting the tears fall onto the chest, washing the years of dirt from it.

At last the tears are spent and, with Anubis, you open the chest. Within is Osiris. No mark of decay mars his body. It is as if he were asleep. With the help of Anubis, the body is laid upon a slab of stone. It is washed and oiled and dressed in royal robes that you have carried with you all these years with this moment in mind. All your powers of magic must be spent on this one last act. For this, you have trained Anubis, your guardian, adopted son, and successor in wisdom.

All through the long hours, you pray to the gods and summon the strength to do what must be done. Anubis moves about the stone on which his father's body lies, building up a ring of power that encloses the whole temple. Then he summons the great gods from the Boat of a Million Years, Ra and Nuit and She, Thoth and Geb and Hathor, the Goddess of Love. Khnum, the potter who spins the bodies of men and women, and great Ptah, the God of Life who fills those bodies with breath. Around the body of Osiris, the Great Ones gather. And Ra, the Sun God, speaks:

"Who summons the gods from their places, and why?"

You step forward, around you a cloak that you once wore in the halls of the Palace of On and on your brow, the royal uraeus crown.

"I, Isis, summon the gods. By my power, I summon thee, Great Ra. I hold the secret of your true name and, by that name, I ask for the life of Osiris to be returned to him."

Ptah steps forward:
"Once the breath of life goes forth, it cannot come again, but this I may do. I may give him one full day of life, then he must return to the underworld. But in that time, I will breathe life into your womb, and Khnum will fashion the body of a son to avenge his father's death."

Ra speaks again:
"Osiris and you, Isis, were sent into human form by the gods that man might be taught new things. Because of your faithfulness and the goodness of your work, I will set Osiris as the Lord of Death and Rebirth. All men shall come before him to be judged and he will have life forever beyond Earth. I shall give my own symbol of the hawk to the son of Osiris, and he shall fight the darkness unceasingly, until the end of time when all things are balanced. Anubis shall be the guide of the newly dead and he shall weigh the hearts of men in his father's hall. He shall teach men the art of preserving the dead, and he shall walk in two worlds without fear, and with great power. To him will be given the guardianship of the Mother, and to all who seek the inner life he will be a guide. His half brother shall be seen in the Sun, and he will light the way of men in the world, as Anubis shall light the way of men after death."

The gods grow brighter and brighter until they are seen no more. Only you and Anubis remain. There is a new sound in the temple, the sound of a man breathing deeply, as if waking from a dream. Osiris opens his eyes and looks around. With your help he sits, then stands. In a few minutes, he is once more the husband you remember and love. Anubis greets his father with joy, then, having knelt to offer him his service, he leaves the two of you together. You have one day and one night together, and then Osiris must return to his own place as Lord of the Underworld. In that time, your son, Horus, will be conceived. When he has grown to manhood and avenged his father, you will be able to loose your hold on life and take your place among the immortals.

The Birth of Horus

This pathworking, in essence, carries on from The Sorrows of Isis and was designed to complement that pathworking and to extend it. It is advised, however, that the two should not be worked one after the other, unless those working them are of advanced training and preferably doing them under lodge conditions. This is not an idle piece of advice, nor is it meant to "whet" the appetite or encourage newcomers to do the very thing they are being asked *not* to do.

Both these pathworkings may have a very real and decisive effect on the physical, astral, and mental levels of those undertaking them. To avoid placing newcomers under more stress than necessary, it is advised that these pathworkings be done at least five, and preferably seven days apart.

A woman doing either of these workings should identify with Isis as deeply as possible. A man may alternate between the characters of Osiris, Anubis, and Horus. The "Sorrows" pathworking ended at the point at which Osiris was given twenty-four hours of physical life to spend with his sister-wife, Isis, in order that a son might be conceived who will avenge his father's murder by Set, the child's uncle, Osiris' brother. Originally, it had been planned that Osiris/Isis would formulate the positive side of manifestation, and their twin siblings, Set/Nephthys, would manifest the negative. This would have meant a perfect balance of positive good and negative evil (evil being seen here as a balanced opposition), the two being the black and white pillars that support the cosmos. However, a flaw in the character of Set produced a positive evil in him and the plan thus reflected that flaw. Other means of balance had to be sought.

Anubis spearheaded this plan, since he was the son of Osiris by his sister, Nephthys, taking the place of the son the gods had denied to Set. It is the task of Anubis to be heir and successor to Isis in the realms of magic. Because of his loyalty and faithfulness to his foster mother and his aunt, Isis, the gods have made Anubis their messenger, the Walker in the Two Worlds, the Weigher of Hearts before his father, Osiris, in the Halls of Amenti. He is also destined to be the dog-guardian of his foster mother. He opens the ways of the gods to mankind, and is the sacred nephew and half brother, the one who will act as forerunner to the young Horus.

Horus, the Golden Hawk, is born of Isis and Osiris. He is golden of skin and eye. This is due to the fact that Isis replaced the phallus of Osiris, lost when Set castrated the dead body of his brother in an effort to deny any chance of an heir who might oppose him, by a phallus made of pure gold. The gods, called by Isis and Anubis, have endowed both the man and the replicated genitals with twenty-four hours of life, taken from the willing Anubis.

The Sorrows of Isis ends on an island in the middle of the Nile River. On this island, there is a ruined temple, old even then. Anubis has left his father and beloved foster mother to themselves, knowing that their time together is short. He walks down to the river and sits down at the water's edge. The pathworking moves on from this point.

Anubis is sitting at the water's edge. The Sun is now above the horizon and the warmth is welcome. Much energy has been expended by the young man in the great ritual enacted during the night. He has been the polarizing influence for his foster mother's magical powers. Only with his help was it possible to call the gods from their unceasing journey in the Boat of a Million Years. But to grant Osiris a day and a night of life, the gods have drawn the necessary life-force from the manhood of Anubis. It has been given willingly and with love. Now, Anubis, endowed with the wisdom and understanding of his much-loved foster mother, sits in contemplation of what the gift will mean, and the far-reaching results it will have in the great pattern of the cosmos.

His father, Osiris, gave him life, seeding him in the body of his mother, Nephthys. Now he has repaid that gift of life and it fills the body of his father once more. But the wisdom of Anubis sees further than this. He knows that, because it is his life that fills Osiris, the seed that fills the womb of Isis will hold part of him, Anubis. In repaying the life given him by his father, Anubis has become one with Osiris, and they now share the same energy. They will also share the seeding of Isis and will both be part of the child that will be born.

Anubis looks up at the Sun as it climbs into the heavens. He stands and holds out his arms to either side, letting the power surge through him. His body transmutes with the ease of long practice and a great eagle soars into the Sun's rays. Up and up Anubis flies, letting the heat of the Sun soak into his feathered pinions.

With fierce golden eyes, he looks directly into the Sun and sees into the heart of the pattern. He sees and understands the great blend of life that will occur: Osiris, Horus, and Anubis, one, each in the other, together yet apart. The father, the son and that which will bind them together for eternity, the soaring spirit that is Anubis, the Opener of the Ways. He sees further still and, with sadness, beholds how that Three in One will be misunderstood and abused. He sees the Sacred Cup of Womanhood, that is a blend of Isis, Nephthys, and Nuit, cast down from its rightful place and despised. He knows this will leave the Three in One with no point of manifestation for long ages, until the Sacred Cup incarnates once more in the Age of the Two Fishes.

All this he sees and understands as he sees beyond the Sun into the heart of the cosmic pattern. Then weariness overcomes him and he sinks to Earth and lies at the water's edge. He sleeps deeply and dreamlessly, free for a while of the great responsibility that the gods have laid upon him.

In the quiet and cool of the ruined temple, Isis and Osiris sit close together. As yet, few words have passed between them. Their need is simply to know each other's touch. The years since their last meeting have been filled with weariness and sorrow for the queen. For Osiris, they have been a dream filled with his love for her and his son, Anubis. In those dreams, he has been close to them, but never with enough power to do more than strengthen their hearts against despair.

At last, Isis stirs from her place against his heart and begins to tell Osiris of all that has happened. The Sun climbs higher and the precious minutes flow away like the river that surrounds them. The story told, there is a space of silence. Then Osiris speaks. He tells his queen and sister what must be done to train the young Sun Hawk who will be his father's emissary on Earth. Halfway between life and death as he is, Osiris can see into the future even further than Isis, for all her magical powers. She listens, her eyes adoring his face, as her mind assimilates his words.

At noon, Anubis comes with food and wine. His sleep has refreshed him and he is no longer weary. Osiris looks upon his son with pride and love, and bids him sit by them as they eat together. Questioned by his father, Anubis tells him of the old king and that, soon, a child of the line of Osiris will be born in the royal household, a child destined to sit upon the throne of the city-state. This pleases Osiris greatly and he promises that, from his hall in Amenti, he will watch over the young king. He sees himself at the same age in the strong, handsome Anubis and rejoices that the line will continue on Earth in physical form. Isis also gives a promise that this line will never fail until the end of time, and with the bloodline will go the powers of Anubis himself.

Osiris now draws his son aside and they speak together. Anubis tells his father of his vision in the Sun. Osiris confirms what he has seen and places the physical training of the Sun Hawk in the hands of Anubis. It will be a special relationship, encompassing within it the bonds of father, brother, and nephew. The child must be kept safe, trained as a warrior, and taught of his mission. Anubis kneels before his father, placing one hand between his father's hands and one hand on the golden phallus. Thus, he swears physically and spiritually to undertake all that is required of him. Osiris raises, blesses, and kisses him. Then Anubis seeks out Isis and kneels to her as the Cup of Life that will soon be filled. He asks for her blessing. This she gives with love. In her wisdom, she knows of his vision and understands that the child she will conceive will be fathered by both Anubis and Osiris, and, being part of both, will also father himself. Herein is a mystery explained for those who can understand.

The three bathe in the river in the heat of the day and, for a little while, they are a family again. Then, as the Sun starts its downward journey, Anubis leaves them again and returns to the river's edge. There, he changes his form into that of an eagle and soars into the cooling air, turning toward the city where a young girl who carries his child within her awaits.

So intent is he, that he does not notice the small party of men wearing the colors of Set gathering on the far side of the river. For once, his watchfulness sleeps and he thinks only of the satin skin and lustrous eyes of the young queen, and the soft, burgeoning shape that encloses a future king.

On the island, Isis lies in the arms of her love. The years of emptiness are now forgotten and there is only the sight, the touch, and the scent of the man above her and within her. The birds and the animals of the island, drawn by the intensity of their love, creep close to the godlike couple. The Sun's last rays caress them in their joy. The wind on the river holds its breath to hear the love cries of Isis, and echoes the deep sigh of Osiris as he sinks down upon her breast.

As they sleep, the Moon, the silver symbol that Isis has made her own, rises, hiding shyly behind a gauze of gray cloud, tinged faintly with the last touch of a setting Sun. Deep within the body of Isis, a speck of life moves toward its destiny. A smile curves the lips of Isis and is echoed on the face of Osiris as, in their dreams, they watch the unfolding drama of conception. Beside their sleeping bodies, the two who will become gods of the future, watch the beginning of the life of another of their eternal kind. As the moment approaches, they feel the mind-touch of Anubis as he, too, watches from his place beside a sleeping girl. The fusion, when it comes, encloses and involves all three of them, and suddenly they are more than three—they are four.

The thoughts of Nephthys join them and, soon after, the awesome presence of Nuit makes it six. The tiny, fluttering speck that will become a child is lovingly surrounded, nurtured, and blessed by the five great ones. Then the three women draw aside and, from the center of the Great Pattern, far beyond the brilliance that is Sirius, comes the identity that will become the young Sun Hawk, just as that which is Anubis came from beyond the Dragon Star. The newly formed essence joins its composite father, brother, nephew, and cousin and the blended souls form a spiral echoing the far-off Pattern at the center of the cosmos. The minds of the three goddesses form a triangle of protection about the precious material, containing it like wine within a cup.

All through the night, the work goes on, the young Sun Hawk growing stronger with every passing hour. All the minds in communication are now aware of the approaching danger. Set knows of the newly arisen Osiris and, even now, he and his men draw near the island. Far away, Anubis rises from the bed of the young queen and takes on his eagle form, flying swiftly toward the island. The outcome is known and accepted, the sacrifice will be made. The sleeping forms of Isis and Osiris dream on, their higher selves keeping the lines of force taut between them and their helpers.

As the predawn light heralds the Sun, Set and his men reach the island. Isis and Osiris awake. Calm and unafraid, they make their farewells. Nephthys and Nuit withdraw. The face of Isis is calm, though her heart is torn with inner grief as she leaps upward in the form of a white dove. A few moments later, Osiris falls beneath the sword of his brother and the first rays of the Sun mark the end of the allotted time.

In a fury, Set hacks the body of Osiris to pieces, but, as he raises his sword to smash the golden phallus, an eagle swoops out of the air to snatch it away. The eagle mounts up into the sky toward the Sun, the gleaming phallus held in one mighty talon. In the other, held with all the gentleness of love, lies a snow-white dove that weeps tears of crystal. The eagle flies north over the sea, carrying the mother and the child. Behind them, Set gives orders for the body of Osiris to be scattered over the land of Egypt.

Time has passed. In a small cave on a mountainside lies Isis, awaiting the birth of her son. Anubis has made a bed of scented herbs and flowers for her and now goes to fetch Nephthys to be with her sister at the birth. In his eagle shape, he flies toward the royal palace where Set now rules. Nephthys waits on the flat roof. The eagle descends and Anubis stands before her, a man now in every sense, tried and tested through grief and joy, hate and love, giving and taking. She smiles, placing her long, narrow hands on his shoulders. She, too, has known the sacrifice of giving. This son of her body, though he honors her as his natural mother, gives his allegiance to Isis. This was meant to be. For this, the Great Ritual was enacted between her and Osiris. She is content knowing that she has had a part in the pattern of the future.

In the evening sky, an eagle mounts into the air. Held securely in his talons, a small field mouse lies quietly and at rest. The land flows beneath the beating wings as they fly through the deepening night. Their thoughts go ahead, reaching out to Isis in her pain. The Moon is high when they enter the cave and begin to prepare for the birth of the Sun Hawk.

The night is soft and dark. Only the Moon's light fills the Temple of Birth. As the hours pass, the animals of the mountains and the plains gather at the entrance, waiting with patience for the morning and the new Sun/Son. The birds gather on the sparse trees outside, their bright eyes glinting in the moonlight. Inside, Nephthys moves to and fro, preparing scented oils and herbs, pausing now and then to minister to her sister. Anubis sits with his foster mother's head on his lap, his hands holding hers, pouring his strength into her as each wave of pain threatens to engulf her tired body. As the pain recedes, he wipes her forehead with a cloth dipped in cool water and moistens her lips.

A little before dawn, the pain takes on a new intensity and Nephthys brings soft linen cloths to wrap the child and oil with which to anoint him. Anubis yields his place to Nephthys and, with his own loving hands, eases his brother, son, and cousin into the hushed dawn of a new day. He smiles as the child's first cry fills the cave. From the waiting animal life there comes an answering cry as the younger brethren of the world welcome the young Sun Hawk.

As the cord of life is cut, the first rays of the Sun illuminate the cave, the child, and those around him. Anubis lifts the babe and carries it into the light of the Sun. There, holding the tiny body above his head, he offers the new Sun Lord to the old. The rays form a nimbus about his tiny head. One by one, birds and animals go past, bending their heads as they pass, until all have paid homage and returned to their places.

All through the day, Isis rests, nursing her new son, tended by her sister and nephew. Then, with the setting of the Sun, come the great gods of Egypt. They gather in the cave. It becomes a vast palace of carved and weathered stone that accommodates their lofty forms. Anubis takes the child in his arms, for it is time for son and father to meet. The gods form an avenue and, with their auras of power, build a shimmering bridge between this world and Amenti. Over the bridge strides Anubis, the messenger of the gods, carrying in his arms his brother-son-cousin. The child shines like a ray of sunlight, lighting a way through the underworld. The shades of those that have left the world draw close to share in this light and are blessed by it. On, to the throne of Osiris in the Halls of Judgment, Anubis takes his precious burden and lays the child at his father's feet.

Osiris blesses the child and holds it close to him for a few moments. He then returns it to Anubis, who places the tiny body in the scales opposite the Feather of Truth. Heaven and Earth wait with bated breath. The great scales move and balance exactly. The Sun Hawk is without blemish. Anubis returns across the bridge in his eagle form, holding in his talons the tiny hawk chick and, as Anubis places Horus once more within the circle of his mother's arms, he also brings a message for Isis from Osiris that he delivers with a gentle kiss.

Nephthys gives them a list of the places where the parts of Osiris' body have been scattered, and the three talk together, planning to seek out each sacred piece and raise above it a temple to hallow the spot. Then, as the first night of the Sun Hawk's life draws in, Isis sleeps, her son close beside her.

Anubis leaves her in the care of Nephthys and flies across the mountains to a small stone palace. There, he stands beside another sleeping woman with a newborn son beside her. In her dreams, she sees him and smiles, lifting her face for his kiss. He blesses and anoints the child with the same oil that bathed the Sun Hawk. He leaves beside the child the miniature sword that Osiris gave to him when he was a boy and bids the young queen send the boy to him when he is grown, saying he will teach him all that he should know. He will take him to Horus to swear allegiance, and over the Bridge of the Gods to be presented to his grandfather, Osiris. He will rule long and wisely, and, when his time comes, his father will lead him into the halls of Amenti.

It is time to leave the Land of Khem. Anubis flies back to take up his role as guardian of the mother and child, a role he is destined to play in many ages. Isis sleeps, watched over by her sister. But the young Sun Hawk is awake and watchful. Already, the man within is aware and making plans. When Anubis enters, the little head turns. The eyes hold his, the mouth smiles, and a small hand reaches out to be enfolded by the strong, dark hand of his brother-father-cousin. They pledge each other in silence, the Hawk and the Eagle joined in the eternal battle for the light.

2

Greek Pathworkings

In many of the world's pantheons. there is a well-defined line between two mythological ages, a time when older gods were supplanted by newer forms. Often the newer gods were taken over from conquering tribes or brought in by traders and immigrants from other areas. In time, the new gods became part of the old myths. One of the best examples is found in the Norse tradition, where there is an obvious line between the Vanir and the Aesir. There is a similar line between the gods of "The First Time," the Zep Tepi, and those who came later, to be found in Egypt. In Greece, this transition was seen as a battle for supremacy between the Titans and the Olympians.

In these workings, I have tried to portray the feeling and power of the god or goddess within the visualizations. Some of these workings require the assumption of the god-form itself. This means they are for experienced students of the occult, those with a working knowledge of the art and practice of assumption techniques. With any form of pathworking, dim lighting, quiet, and privacy are recommended. With the higher forms of this technique, this is not just a recommendation, it is a requirement. When working with the god-forms portrayed in these workings, you can either stick to your own gender or change over. Despite the tales of their sexual adventures, the Greek gods, like the gods of any tradition, are beyond sexual characteristics. They are archetypes and have both male and female attributes. Greek pathworkings often have a lighter feel than the Egyptian. For the most part, their gods were closer to the human species. Bear this in mind when working them.

Apollo, God of the Sun

Relax and slow your breathing as much as you can with comfort. Allow your mind to drift in a warm, soft darkness that has the feel of the last few moments of sleep before waking. Build before you a sea of intense blue, with small green islands here and there. One island is filled with white temples that gleam in the predawn light. The astral self descends and walks on the green grass. All around you is silence and an overwhelming sense of great power.

This is Delos, the island of Apollo, lord of prophecy, music, and healing. It is here he comes to rest and sleep through the night when his twin sister, Artemis, rides the night sky in her silver boat. The air is full of the scent of wildflowers and the sound of the sea is all around you. You walk across the small island to its far side and there you see a cave from which there shines an intermittent light. You approach cautiously.

Before the cave entrance stands a chariot of pure gold. It looks so light that you wonder how it remains on earth at all. Close by, cropping the lush grass, stand four pure-white horses—the Gammadion, the four who pull the Sun chariot across the sky. You walk closer to the entrance of the cave and look inside. The rock has been touched by the power of the sleeping god and has been transmuted into gold, so that Apollo rests within a golden cocoon. He lies sprawled in sleep on a mound of soft fleece, his limbs relaxed, his face at peace. The beauty of his form and features are a wonder to mortal eyes and it dazzles you. But time is short. The goddess Eos, the Dawn, is racing across the sea toward the island to wake the Sun God and set him on his journey. You can hear her feet as they lightly touch the wave tops. It is time for the sun to rise.

Look at Apollo. Draw nearer to him. Settle your astral body over his and allow it to sink down into the immortal form. Not a moment too soon, for here is Eos. She catches the white horses and links them to the chariot, then steals into the cave to awaken Apollo, to awaken *you.*

Let yourself feel the power and grace of the god-form as it stirs and begins to wake. Feel the strength and sleekness of muscles and sinews as they stretch and loosen. As the eyes open, you must look through them and see the laughing face of Eos as she bends over you. Catch her hair, draw her face down to yours, and kiss the morning awake.

Sandals are at your side, ready to put on, and a swath of golden silk, as light as the breath of Eos herself, is wrapped around the godlike form. Keep looking through the eyes of Apollo as he emerges from the cave and greets his horses with a gentle hand and a palm full of sweet clover for each one. Before the cave lie offerings made by the priestesses of the island: fruit, honey, bread, and cheese, and wine to drink.

Time to be gone. Mount the chariot and take up the reins. Turn the horses toward the running form of Eos as she leaps into the air to act as your herald. The horses throw their strength into the harness and the chariot wheels over the grass to the cliff top. For a moment, it hangs in the air as the horses leap, then it mounts upward, wheeling into place, and seemingly bursts into flame as the Sun rises ready to start the day.

Higher and higher you climb, until Earth lies far beneath you. Eos turns and waves farewell, then, her task completed, returns to Olympus. You/Apollo laugh with sheer joy and urge the horses onward. Feel the pull on your muscles as they maintain their heading and light the day for those on Earth.

Far below, the clouds drift and change, flowing from one form to another as the four brothers, the Winds of Heaven, blow them this way and that. You ride so high that nothing is hidden from you. You have the sight of Apollo, as keen as that of an eagle and can see the smallest object far below. You can see children bathing in the rivers and the fishermen putting out to sea. Farmers are already in the fields and the women are making their way to market. Birds ride the air currents below you as you ride over the seas and the valleys and the tall mountains.

From time to time, your eye is caught by the face of a beautiful woman and you laugh down at her, turning her skin to gold with your glance. You race over the fierce desert and watch the caravans making their way to the East and the Silk Road leading to Khangar, Samarkand, and Cathay.

You pass over Olympus and wave to your peers as they walk amid the flower-strewn paths of their halls and palaces. For a while, your half brother, Hermes, races alongside you, carrying a message from great Zeus to his brother, Poseidon. Then he flashes a grin at you and easily outdistances your horses as he speeds away to the West. By noon, the chariot is at its highest point and all below are seeking shade from its brightness. You/Apollo draw the horses to a halt and, leaving the chariot, descend to Earth along a sunbeam to where a dark-eyed girl waits to welcome and gift you/Apollo with wine and food and the passion in her soft, young body.

But the Sun cannot be still and you must take your place in the chariot again and drive the horses on toward the west. As the day wears on, the horses begin to tire and go more slowly, so the chariot burns less brightly and the heat is not so fierce. You/Apollo turn to look at the softer glow of the celestial globe on Earth below, and your thoughts turn toward the green glades of western Greece and the long shadows upon the grass. The fiery steeds know the way through the halls of Hades, where the chariot becomes the Sun at midnight, and their way back to Delos. Apollo leaves the chariot and drops down through the twilight to a meandering river where a group of nymphs and satyrs enjoy the last rays of the Sun Chariot as it sinks in the west. They greet you with wine and laughter and offer to dance, if you supply the music.

You take up the lyre offered. As dark-robed night hastens across the sea, you play and sing, until the last of the light is overcome and your sister's moonboat rises into the sky. The last note dies away. You look at the sleeping forms and the power of prophecy arises in you. You look into the future and see your temples in ruins and strangers treading on sacred soil. There are no nymphs to dance to your music, no satyrs to chase them. Earth is a noisier, sadder place, with no room left for the gods. You look further still and see strange shapes in the sky—not your chariot or your sister's silver barque, but man-made carriers of death and destruction. Yet, as you look with horror upon all this, you hear, as if from far away, the sound of voices singing and music playing.

You cross the sea toward the sound. It is not Greece, but they chant the old invocations and dance in a temple unlike any you have seen. They worship the glory and power of the Sun. Your heart lifts in pleasure. The old ways will not die completely; a small part will remain. Make your way across the dark sea to Delos and seek out the golden cave that is your resting place. You know that one day you will come here and fall asleep for long ages, until strange voices awaken you to the return of the old ways. Apollo rests. Rise from his form and take back your own shape. Look upon him as he sleeps and remember. Return to your own form and awaken gently.

Hermes, the Messenger

Using whatever format you prefer, pass into the space between the worlds. You are wrapped in a soft, safe darkness that gradually lightens. You feel you are awakening from a deep and refreshing sleep. Open your eyes and find yourself lying on a bed of brightly painted wood. The mattress beneath you is filled with soft feathers. There is a pillow of the same. A thick square of tightly woven wool covers you.

Slowly, you raise yourself upon an elbow and look about the room. It is large, with walls of white painted with shadowy figures in pale blues and grays. The whole place feels light and airy. There is a scent of apple and orange blossom in the air. Several painted wooden coffers and a few chairs stand around the room and one wall is open to the elements. You rise from the bed and step out onto a balcony looking out over snow-capped mountains, range upon range of them sweeping down into a distant valley.

Returning to the room, you see a doorway leading off to the right. There you find a pool of clear water sunk into the floor. There are steps leading down into its warm depths. Around the edge are marble benches, on which can be found phials of oils and a pile of soft linen cloths. You lie down on one of the benches and from another room come a boy and a girl, both about 16 years old. Together, they oil your body and work the sweet-smelling liquid into your skin, making it supple and taut. When they have finished, you rise and step into the water, pausing to look at your reflection.

You see a tall, slender, but well-muscled young man with a pleasant open face, tightly curled hair of warm honey-brown, and eyes that are both green and gold. You smile at your image and see the answering wide grin on the face of your reflection. You wash away the remaining oil and, wrapped in a linen cloth, you return to the first room.

Lying on one of the chairs is a Greek lyre made from tortoiseshell. On another lies a tunic of delicate silk in a soft cloud-gray. Beneath the chair, a pair of sandals lie, one on top of the other. They have small wings attached to either side of the heels, though, at the moment, they look limp and bedraggled, as if they were worn out. You smile, knowing that they are more than they seem to be. You give a soft whistle. The wings of the topmost sandal flutter slightly. You whistle again and they lift themselves and stretch as if they were easing their feathers after a long flight. Then the sandal hops across the floor to your feet, the second sandal following more slowly. Side by side they sit, waiting. You pick one up and slide it on, tying the leather strings firmly. Now the second one. You stand and walk across to where your tunic lies and slip it over your head. It wraps around you and, like the sandals, it gives the impression that it has a life of its own.

You look around, searching for something. The sandals tug at your feet and lift you smoothly from the floor. Walking some fifteen inches above it, you go out onto the balcony. Before and below you is the Olympus range. The air is crisp and tangy and it fills you with delight. There is a clattering sound to your left. You turn your head.

Perched on the edge of the balcony is a staff, topped by a pinecone and supported by another pair of wings. Beside the staff is a shallow, bowl-shaped hat, again, winged. When you turn back to the room, the staff and hat hop down from the balcony and follow you. At the foot of the bed, two serpents are drinking from a bowl of milk. You wait until they have finished, then/whistle. They glide to the staff and climb it, to position themselves in their usual place. There, they freeze and become like stone.

"Hermes, my son, come to me. I have need of you."

It is the voice of Zeus, your father and the ruler of Olympus. You snatch up the hat and staff and leave at a run. You head for the balcony and, as you reach it, you leap upward. The wings of hat, staff, and sandals take the weight of your body and lift you up into the thin air of the mountains. You run, using the clouds as a pathway, swift as a thought, and laughing with sheer exhilaration of flight. Within seconds, you see below you the great marble and gold hall of Zeus. Descending, you land like a feather on the floor of decorated tiles.

Walking forward, you sink gracefully onto one knee before your exalted sire. You are conscious of the cold gaze of Hera. She resents your status and the fact that you are not her son. But she tolerates you, for you are useful to all the gods. Unlike the others, you never take sides, never quarrel with your peers, and never appear to notice what goes on. But you see and hear all.

Your father towers over all the other gods, with golden skin, gray-gold hair and beard, and eyes of amber flecked with green. He appears to be of mature years, but with an air of virility and strength about him. He leans forward and beckons you near. You are given a rolled parchment and a soft leather bag. He speaks some words in your ear. You grin and nod your head. You turn to Hera and bow low to her, then turn and leap into the air. In a second, you are out over the dark-blue sea and heading for the West. Your destination is the fog-bound, rain-filled island of Erin at the edge of the Western Sea.

You run easily, enjoying the feel of smooth muscles working as if oiled, and the heat of the Sun on your back. You look up and see the solar chariot moving across the sky. Your half brother, Apollo, waves as he guides his steeds toward the west and sleep. You wave back and smile, remembering how you stole his sun cattle when you were only a few days old. Nevertheless, you are firm friends now.

You drop down to the surface of the blue Aegean Sea and, for the sheer fun of it, you run across the tip of the waves so lightly that no trace of your passing remains. You pause to rest on the top mast of a passing ship laden with spices and bound for the cold northern islands of the uttermost west.

Far above you, you see the trailing rainbow gown of Iris, messenger of Hera, and rise to run alongside her, smiling and teasing her until she bids you be on your way. Far below, an island gleams in the rays of the Sun. You swoop downward and alight gently on the soft green grass. You walk toward a group of trees that cluster about a pool of clear water. Sitting beside the pool is a beautiful young woman. Her hair is the color of a burnished leaf in autumn and her eyes as green as the grass around her. She turns her head as you approach and smiles. She has been expecting you.

You offer her the rolled vellum, which she reads. Then, blushing, she takes the leather bag. When opened, it reveals a necklace of gold, amber, and pearls. You recognize it as the work of Hephasteus, the master smith of Olympus. She clasps it about her neck and admires herself in the mirror of the pool. You smile slyly, knowing that this is another of the loves of your father, Zeus. Bidding the girl farewell, you leap upward, turning toward the east and Greece.

Along the way, you stop at a small town to watch with interest as a thief is chased by angry street vendors. You hear his breathless prayer to the God of Thieves—*you*—and you swoop down to cover him with a cloud of mist that hides him from those pursuing him. You are, after all, simply answering a prayer. You have a soft heart for those who live by their wits. Finally, you see below you the white-capped top of

Olympus and drop down to tell your father that the mission has been accomplished and that his proposition is agreeable to her. For a while, you stay with the gods, drinking and eating with them. Apollo pauses on his way home to his island of Delos. Artemis, his twin sister, leaves to prepare her moon chariot for its night ride across the starry sky.

You walk out onto the wide balcony, your staff hopping curiously behind you, and look back at the crowded hall. Suddenly, you feel the need for solitude and, setting down the chalice of wine, you take hold of the staff and leap into the air. For a while, you run alongside Artemis and her pale horses, then you leave to follow a trail of twinkling lights far below. It is a procession setting out from Athens to walk along the Eleusian Way. You amuse yourself by donning a disguise and walking with them for a few miles.

From among the procession, a young girl catches your eye and you walk beside her, making her laugh with your wit and quicksilver tongue. Finally, you tug her into a flower-filled meadow and tumble her on the sweet-smelling blossoms. She will never know that the handsome young man who stole her innocence is Hermes, the son of Zeus. Later, as she sleeps among the flowers, you leave her to her dreams and make your way back to your own hall. There, you slip off the sandals and watch with a laugh as the wings flop wearily to the floor. Likewise, your hat flutters to a table and there settles down for the night. Your staff lies inert, wings a tangle of white and gray feathers. The snakes are drinking from their milk bowl. You lie on the bed, relaxed and open to the touch of Morpheus when he offers sleep on his way across the night-time world. Smiling, you accept the dreams the God of Sleep offers.

Outside, the stars dance through the night. Artemis peers in and smiles to see Hermes sleeping soundly, then continues her ordained pathway across the dark sky. The mountains hide themselves in the dark cloak of night and take up their watch. Gods and men alike need the blessing of sleep, and dreams.

In a shadowed corner of the room, the wings of the sandals flutter slightly and then settle down again. The night moves on toward the dawn and all is quiet. In a far-off town, a thief gives thanks to his patron god, Hermes, as he counts his gains, and a young girl dreams of the strong arms, golden limbs, and laughing eyes of a handsome stranger.

Athene, Goddess of Athens

See before you the image of a full-length mirror. It is black and mysterious and has a liquid quality. You step close to it and put out a hand to touch the surface. The hand sinks into the mirror and the arm follows. You step closer still and, now, your arm, up to the shoulder, is inside the mirror. You step forward and the dark surface silently swallows your form.

You emerge on the edge of a high cliff overlooking the Aegean. Below you, the sea is dark blue and foam-flecked with white. You wear an ankle-length robe of pleated white linen so fine it is almost transparent. Over this, a heavier tunic of dark red acts as a foundation for a breastplate of bronze. This covers you back and front, laced at the sides with leather straps. About your neck and covering your breast is the silver image of a goat's head. This is the protective Aegis given by Zeus to his daughter. Self-begotten, sprung from the head of the king of the gods, his dream, his ultimate self, his Athene.

About your shoulders is a cloak of thin wool fastened with a golden pin. You wear sandals of the finest leather studded with gold. Behind you on the green grass lie a shield of heavy bronze and leather embossed with a lightning flash, a helmet of similar material crowned with a white horsehair crest, and a tall spear, one of Hephasteus' finest creations.

With a final look out over the wild sea, you turn and gather up your belongings. You begin to walk over the grassland and, as you do so, you visualize your father's hall and your form fades from view, had anyone been there to see it. You keep walking and reappear in the entrance to the Hall of Zeus.

The first thing you see is the fierce cold look of Hera's face. She has not forgotten that your august father chose to bring you to birth all by himself. She hates you, and only your wisdom and power keep her from challenging you. Zeus calls you to him and you speak together. He tells you the Greeks have built a new and beautiful city on Earth and have asked that you become their patroness. It will be called Athens, after you. If you agree to be their guardian, they will build you a temple second only to that of Zeus himself on Olympus.

You agree to go to see this new city and, with a cool bow to Hera and a much deeper one to Zeus, you walk from the hall and into the agora (market square) of the new city. You take on the disguise of an old woman begging for bread and walk around, looking at the people who have asked you to become their patroness.

They are a proud and beautiful race and you see far beyond their physical beauty to the quick, fertile minds behind their eyes. You know you can guide them to greater things, given the chance. You look up and see upon the high hill overlooking the city the outline of a temple. Quietly, you disappear and reappear, invisibly, before the half-built temple on the summit.

It is breathtaking. Made from the finest marble, with pillars carved by skillful hands and minds. You look into the future and see it finished: the wonderful carvings, the inlaid floor, the brilliant colors, and, above all, the statue of yourself, three times the size of the tallest man, with your shield and spear at the ready. You see the crowds come to worship and pray in the beautiful temple high above the city that bears your name. You seek a way to let the Athenians know of your pleasure in the honor they offer to you.

Hearing voices raised in disagreement, you approach unseen. The builder and the sculptor are arguing. The builder wants the statue built and in place before the last wall is in place, because it will be too big once the wall is up. The sculptor is in despair because he cannot envisage the form or face of the goddess and cannot begin the carving. He shows the builder drawings, but says they do not convey the majesty of Athene. The builder protests that one cannot carve a god from life . . . and you laugh to yourself. You influence the sculptor to walk into the temple to the place where a huge block of marble stands. He has chipped out the outline of the form, but can go no further.

You speak quietly in his mind, telling him to look to his right and to carve what he sees. He does so and, to his amazement he sees Athene in her glory as a goddess. Stunned and awed, he drops to his knees and bows in prayer. You tell him to get up and to carve what he sees from life. You tell him you will come each day until the statue is finished, but that he is to tell no one, and that only he will be able to see you.

Eagerly, he grabs his tools and begins to work. You sustain his human strength through the day. When he can do no more because the light has faded, you leave, promising to come again. Each day, you pose for him and, each day, the statue grows in beauty, power, and strength. Workmen gather to watch, people climb the hill to see the inspired work and whisper that such is the power of the work that it is inspired by Athene herself. You use their energies and prayers to empower both building and statue, so that it may become a thing of inspiration for all to see. As the work progresses, you empower the statue with your own grace and wisdom.

Finally, it is finished. The builders can now put the final wall in place. A long time has passed and those that began the temple have gone to the Elysian Fields. Athens, below, has grown into a city of wealth and power. Great men and women walk and talk and live out lives of wisdom inspired by the goddess Athene. You continue to visit the city, to wander unseen and unknown among its people. You feel a passionate love for this place, this time, and this race that will one day become synonymous with culture.

You watch the crowds come to make offerings and worship the goddess. Listen as they pray to you. Sometimes you are moved to grant their wishes and see their joy. Let your love and wisdom flow out over the city, knowing that it will one day fall into ruin and your name will be forgotten. But here, in this time, let your power lift their hearts, for you are Athene, epitome of wisdom.

One day, as you stand watching the crowds about the feet of your statue, the sculptor, now an old, old man comes wearily to kneel before his greatest creation. He remembers how the goddess herself posed for him so that the statue might be a true likeness. In all these years, he has kept his promise and told no one of this grace and favor of wisdom's daughter. Now, he feels his life drawing to a close and comes one last time to look upon the face of his beloved Athene. He kneels slowly and painfully on limbs grown stiff and swollen, and bows his head. As he prays, he hears your voice as he heard it long ago. He lifts his head and, with eyes no longer dim and unfocused, sees you in your full glory.

His face lights up with joy. Trembling, he tries to rise, to reach out to you. Gently, you take his hand in yours. Those near see the worn-out body slump to the floor, but its spirit is no longer there. You lead the awed and trembling soul into the sunshine, where it becomes young and handsome again. Disdaining the help of Hermes, who has come to lead him to the Fields of Elysium, you, Athene, take him and personally deliver him into the gentle hands of Persephone, the Goddess of the Underworld. Release the form of the goddess and return to your own time and place, and rest.

Pluto, Lord of Hades

As the warm, comforting darkness of inner space closes about you, there is a sensation of something momentous about to happen. You are drawn across starlit space toward a darker area where there are no stars, just a deep blackness that swirls like a whirlpool. You are caught up in this and feel a pull of enormous power drawing you down and into the blackness. You travel at enormous speeds through worlds of color, sound, and shapes that bear no resemblance to any that you know. Momentarily, you pass through areas that resemble your own galaxy, but then are immediately plunged back into the swirling darkness.

Gradually, you slow down and feel your journey coming to its appointed end. Abruptly, you are shot from the darkness into bright sunlight. Your landing is on soft grass and you are not injured. Overhead, there is a brilliant noonday Sun; around you on three sides there are trees, grasslands, and shrubs. On the fourth side is a cliff face, at the foot of which you can see the entrance to a cave.

Beside the cave stands a figure wrapped in a dark cloak. It beckons and points to the cave entrance. You understand it is saying you must take this path leading away from the light of day and the bright, warm sun. You are reluctant to do this and turn away, but the figure comes toward you, its face hidden by the hood of its cloak, and places in your hand a small coin. It lays a hand on your shoulder and whispers, "Come." You turn and follow it across the green grass filled with wildflowers. At the entrance of the cave, you turn and look at the color, the warmth, and the sunlit scene before you. You tell yourself that you can be strong and get through this. Then you turn and pass into the darkness. At first, the light from the entrance makes it easier, but as you go further in, the darkness closes around you. You put out your hands to feel your way. On either side, there is a damp and rather slimy stone wall, in front of you, emptiness. You feel with your feet, sliding one foot in front of the other, trying to discover if it is safe. Then, without warning, you bump your head—not badly, but enough to let you know the ceiling is much lower here. You bend, until you can walk forward again.

With one hand held high to let you know if there are any further surprises, you crawl farther and deeper into the darkness. After some time, the ceiling opens up and you can stand straight again. While you ease your aching back, you take time to wonder why you are doing this.

After some deliberation, you admit that it is because, as a student of the ancient mysteries you *know* it is something important and that you must go on. You take time to collect your thoughts, to reach within yourself for courage, strength, and hope. Then you move on.

The walls begin to close in and the way is narrow. Soon, you have to force your body along the path. You long for the feel of cool fresh air and become all too conscious of the fact that the green fields and the bright Sun are far above you, that between you there are tons of rock and earth. You stop and, once more, reach within to find the determination to go on.

You begin to hallucinate. The walls glow and flash with color. Then you see them studded with gems that give off their own light. You can smell damp, wet earth and the stench of rotting plant life. You think you hear voices chanting ancient, long-forgotten hymns of praise to a god also long-forgotten. By now, you are simply putting one foot in front of the other, too tired to do anything but carry on. When you think of how long it will take you to return to the upper world you begin to weep silently, the tears offering a blessed coolness on cheeks that are feverish.

Ten more steps, you tell yourself, then you will turn back, then another ten, and another. Finally, your body rebels and your legs give way beneath you. It is too late to turn back. You no longer have the strength.

You lie on the damp earth, dreaming of rain, soft and cool, filling your mouth with sweet water. You can hear it drumming softly on the leaves over your head. You can hear a river close by. You think it is a dream. But the presence beside you is not a dream. It places a warm, strong hand over yours. A deep quiet voice bids you take heart, saying that what you have come seeking is within your reach. The hands help you to rise, and hold you steady while you find your feet. Grateful for the help, you lift your head and find yourself looking into the face of a god.

Pluto is tall and dark, with hair the color of a raven's back. His eyes are gray and full of wisdom, understanding, and humor. The broad shoulders take your weight and he helps you toward a dark, fast-flowing river where another, even bigger, man awaits. Pluto tells you to give him the coin you were given. Then you both take your seat in the boat and Charon rows you across the Styx. On the other side, there is an iron door reaching from floor to ceiling. Pluto raises a large fist and pounds on it. The door opens and a large, black dog hurls itself upon him. It leaps and barks and fusses around him like any dog welcoming its master. But this dog has three large heads, and three mouths, all filled with teeth.

Pluto leads you forward, then stops and urges you to go forward on your own. You do so and then stop, filled with wonder, awe, and a great joy that unfurls from within your soul and rises up in a shout of astonishment. Before you is a seashore of fine white sand. On either side stretch green trees filled with blossoms that scent the air. The ocean is a deep blue, like the wing of a hummingbird, and the waves, white-tipped, surge and ebb with the pull of the tide. Above you, there is a brilliant sun, not golden, like the Sun you know, but white-hot with a tinge of blue. Only one thing is different: this sun burns in a sky of utter blackness, studded with stars that shine with a brilliance you have never seen before. You look with eyes filled with wonder as you realize that you have the whole cosmos at your feet. You turn with questions on your lips.

Pluto comes and, with a hand on your shoulder and Cerberus bounding in front, you walk along the shores of the Sea of Dreams in the Land of the Summer Stars beneath the Sun at midnight. There are many things to see and learn here. Never again will the way be so hard and so fear-filled. There is a whole world to explore and Pluto will be your guide. As Apollo is to the world above, so Pluto is to the world below. In ancient times, he was the God Within, as Apollo was the God Without.

Learn to balance these two powers and you will have set your feet upon the road to divinity. If you visit this place often, you will come to know it well and, when the time of your physical death approaches, you will know that it is not what you feared, but simply a crossing of a bridge between the worlds. It is something you have done often. The way ahead is known to you. Remember this and you will *never* lose what you know and love. You cannot be separated, because you are part of a cosmic wholeness.

Before you is a small door of black and silver. Pluto gives you a key. Through this door is your own time and place. When you desire to come again, you will find the cave is now a door, a door to which you have the key. Go through it and awaken.

Pandora's Box

Think of a door that you know well. It can be your own front door, or a door leading into a garden. It can be the imposing door of a church or a library, or it can be a door that simply leads into your office at work. Build it in your mind with as much detail as you can. Mentally reach out and touch it, feel the wood. Take hold of the handle or doorknob and feel its smoothness. Now open the door wide.

You are looking into a landscape of great beauty. Soft green hills and wooded valleys. High mountains to the right side and a blue ocean to the left. This is the Greece of long ago before it was given that name, before the land was damaged by being overgrazed by sheep and goats, before wars had ebbed and flowed across it. Long before Atlantis plunged to its destruction. This is the western side of Greece, a place once known as Arcady. Step over the threshold and, as you do, feel yourself change.

Turn around and you will see that the door on this side is a mirror. You see a young girl with long light-brown hair twisted into a mass of curls on top of her head. Her eyes are brown and full of the joy of youth. She is classically beautiful and charming, with a smile that would lighten any heart. Her dress is of fine linen in a shade of the palest lavender. A cord of gold holds in the waist and, on her feet, she wears soft leather sandals. Around her neck is a string of pearls and coral beads. Look at yourself and take time, not just to look, but to feel the essence of the person you have become.

You are Pandora, created by the gods as a gift to mankind. But you are also a test for this newly created world. You have been given a box and told that, no matter what happens, it must never, ever be opened. You see it at your feet now, made of wood and carved with symbols covered with gold leaf. When you pick it up, it feels heavy and you wonder what is in it and why mankind needs to be warned about its danger.

You think about this as you look out over the valley. You are but newly created yourself and there are many things you do not understand. But you place your trust in the gods. You pick up the box and begin to walk down into the valley.

Time has passed and now you sit in a house, looking out of the window over fields of ripe corn. Several years have gone by since you first came here. You are now married and have two small children. Your husband is an important man and you have everything you could wish for. But your husband keeps asking you about the box and its contents. When you first arrived, he was content with your explanation that the gods did not want the box opened. He looked upon it and its mysterious contents as a dowry. But lately, he and his family have tried to persuade you to open it. They are certain it contains gold and jewels that you are keeping for yourself.

You sigh and call your servants to you. There is a feast tonight and many important people will come to eat at your table. As always, your husband will place the box in the center where people can see it and wonder. He feels it makes him more important in the eyes of his neighbors. He is a greedy man.

With your servants, you arrange the table and the long couches where your guests will lie as they eat in the fashion of the times. The dishes are arranged with bowls of flowers and fruit in between them. Fish baked with herbs, creamy cheeses, and freshly baked bread. Meat cooked in wine and spiced with small hot seeds. Bread dipped in honey and covered with sesame seeds are placed next to bowls of perfumed water for the cleansing of hands and fingers. Wine and cups are placed on a separate table and young girls wait to pour it for your guests.

Now they begin to arrive, led in by your husband. His eyes go immediately to the box set up in the center of the table. Everyone is seated and the feast begins. The wine flows freely, for your husband is a wealthy man and likes his wealth to be seen. The evening passes and the torches are lit. The guests are flushed with their feasting and you, as always, watch quietly. You care little for such displays of excess. You eat sparingly and drink little, contenting yourself with seeing that your guests have all they need. You hope that your husband will not mention the box, but that hope is soon dashed as he rises to his feet, his cup held high.

In a loud and somewhat slurred voice, he invites everyone to look upon the treasure of his house. It is taken down and passed from hand to hand. This has happened so many times that you ignore it. They cannot open it. Only you know how to do this. As always, the conversation turns to the subject of what the box contains. But tonight, your husband is determined to know. He catches you by the arm and pulls you to the table. In a loud voice, he demands that you open the box and display the wealth he is certain lies within.

You struggle against his strength and protest that the gods themselves have warned you about opening the box. He brushes aside your words and boasts that this is his house and you are his wife and your duty is to him and not to the gods. In vain, you plead with him. The drunken guests take up the chant of "Open the box." Your arm is twisted up behind you and your husband's voice is low and threatening. "Open the box or I will kill you and take another wife."

You think of your children, left to the mercies of another woman, and bow your head. You breathe a prayer to the gods, asking forgiveness for what you are about to do. As you take the box in your hands, a silence falls upon the revelers. They lean forward, eyes bright with anticipation—the women licking their lips in thought of the jewels they expect to see, the men hoping for gold or maybe some magical gift that the gods have withheld from humankind.

In your heart, you know that this is a moment when time itself stands still in horror. With a few deft movements, you unlock the box. Your husband snatches it from you and opens it with a roar of triumph. For a moment, he makes no sound as he looks into the empty interior. Then, from the box comes a hum, as if a thousand angry bees were swarming. A great cloud of darkness erupts from the box and fills the room.

You call for your children, and sweeping them up, you run from the house, running from what you know will be destruction. You make for the temple, the only place where you can hope to find refuge and safety from the destruction that is about to engulf your town.

Behind you, the house echoes with screams of fear, anguish, and pain. People stagger from the doors, covered with sores and boils, and spotted with fever. The cloud of fear, disease, epidemic, and death follows them. It covers the whole town and then moves on to spread throughout the whole world. In the temple, you weep and cover your terrified children with your cloak, praying to Zeus to forgive you. The night of terror passes and the dawn breaks over a silent town. What had been a thriving community, is now a place of death. Those who have been spared walk numbly among their dead. Those who screamed for you to open the box now scream at you for doing so. A few take up stones and throw them. It is no longer safe for you here.

You take your children and walk back to what was once your home. The streets are full of bodies. People who tried to flee from the cloud of death were overtaken even as they ran. You enter the house to find chaos. Your husband lies dead, the box now closed again beside him. His face is twisted with anger and fear. The servants lie where they dropped. It is the same all over the town. As you prepare to leave this place of death, you hear a voice calling your name. It is coming from the box. At first, you ignore it, in case something even worse is trapped inside. But the voice is insistent. Finally, you open the lid.

From within, there comes a small winged figure that grows larger, until it is seen as a Being of Light. It hovers before you and speaks gently.

"Have no fear. It was inevitable that this would happen, for mankind must make many mistakes before it learns to trust. You kept your promise for as long as you could. Because of this, you and your children will live. I am the spirit of Hope and the gods placed me in the box so that I might lessen the fear that it contained. From now on, I shall dwell with humanity and, in me, they will see the promise of the future. Have no regrets, for what is learned from this will shape the future of the whole world. Go now, Pandora, and take your children into that world. Live your life as best you can. There is nothing that can imprison what has been set free, but look upon me, Hope, and know that all is not lost while I am in the world."

You bow your head in acceptance and take up the bundle of provisions. With your children, you make your way up the valley toward the doorway through which you came. As you walk, your children change and become grown. They grow old as they walk beside you, then disappear to become part of the land. You walk, until you see before you the doorway through which you entered. You pause and look back over the valley. You have learned that you must have no regrets. It is part of the ongoing lessons of life. Pass on through the door, into your own world and your own time.

The Healing Spring
(Women only)

Relax and allow your body to talk to you. Begin with your feet: feel them, flex them, ask yourself if they hurt, ache, or give you any kind of discomfort. If so, note how it feels and move on to your ankles, legs, and knees. Again, note any pain or discomfort. Now, move on up to the thighs and hips, taking particular note of the joints. Women suffer more than men in this area, perhaps because their legs are attached to the hips at a slightly different angle.

Now, look at the genital area. This includes the uterus, ovaries, etc. Note even the smallest thing, then move up to the abdomen and the area covering the spleen, pancreas, liver, and stomach. Take your time and allow your body to tell you where to look and to feel. Next, the lungs, heart, breasts, followed by the hands, arms, shoulder joints, and neck. Don't forget to look at the length of the spine separately. Finally, the head, covering the ears, eyes, nose, and throat and the hair, as well as the more obvious brain.

Go over anything you have noted that may need healing, easing, strengthening, or just rejuvenation. Keep the information tucked away inside your head. Now, let yourself float, as if you were on the verge of sleep. Gradually, become aware of the scent of the sea, the sound of waves on a beach, and the cry of seabirds. There is a breeze on your face, its coolness taking the sting out of the hot sun.

Open your inner eye. You stand on a beach. The sand is warm beneath your feet and the sun hot on your skin. Overhead, the sky is brilliantly blue, with small clouds floating like white swans on a blue sea. You walk along the beach with your feet in the water. It is warm and soothing, so you lie down and let the warm waves flow over you and caress your whole body.

Far above you, a seabird calls and you sit up and look around. The beach is horseshoe-shaped, with high cliffs surrounding it. One has to either swim or sail into it, for there is no other way in. You get up and begin to walk toward the cliffs. As you get nearer, you see traces of an ancient stairway cut into the rock. In places, the steps have almost been worn away, but it looks inviting. Slowly and carefully, you begin to climb.

As you get higher, you see carvings cut into the rock. Shells, leopards, fish, birds, and strange symbols that mean nothing to you, but seem to be older than the others. The beach is now far below you and it makes you dizzy to look down. From here, you can look out over the sea toward other small islands. Most are rocky, but some contain grass and flowers and small trees. You begin to climb again. Suddenly, the steps are less broken, firmer, much easier to climb. Soon, you can see the outline of a cave above you and the steps lead toward it.

When you reach the cave, it smells damp and salty and looks rather uninviting. The floor slopes downward but is covered with fine sand and is gentle to your bare feet. You hear a woman's voice singing, but you cannot be sure. Ahead, there is a dim green light, as if the light were coming from under the sea. You can also hear the sound of fast-moving water.

You see a pool ahead fed by a waterfall. Beyond that, through a small opening, you can see another pool in the sunlight, but there seems no way to get to it. The path leads directly to the pool and, as you look down, you can see that, beneath the water, there is an opening through which sunlight is filtering. This is the way to the other pool. With no hesitation, you dive in and swim down through the clear water toward the sunfilled opening far below.

It is very cold, almost numbing. But in the green semidarkness, you feel the presence of other beings. Small but strong hands gently guide and push you toward the archway. The flow of the water helps you and you duck under the rocky arch and rise up to the surface. The water, though cold, has a cleansing effect on your body as you rise.

Your head breaks the surface close to the rock face behind another waterfall. You float on the water, supported by the gentle hands of the sea nymphs. They press and massage every part of your body. Sometimes, it feels as if their hands actually enter your body and heal it from the inside. But the coldness is telling on you. They pass you from hand to hand and, with a quick push, send you through the waterfall and into much warmer water.

This second pool is very different from the first. It is part of a small crater, long extinct. Its waters are warm, slightly carbonated, and pinkish in color from the iron content. They have an herbal scent to which you cannot quite put a name, strong but not unpleasant. They soothe and calm you. All around the pool rise sheer cliffs except for one spot where a series of flat, smooth lava flows form a natural resting place.

You swim to these rocks, lift yourself from the water, and lie in the sun, soaking up the light and warmth. Seeds brought by birds have fastened in the crevices of the rocks and their flowers form a curtain a brilliant color that softens the rock face and fills the air with fragrance. The sun eases the last of the icy coldness from your bones. You feel full of light and a sense of well-being. After a while, you slide back into the water. It has a healing quality that soaks into every part of you. You can feel your body easing, straightening, healing, and growing stronger.

Your breasts grow firmer, your skin smoother, your hair is thicker, and every muscle tightens and lifts. More than this, the very core of your womanhood is revived. The womb and uterus lift and grow firm, the pelvic muscles and the vagina become as they were when you were young. You sink below the surface, allowing the water access to every part of you, cleansing and clearing.

When you rise to the surface again, you find you are no longer alone. Sitting on the rock is a woman. In face and form, she is perfection. This arouses no jealousy within you, for you know her. She is your goddess, the immortal Aphrodite herself. You were brought here at her request that she might give of her bounty to you. You lift your hands in supplication and hail her.

"Hail Beauteous One, Hail Aphrodite, Goddess of Love, giver of pleasure and joy. Pearl of the Ocean, Hail."

She smiles and accepts your praise and beckons you to join her. Together, you sit and she teaches you many things. Tell her of your problems and she will counsel you. The long hours pass, filled with the joy of being near her. At last, as the shadows lengthen, she gives to you a small golden whistle in a fine chain. This she hangs about your neck. It will be invisible to all but you. When you wish to return to the pool, blow it and her chariot will come for you.

You put it to your lips and blow. A sweet note echoes back from the rock cliffs. You hear the beating of wings and there, descending into the crater, is a golden chariot drawn by four graceful leopards and surrounded by a cloud of snow-white doves. You and the goddess step into it and are drawn up into the sky, now filled with the golden glow of sunset.

Far below, you can see the little beach where your adventure began. You also see that the pool cannot possibly be reached in any way other than through the inner pool or by the chariot. You fly over the sea toward the bank of dark clouds that herald the onset of night.

Aphrodite turns to you and tells you not to forget what she has told you, that you may return to the pool whenever you have need of its healing qualities. She may not always be there. She may be needed elsewhere. But you are free to use the pool. You may even bring along a friend. She tells you to place your trust in her, and asks you to jump from the chariot. There is a brief hesitation and then you comply. You fall gently, slowly, head over heels, through the clouds. It feels as if you are flying.

You look toward the setting Sun and marvel at its colors reflected in the clouds and sky. Birds are winging homeward to roost and you must return to your own time and place. For a moment, you fall into a soft warm darkness and then you are back in your physical body. Stretch your arms and legs, wriggle your fingers and toes, and slowly come back to reality. If you wish to return to the pool for healing, go through the icy pool, for that helps to cleanse the body. If you simply wish to relax, then call the chariot.

3

Alexandrian Pathworkings

If ever there was a golden age, chances are it would have occurred in the heyday of Alexandria. The destruction of the Great Library was one of the most devastating acts of vandalism ever perpetrated by fanatics. There have been others, but this one act destroyed knowledge we will never be able to reassemble.

It was a time when many traditions walked and talked together, if not in complete harmony, at least in an agreement to differ. It was a meeting place for the old, the new, and the potential. Many gods had their temples there, and over all of them stood the great Serapeum. To study there, all that was required was an open intellect and an open mind. The past, the present, and the future met and mingled there in harmony.

Alexandria was the dream of Alexander, the city of Cleopatra and Mark Antony. Rich in treasure and ideas, its glory was the Pharos, a light that guided ships to safety. Its library was such a light for the mind; its teachers were a light for the soul. Alexandria's predecessor was Heliopolis, and much of its library came from there, including the famous scrolls concerning Atlantis shown to Solon hundreds of years before.

I have chosen three pathworkings to represent this era. The first concerns the finding of a great seer of Apollo, a rare event and one filled with emotion. The second deals with the lost tomb of Antony and Cleopatra and is pure speculation, though it is believed that Antony's tomb exists beneath the modern city. Others believe the tomb of Alexander himself may yet be discovered. The last working concerns the feelings and emotions of the last priest of On (Heliopolis) as he closes the door of his temple for the last time and walks away.

The Choosing

Sit comfortably in your chair and close your eyes. Slow your breathing gradually, making each breath longer, deeper, and slower. As you do this, imagine that you can feel the heat of the Sun on your face and body. Feel it through your clothing, as if you were outside on a very hot summer day.

Now, with your eyes closed, begin to listen, now and then checking back to feel the heat of the Sun. Listen for sounds you would hear in a busy harbor: voices shouting, water slapping against wooden hulls, the rattle of chains as anchors are weighed, the rumble of wheels as wagons are driven past you, and the lowing of the oxen that pull them.

Time now to bring in the smells. First, the salty sea air, the breeze laden with a new, strange, and spicy scent. The smell of wet sails drying in the sun, and the smell of the oxen and their droppings. Add to this the smell of human sweat of many people working hard for long hours.

With your eyes still closed, begin now to feel. Feel the smoothness of polished stone beneath your hands and your buttocks, the feel of coarse linen garments on your body and the heaviness of leather sandals on your feet, the feeling of fullness in your stomach and the sharp taste of fruit in your mouth, as if you had lately eaten.

Now, open your eyes and take in the scene around you. It is within a few hours of noon and the Sun is hot and bright. Its rays bounce off the deep blue of the water that almost surrounds you, dazzling your eyes. Before you is a busy harbor, with ships being loaded and unloaded by sweating laborers. Here and there stand others who look like soldiers, with short white kilts and leather breastplates and helmets. They carry round shields and are armed with long spears and short swords that hang at their sides.

The sails of the ships carry painted designs, some of which are familiar, others not so easily deciphered. You are sitting on a wall of white stone running alongside the main jetty. Directly opposite, on the other side of the harbor is a breakwater of the same white stone. At the end of its considerable length stands an enormous building towering up in three distinct levels. On the very top is a small domed building pierced with arches. From this distance, you can see only clouds of smoke coming from it, but you know that, at night, a great fire can be seen that throws out light to the incoming ships on the dark seas. You also know that you are in Alexandria, that you are a first-level initiate of the Great Library, and that, if you do not hurry, you will be late for a very important ceremony.

You jump from your perch on the wall and hurry to where a narrow street begins. It is thronged with people and you have to push your way through. How could you have been so stupid as to forget what day this is and go dreaming by the harbor?

Many people here are going the same way, to the big open square facing the steps of the Great Library. You break into a run and soon come out into the square itself. It is packed with people, but you duck down a side street and head for a small door set into the stone wall that surrounds the library. As you hurry, you go over what you know of this body you are using.

You are young—barely 19 years old—and you have lived in the library and temple since you were 7. It was then that you were brought by your parents and the local priest to be assessed for your fitness to enter the famous school. You had been dreaming true dreams since you were 3 years old and the priest persuaded your parents to bring you here.

When you were chosen, you cried, for you knew you would not see your parents again for many years. They were long lonely years, for you do not make friends easily. Neither are you a very good student. You tend to dream too much and forget your duties as a priest of Apollo, the god of the Sun, of healing, but most of all, of prophesy.

You have dutifully told your dreams to the teacher each morning, but you cannot keep your mind on the mundane work you have to do. You would much rather watch the nature spirits that are so clear to you, or play with the water sprites in the fountains. You enjoy working in the gardens and helping to increase the energies of the plants and herbs that are grown there. You like lying in the sun and thinking about the great god that drives its chariot across the sky.

Sometimes, he speaks with you and you laugh together. Once, in a dream, he showed you how Earth looks from his chariot. You know him, not as a bright shining god, but as a friend, and you love him dearly. But you are clumsy and awkward and forever dropping or spilling things, and you know you are the despair of your teachers.

Today is special for many reasons. First, it is the day when many of your friends will be accepted into the next level of the priesthood. You are pleased and happy for them and, although you know there is no chance you will be selected for further training, you are content and hold no jealousy, but wish them well.

Also, your parents will be here at the invitation of the priesthood, along with the parents and families of your colleagues. This will be only the third time you have seen them since you entered the school. They live many days' journey away and cannot easily leave their little farm. But most of all, it is a day for rejoicing. The High Priest has let it be known that a true Apollonian seer has been found in the priesthood and today will be installed at high noon in the Serapeum before the assembled throng of people and priests.

You are now hurrying down a corridor to the little dormitory you share with five others. The room is empty, so they have already left. In a panic, you wash your hands and face and throw off your plain linen robe, now badly stained with tar, mud, and dust. Sandals are kicked under your narrow bed and you hastily rummage through the wooden chest by the bed for your temple robe.

It is of fine linen, fringed with blue on the sleeves and the hem. About your waist you knot a blue cord, thrusting your feet into your best sandals as you do so. Then you rush out of the door and along the corridor toward the Great Hall. You can hear the chanters beginning the invocation and the sound of the drums, harps, and flutes. The ceremony is starting! You round the next corner at a run and almost knock down an old priest coming the other way. Breathlessly, you help him to recover his balance and mutter apologies. He rolls his eyes to heaven and shakes his head and looks after you as you scurry into the antechamber with seconds to spare.

Your companions silently make a place for you and you try desperately to control your breathing as the hymn to Apollo begins. Your heart is still racing as you enter the hall and process through the rows of columns toward the golden statue that stands at the far end and is reached by a flight of marble steps. The public crowds together at the near end, the chanters and priests of the lower ranks take their places in the middle facing the altar, with the higher ranks facing each other across the wide floor with its mosaic of the Sun God in his chariot drawn by four fiery horses. And so the rite begins.

As always, as the ceremony moves on, you feel your attention drawn toward the translucent forms that gather above the heads of the people. Beautiful beyond description, these beings are made of pure light and always appear when any ritual, no matter how small, is being performed. Entranced, you watch them join with the humans as they chant and pray and invoke the presence of Apollo.

Now is the moment when the Master of Novices will summon those deemed worthy of advancement to the altar, there to receive the white robe with its gold-embroidered collar and the golden cord that will proclaim their full priesthood. Slowly, the Master walks along the line of bowed heads. Now and then, he stops and taps a novice on the shoulder. Immediately, they step forward, shaking with excitement. Then the Master of Novices leads them in a dignified procession around the hall to the shouts and cheers of the people and the gentle smiles and approving nods of their peers.

You join with them in wishing your friends well. You know in your heart that such honors are not for you. You are too clumsy, too distracted by the beauties of the inner world to be worthy of the golden collar. Now, the newly made priests have taken their places in the higher ranks. It is time for the High Priest to make his announcement. It is almost noon and the Sun approaches that time when its rays will shine directly through the opening in the roof and light up the golden statue. Standing on the steps, the highest priest in the land speaks to the people, telling them that, after almost a generation, a true Apollonian seer has been found, an oracle who will speak for the Golden God. One who will, from now on, guide them on life's road.

At his behest, all bow their heads and fold their hands. You obey with the rest, your heart beating like a drum and full of adoration for Apollo. You wish the unknown seer well with all your heart, for it will surely be a hard and lonely role. You vow to pray for the seer every night and morning and to make a special offering to Apollo to help this chosen one.

The High Priest descends the steps and begins to pass the ranks of the priesthood. When he passes the highest rank without choosing, there is a low murmmer of amazement, for this means the seer will come from a lower rank. When he continues past the next level, wherein stand those newly raised, the murmur becomes a buzz of breathless excitement as speculation grows.

But you are alone with your thoughts and prayers, eyes closed as you profess your love and willingness to serve the one chosen. You do not see the High Priest pause before you. Only when you feel the touch of his hand do you open your eyes and see him smile and hold out his hand. He speaks your name three times and calls you forth from the ranks of the most humble level of the priesthood.

In a daze, you stumble forward, shaking your head and whispering that it cannot be you, it cannot be, cannot be. The god must have someone of power and worth, not a clumsy fool. But the High Priest takes you by the hand and leads you firmly toward the flight of marble steps. There, he lets go of your hand and steps back, pointing to the statue above you.

You look up, your heart in your throat. This cannot be true. Silently, you beg the god to speak to tell them it is a mistake. Then, you see the statue change and become a young man, golden of skin and hair. Smiling, he beckons you to him and you mount the steps one by one, your hands held out to the wondrous being that is calling you to him. You can see and hear only him.

Below you, the crowd is cheering and shouting your name, calling for a blessing from the new great seer. Apollo whispers in your ear and you turn around to face them.

At that precise moment, the Sun strikes down through the opening and invests you with light, surrounding you with an aura of flaming gold. With a single gasp of wonder, the crowd falls silent, mouths agape. Then as one, they kneel.

Bathed in sunlight, you and the statue have become one and even the priests bow down, awed into silence by what is happening. In the midst of the crowd, an elderly couple hold hands and watch, with tears running down their cheeks, as the person that was once their child, their little son, takes on the burden of the seer of Apollo.

You look out over their heads and time seems to stop as you look into the future unrolling before you. Your senses reel at what you see. You see the wars and the intrigues, the fall of the Great Library and the burning of its treasures. You see Rome rise to become a great power and fall, to rise again. You see darkness and despair settling over the ancient lands and the coming of new gods, new faiths, and new religions.

You see a gentle man nailed to a cross because he spoke of love. You see those who follow him killed and tortured and yet conquering in their turn. You see changes sweeping across Earth, the joys and fears, the suffering and the progress. Men fly in machines and travel beneath the sea. They circle the globe at the speed of Hermes the Messenger. They touch the surface of the Moon and look beyond it to the stars.

Suddenly, you understand the real burden of the seer. It is not what you can tell them, it is what you do not tell them. You must prepare them for what lies ahead in their time only. The rest must be kept for a very few. Your first task must be to see that every single scroll and book is copied. Then a place must be found where this knowledge can be hidden until it is safe for it to be given out once more. This is the single most important task that you must complete. In the meantime, you must speak to those who now wait before you, hoping for a prophecy of peace and plenty. For a while, you can give them this reassurance, but only for a little while.

The Sun's rays lessen and pass, the presence leaves you with words of comfort and the promise that it will always be with you. You lift your head, your shoulders straighten to take on the burden. In the distance, you can see the awed faces of your parents. You begin to speak. Gently, let go of this persona and return to your own time and place, and rest.

The Tomb of Antony and Cleopatra

Make yourself comfortable and prepare to enter the space between the worlds. Close your eyes and concentrate on your breathing, slowing it down, deepening the intake of air until you are fully relaxed. After a few minutes, open your inner eye and find yourself in Stygian blackness. Do not move. Allow your senses to speak to you. It is very cold. Feel the prickle of your raised flesh and the icy feel of the faint draft that reaches you from somewhere far ahead. The air has the smell of dampness and the taste of ancient dust.

The only thing you can hear is the slow drip of water close by. It has a hollow sound and from this you surmise that you are somewhere underground with a lot of space. A cave perhaps. There is no fear, you are content to wait until something happens. You know you cannot be harmed, that around you there is a protection that cannot be breached unless the threat comes from within you. You also know intuitively that you have come here to this place for a specific purpose.

Somewhere ahead of you, there is movement. You can hear the slow, steady tread of one who knows the way. In the distance, you see a pinpoint of light that moves from side to side and grows larger with every second. The footfall is firm and sure. Then a voice splits the silence with a suddenness that makes you jump a little.

"Take heart, traveler. I am almost with you."

As the light comes nearer, you begin to see more of your present surroundings. It is indeed a cave of considerable proportions and great age. Around you are the remnants of an ancient building, the stones and pillars tumbled and broken as if by a tremendous force. Here and there is the gleam of gold, a chalice, a statue, a broken marble table, all shattered. It is as if Earth had opened and the building had dropped into it. Though very cold, it is not freezing. This accounts for the water dripping from the roof far above your head.

Out of the darkness, carrying a torch, comes a man, not too tall, but sturdily built. He wears a thick robe of dark-blue wool that he has caught up with a leather belt in order not to get the hem wet. Around his shoulders is a cloak of the same thick weave, and, praise be, he has another one for you. As he unfolds it and throws it about you, you see that his face is somewhat round and his eyes show the corner wrinkles gained by looking into far distances and against the Sun. His hair has receded until it is just a half-circle about his head. Though no longer young and trim of figure, he carries himself like a soldier, with the slightly rolling gait of one who has ridden a horse for most of his life. On his forehead, faded but still visible, you can see the mark that declares him to be a follower of Mithras.

"Now come, we must make the best of the time we have," he tells you.

"Why am I here?" Your voice echoes in the darkness.

"Why, to see the tomb, of course, the tomb of Mark Antony and Cleopatra, Queen of Egypt."

He leads you back the way he came, following a straight corridor cut from the living rock. The ceiling is not very high and carries the mark of the torches used to light the way for strangers for many hundreds of years. As you walk, your guide talks, telling you what you have been brought to see.

"A remarkable tomb and seen only by those who have been chosen by the Collegia Sancta. You are most fortunate. They have not sent anyone here for a long time. Tell me what has passed in the world above since I took up my duties?"

Perhaps it is the tone of voice, or the way the question is phrased. You feel impelled to ask how long it is since he became a "caretaker," which he obviously is. He chuckles and shakes his head.

"A long time, a very long time."

You persist in your question, so he stops and turns to face you.

"I was his body servant, his right hand. I held him as he died. Then I brought his body to the queen and I laid him in her arms and wept with her."

The words are quiet and simple, but mind-blowing. You draw a breath and try to formulate your next question coherently.

"Mark Antony died before the birth of Christ. Are you saying that you have been here since then?"

"I offered myself as the tomb guardian of two people I loved more than life. The gods heard my prayer and granted it. For a while, I lived 'up there.' But over the years, fewer people came to see the tomb and make offerings. Then, one day, Earth quaked and the ground sank beneath me and we went down together, the tomb and I. As you have seen, everything was broken, destroyed, only the tomb itself was intact. I saved what I could, and for a long time, I worked to clear the debris and make some semblance of a sacred space about them.

At first, I grew a little older, but then time stopped for me. I no longer needed to eat or drink or sleep. I just . . . waited. I know one day it must end, but I do not know how. Maybe the tomb will be discovered and my task will be ended. Maybe it will all be destroyed completely and myself with it. Who knows? Only the gods."

You come to a strong wooden door set into the wall. The guardian takes out a bunch of keys and opens it. Pushing it open, he indicates that you are to enter. The space is not very large, but it has been kept meticulously clean and well-preserved. The guardian hastens to light more torches and you see before you a curtain of royal-purple silk edged with intricate gold embroidery. With reverent hands, the curtain is drawn back to reveal the tomb of legend. Whatever it was that you had expected, it was not this—this magnificent tribute to an eternal love.

The tomb itself is a couch covered with the same imperial purple as the curtain. On it lie two figures. The clean-shaven man is of medium height, broad in shoulder and chest. His arms are those of a man used to fighting, well-muscled and corded with veins. He wears a simple white tunic bordered and belted with gold. His light-brown hair, lightly sprinkled with gray, is curly and cut short to fit beneath his helmet. He lies on his back, his head turned toward his love, his well-formed lips smiling even in death.

She lies on her side, held within the circle of his arm, her head resting upon his shoulder, one leg lifted to lay over his. Her hair is as glossy and as black as it was on the day her world came to an end. It flows over her like a curtain and one lustrous strand is caught and held by her beloved Antony. She seems, they both seem, only to sleep. Surely in a moment she will open her eyes and lift herself, bending over him to kiss his lips and waken him to life and love.

Her light robe, like his, is simple, the color of the Nile at dawn, and embroidered with small golden fishes. A silk coverlet lies across the foot of the couch and curled in a corner lies a sleek black cat. At head and foot, two more figures complete the scene. Iras and Charmian watch over their queen in death.

Over the whole group is a dome of pure crystal, enclosing and encompassing Cleopatra and her Antony as they sleep forever. Below the steps on the right side of the tomb are displayed Cleopatra's royal robes, her jewelery, the vulture crown topped with a circle of twelve royal serpents, and the crook and the flail of majestic power. On the left, a wooden stand holds Mark Antony's golden armor, a scarlet cloak draped across it. His sword and shield lean against a small marble table on which stands his helmet with its white plume.

It is right that this should be hidden from all but those who have earned the right to be here. This is not for the eyes of the masses, an object of curiosity, whispers, and glances. Here the nobility of royal death is seen for what it really is. The silence holds the dust of eternity. *[Narrator pauses here for 2 to 3 minutes.]* After a time, you turn and ask the guardian a question.

"Why was I brought here?"

"Because you need to know and understand how powerful love can be. It is the first, last, and most enduring law of the cosmos. It creates miracles in its own name. There was no embalming of my master and his queen, their love keeps them uncorrupted. It keeps me here, undying until the gods decide it is time for it to end. If you are ready I will escort you back."

He picks up a torch and lights it, with a backward glance to see if you are following. He leaves the little temple and the sleeping lovers. You follow him down the dark corridor, noting how different it is from the warm, dry atmosphere you have just left. As you follow your guide, you notice small marks incised in the wall. There are so many that you cannot count them. Every now and then, there is a circle instead of a mark.

"What are these markings?"

He answers without turning his head. "They are the days I have spent guarding them. From the beginning, I have marked each day and each Full Moon. On that day, I pray and offer thanks. On other days, I just . . . remember. We are here."

You ask one more question. "What is your name, Guardian?"

"Once I was Flavius Quintus, but that was long ago."

"Be blessed now and forever, Flavius Quintus. All honor to thee in thy service of love."

He smiles and bows, accepting your blessing. The torch flickers and dies, leaving you in darkness. You wait, knowing that all will be well and remembering the examples of love you have been shown—the love of two people whose physical love transcended the four worlds, and the love of the faithful servant. After a while, the darkness lightens, the air becomes sweeter and warmer. You feel the chair beneath you and your feet upon the floor. You know, without being conscious of it, that you have crossed the centuries and come safely to your own time and place.

The Last Priest of On

Close your eyes and begin to breathe in a four-in and four-out rhythm. Allow yourself to sink deeply into a meditative state, concentrating upon a single white light. Watch it intently and see it begin to enlarge, like the iris of a camera opening up. Slowly, you begin to see before you the blindingly white walls of an ancient city.

With startling suddenness, you are standing before one of the many gates that lead into the city of On. That was once its name, On, or Aun in the Egyptian language. Then the Greeks came and slowly it became Heliopolis, the city of the Sun. This is very apt, for the sun beats down on it relentlessly, making it difficult to see directly.

As you pass beneath the gate, you realize that the walls are at least five to six feet thick and there is a pleasant coolness as you pass into the shade. One might expect that a city such as this would be full of people, a bustling market town, especially since it was famous for its many temples. So it is something of a shock to find the city almost deserted. Everywhere, there are empty houses, most of them falling into decay. Roofs have fallen in and courtyards are full of debris and forgotten household rubbish.

The streets still run in every direction, most, it seems, ending in a gate leading to a temple, some large and others quite small. You venture into some of them. Inside, there are empty storerooms, pieces of broken statuary, pools that have grown stagnant or dried up completely. Within the sanctuaries, most of the sacred statues have gone, a few lie broken. In the inner Adytums, all is empty and silent.

Outside, in the heat of the day, nothing moves. The marketplace is almost empty, with just a few stalls selling vegetables, pottery, and similar goods. Those people who remain in the city are sleeping in the heat of the day.

You walk slowly down the widest street, looking from left to right, peering into houses, shutterless windows, and deserted courtyards. On the roofs, birds have nested, adding to the overall atmosphere of decay. Somewhere a child cries and is hushed into sleep. Camels groan and grumble and goats bleat restlessly.

Is this proud On, city of the Ben-Ben bird, the immortal phoenix? The city of a hundred temples? The place where Solon came to study? Where he received initiation at the hands of priests who came from an unbroken line that stretched back to Atlantis? Where he was shown records saved from the Great Flood? Where are the priests, the acolytes, the wise men and women, the ancient books?

Before you is yet another temple, its gate broken and swinging loose. But this, at least, shows signs of being cared for. The courtyard has been swept clean, the central pool is full of water, and lotus buds are opening in the heat of the day. You cross the empty space and pause before the open door leading into the sanctuary.

A man appears in the doorway. He does not see you, but goes to the pool and, with a small knife gathers and cuts a bunch of lotus flowers. When he returns, you follow him into the temple. Inside, the temple is lit with a few small torches burning in holders on the walls. The light is increased by the flames coming from two tripods standing on either side of a statue of Osiris, Isis, and the child Horus. Incense sweetens the air and flowers adorn the pillars and the altar. All that is missing is a crowd of worshipers making their offering before the altar.

The priest moves silently about his small tasks, feeding the burners with fragrant herbs, renewing burned-out torches sweeping the ever present dust from the floor. The lotus flowers he places in a clay pot at the feet of the gods. Finally, he kneels and begins his prayers.

You watch this lonely man, whose faith alone has sustained him as, one by one, the temples closed and its priesthood left for other, more prosperous, towns. A new regime has arisen in Egypt and the focus has shifted to the Great Library in Alexandria. The libraries and treasures of On, Memphis, and Abydos have been sent to the new capital.

The new dynasties have no Egyptian blood and even the gods are given new names. But here, they are still worshiped as they have been for three thousand years. But the people have stopped coming to the temples and there is little call for the priests, even as healers, and none at all as teachers and trainers of a new generation of priesthood.

In the quietness of the temple, you hear the priest weep for what has gone. He rocks to and fro, calling on the names of gods who seem to have deserted him. Yet his indestructible faith shines through and sustains him. He looks into the serene faces above him and asks for guidance. Far into the night, he prays and weeps. Finally, he sleeps.

The silence is profound; the lights flicker and burn low. A single ray of moonlight finds a broken tile in the roof and steals through to shine lovingly on the face of the sleeping man. It surrounds him with light. As we watch, into that light step two pairs of feet, feet that do not quite touch the earth. The smaller pair shine with a silvery light, the other, larger, pair are golden. In the dimness, beyond the moonlight, we see the two statues have come to life and left their pedestals to stand at the head and foot of their lone worshiper.

The gentle voice of Isis is heard once more in the sanctuary. "Hat-ab-Auser, truly are you named 'House of the Heart of Osiris.' You have been a faithful friend and now, in your loneliness and despair, you seek answers from us. The power we once wielded has been whittled away. But all things return to the point of beginning and we will come again, but after another fashion."

Now, the deeper tones of Osiris as he bends over his priest. "Beloved friend, faithful servant, all things must change, dissolve, and be renewed. Only the strongest are born into such times. You have endured your loneliness with strength and courage and now we ask even more of you. This is our command: Go forth with tomorrow's Sun and travel westward, as if seeking Amenti. You still have a vigorous life-force and with this, my sister-wife and I will establish a bloodline that will endure far into the future."

Isis takes up the thread. "It will not be an easy journey, but we will make it as easy as we can. Go to Alexandria and there look for a boat whose sail carries the Winged Disk. Ask its captain for passage in the name of Isis and it will be given to you. He sails for Rome. From there, you must find a ship to take you to Gaul. You will never return to the warm sun of Egypt in this life dear friend, but you will remain forever a priest of Osiris. In Gaul, you will make a friend, a man with one daughter whom you must take to wife. With her, you will forge a bloodline of seers that will never fail and from this line we will take our future priests and priestesses. Know that we will always be with you and, at the end, I will send my foster-son, Anubis, to bring you to us in Amenti. When you wake, overturn the altar and you will find beneath it our gift to you. Farewell."

The silence returns, the feet shimmer and disappear, and the priest stirs, sits up, and looks around. He jumps to his feet and seizes a torch, whirling it around his head to bring it to flame. In its light, he looks to the statues, but they have gone. The tripods are cold, the incense also. The sacred presence has withdrawn from the last temple.

He goes to the altar and, setting aside the torch, puts his strength against it. Slowly, it topples over and breaks. Inside it there is the shine of gold and jewels. The hidden hoard of a forgotten priest will now be used to complete the prophecy of Isis. For a long time, the priest stares at it, then he sets about making ready for the journey.

A little food, a skin of water, a warm cloak, and, beneath his robe, a leather pouch containing the gift of the gods. This and a stout staff of seasoned wood are all he will need. He puts out the torches and salutes the place where once stood his gods. Now he will carry them only within his heart.

He steps out into the early morning sun, blinking a little in its light. Then he closes the door of the temple and fastens it with a scarlet cord. Then he crosses the courtyard and steps through the gate. He pauses and looks back for a moment, then turns and set his face to the West. The last priest of On goes forth upon his quest.

4

Greco-Egyptian Pathworkings

This section of *The Initiate's Book of Pathworkings* brings together both Greek and Egyptian traditions. The first part is a portion of an actual ritual, but one that is complete in itself. If followed exactly, it will have a deep and lasting effect on the participants. It is not an easy working, but will repay the effort expended on its preparation.

Sekhmet is the "personal" goddess of the writer and has been since she was very young. This relationship began with a visitation by Sekhmet and the gift of a trio of leashed lion cubs. It has continued through the years to maturity. Seldom has the power of the cubs, now full-grown, been unleashed. Their owner is well aware of the consequences and her training has been such that her control of them is well established. This long association with this goddess has brought about strength and courage in adversity.

Aphrodite, though few know of it, can also be equated with the Lion-Headed Lady, for in Egypt, she is also Hathor, the Lady of Beauty and Love. Here she can be worked with in her Greek form to great advantage. Both men and women need the power of Aphrodite, for it balances them within on the emotional level and can bring about an inner healing of the heart center.

The working for Hecate carries a warning. It is extremely powerful and can bring about great changes in those who undertake the path. It is *not* to be used lightly. Read it through several times *without using any power,* before actually doing it. Worked with insight, courage, and common sense, it can change your whole outlook.

The Temple Beneath the Sphinx

This is a dramatized pathworking for several voices. It has been condensed from a larger ritual work by the same author.

Guide:
Companions of the Temple of Isis, I bid thee welcome. Let us prepare ourselves for our journey, a journey that will take us back to a more ancient time and place. We are together in this time and in this place for a purpose: to take the initiates' journey to the Land of Khem and on into the secret chamber beneath the ancient Sphinx. There will we meet one who will reveal to us a great and spiritual truth.

Before us, we see a doorway upon which is painted a picture of the tarot card "The World." This is one of the gateways of Malkuth. We step through and find ourselves in a cornfield. The corn is waist-high—ripe and golden. The sky above us is the deep azure blue of a late afternoon. The sun is warm upon our skins. We feel a sense of great peace and the worries and anxieties of that other time and place fall away from us.

Two figures approach us. Tall golden beings. A man and a woman. They are dressed simply in white linen garments. The man wears the red-and-white Double Crown of Upper and Lower Egypt. The woman has a silver circlet around her brow upon which is a silver crescent. These, O my Companions of the Temple, are the Lady Isis and her husband, brother, and love, the Risen Osiris. They greet us warmly and welcome us to their land, known in this time and in this place as Khem. They beckon us to follow them through the cornfield to a narrow pathway that leads down to a river. Waiting for us is a long reed boat with ten oarsmen ready for us to embark.

Isis and Osiris motion us to climb aboard and wish us well on our journey. As we step into the boat, they give a blessing to each one of us. We take our places. Then, silently, the boat leaves the bank and we begin our journey down the great River Nile. We can hear the dip of the oars and the splash of water. As we make our way, we watch in silence the tall ibis birds in the reeds, the fisherman and his young son casting their nets into the green water. Young dark-haired girls run laughing alongside the bank in an effort to keep up with us. Older women carry baskets and clay pots upon their heads. An old man driving his goats turns and leans on his staff to watch us go by. He raises his hand in salute.

We notice with surprise how green and fertile this land is—how different from the sand and desert we have come to expect. The Sun gets lower in the sky. It is not so warm now. A cool breeze ripples the waters of the river, which has now widened. In the twilight of early evening, we see other reed boats pass us by and hail us.

A shout from one of the oarsmen alerts us and we look up as we round the bend of the river. In wonder and awe, we see the three great pyramids ahead. They stand white and sharp against the evening sky, tipped with gold and orichalchum. They catch the dying rays of the Sun and welcome us with a flash of golden fire. But the greatest wonder is yet to come. The gigantic figure of the Sphinx looms behind the pyramids—not the crumbling, weather-beaten monument of our time, but sharp, every feature outlined and perfect, carved from white stone. The painted face of the Sphinx gazes serenely across his land with eyes of blue lapis. There is the hint of a smile about his painted lips, the lion's body strong, coiled, as if about to spring from his huge pedestal. For the first time, we feel a chill of apprehension run up our spines.

The Sphinx is raised up on a stone platform and the waters of the Nile have been diverted by way of a canal to follow a path to its base. Our boat turns into the canal. On both sides stand Egyptian guards in their short linen kilts of red and white, each holding a flaming torch to guide us. We are expected.

We pull up to the base of the Sphinx. Our oarsmen swiftly and expertly moor the boat to the steps. At the top of the steps, a man waits for us. He is tall, about 60 with white hair and beard. He is not a native of this land. He is dressed in a blue robe and seems strangely familiar to us, although we cannot recall his name. He greets us as we alight from the boat.

Elder:
Welcome to the Land of Khem. Before you can proceed into the sacred inner chamber of the Sphinx, you must seek permission of Pharaoh who rules over the Two Lands.

We follow our strange friend up the steps to a place between the paws of the mighty Sphinx. Here, seated on a small chair under a canopy of crimson and gold, is a young and beautiful man. He wears a blue-and-gold nemyss on his head and, in his hands, he holds the crook and the flail, symbols of his kingship as both the shepherd and judge of his people. Although he appears young to us, there is a wisdom and a thoughtfulness in his eyes and he greets us with a gentle nod. He looks at each of us in turn. Our friend explains to Pharaoh that we have come from another place on a long journey to learn the wisdom of the ancient and sacred site. Pharaoh smiles, but we notice a sadness in his smile.

Pharaoh:
I am Pharaoh, guardian and the king of the Two Lands. In your time, so much has been plundered, so much taken and destroyed from these sacred sites. Our tombs have been robbed, our dead taken from their resting places to be sent away from the sacred soil of their homeland. Our monuments have been desecrated, our temples destroyed, the great statues of our gods dismantled and sold to other nations. Yet such was the greatness and the wisdom of my people that we were given a great gift. That gift lies in the secret chamber beneath our feet. I

give you my permission to journey to the first level, for I can
see that you are travelers, that you come with wisdom and in
the name of light. But know you this: as I am the Crook, so
also am I the Flail. Respect this land, honor our wisdom and
our gods. Seek to understand our ways, even though you may
serve a different divinity. Know you this, that there is but *one
truth* that guides all.

He invites us to partake of wine, fruits, and sweet cakes
with him before we enter the chamber of the Sphinx. Eat of
the food and drink of the wine provided for us by Pharaoh.
As you do so, remember his words to us and recall them as
we take the next part of this journey. In silence, cups of wine
and plates of chopped fruit and small sweet cakes are offered, followed by bowls of rose-scented water for the washing of hands. And now, my brothers and sisters of the Lodge,
we have been given leave to enter into the chamber. Prepare
yourselves.

Close your eyes and listen to my words. We enter into the
secret chamber by way of a small doorway in the right paw. It
is dimly lit by rushlight. There is a long, narrow corridor that
leads downward and we can just make out the faint outlines
of paintings and hieroglyphics on the walls. It is cold and the
air smells earthy and damp. We walk in single file for a little
way. The corridor bears right again and now the path feels
uneven and slippery beneath our feet. We begin to feel disoriented, as if we were indeed in another place and between
worlds.

There is a small doorway ahead of us, a small insignificant wooden doorway. On each side, raised on platforms, are
representations of Anubis in his jackal form. Their black-and-
gold bodies cast long shadows in the flickering candlelight.
We enter. There is darkness. Nothing.

We are now in the secret chamber that links the guardian
to the Great Pyramid. It is here that part of the Greater Mystery will be revealed to us. Be with me as I invoke He who
will guide us to that Greater Mystery and the truth that lies
concealed here.

INVOCATION TO ANUBIS
O Thou, who art the son of thy father Osiris,
Thou who are the beloved of thy mother Nephthys,
Thou who art beloved of Isis—
Reveal thyself to us in this place.
O Thou who wearest the jackal's head,
Who roams the deserts and the heavens,
Thou who hast waited in the darkness and in the light,
and knoweth no fear—
Weigher of Hearts, Guardian of Souls,
Guide of the Dead—
Come to us now in our need for thee.
Bring light to us who stand in darkness;
Illuminate our path that we may understand.
O thou who art known by many names—
Anubis, Anpu, Upuat, Opener of the Ways—
Come, now, to us here.

Anubis:
I am he who is jackal-headed. I am he who walks in the darkness and the light and knoweth no fear; I am the Guide and the Guardian and the Weigher of Hearts, I am the Beloved. I am Anubis, Anpu, Upaut, The Opener of the Ways. I bring the light to illuminate your path. What is your purpose?

Guide:
We are travelers, seeking truth, wisdom, and the light.

Anubis:
Why do you seek these things?

Guide:
Many in our world have lost their way and experience a spiritual darkness. My companions and I have come seeking the light of truth and the path that leads to the source.

Anubis:
Yes, it is time for change. The stars herald the dawning of a new age—the Age of the Water-Bearer—and a new begin-

ning for mankind. Guide, take light and illuminate the chamber for your companions. Know this, all you who have traveled far to this place. You now stand at the very center of the world. The time shall soon come to pass when this secret chamber shall be opened once again to the gaze of all. Yet, what shall they find? Perhaps an empty room? Yet, it was here that the Boat of Millions of Years did come to rest after its long journey between the stars. I and my companions did alight and did teach the peoples of the land how to build the sacred structures of the Pyramids, and to plot the course of the stars. It was in this very place that the first initiates were brought to take their symbolic journey into the underworld to learn the truth concerning their origins and destiny. And in this place, it was also foretold to the priest-kings that a time would come when men and women would forget their true nature and their part in the Greater Mystery.

Now, you who are among the first, have returned to the place of the Beginning and therefore part of the Greater Mystery may be revealed to you. Though you think of my kind as gods, we have walked as men and women upon Earth, as you do now. I knew once what is was to be a man. I, too, have felt the loneliness, the despair, the joys and blessings of an earthly body.

Now let it be said that, when the first initiates were brought to this place, it was revealed to them that all were the children of the First Son. He who in that time was known as Atum Ra. All comes from Atum, who is in the form of the Sun disc, but who is greater than the Sun. Prepare yourselves for the coming of the Sun.

Guide:

Hail to Atum Ra, who in his form as Kephra, rolls the Sun disc into the morning sky. Hail to Atum Ra who is our dawning.

Hail to Atum Ra, who in his form as Ra, the Hawk-Headed One, sails the sacred Sun disc above our heads. Hail to Atum Ra who is strong in his power. He is our noon.

Hail to Atum Ra, who in his form as Tum, the Wise One, ram-headed and leaning upon his staff of gold, begins his descent into the underworld. Hail to Atum Ra, who is our twilight.

Hail to Atum Ra, in his form as the unseen Sun at midnight. He sails the sacred Sun Boat through the dark waters of the underworld. Hail to Atum Ra, who is the light in our darkness.

Behold, Atum Ra, who keeps his promise to his children, has risen again by the power of the hand of Sekhmet. All hail to Sekhmet, who is the Eye of Ra. *[All turn to the west and Anubis, and lower hands.]*

Anubis:
Thus have you performed the Rite of Atum as it was done by the first initiates and the priest-kings. Hail be to Atum Ra, the Sun behind the Sun, who came from the first Mother, the Nun. He is the everlasting light from which there shall be no separation. Prepare now for the second Rite of Atum—the Illumination and the Understanding.

HYMN TO ATUM
O Thou who giveth life to all
From whom all things come forth
To whom all things finally return.
Show to us thy face the true and spiritual Sun.
Hidden by an orb of solar light
That we may know thy truth.

And do all in our power
As we journey into thy sacred light.

O Thou who giveth light after darkness
Who sacrifices himself for our sakes,
Who returns to us with each dawning.
Descend to us that we may know thy light
and rejoice in thy presence.
Behold the One who is known by many names
Blessed is he who is Atum Ra.
He comes to us in the form of the Sun.
All hail to Atum Ra.

Hail be to Atum Ra
Who giveth life to all.
From whom all things come forth
To whom all things finally return.
Hear the voices of thy children raised in adoration
Atum Ra. Atum Ra. Atum Ra.

Voice of Atum Ra:
I am Atum Ra.
I am the first cause.
I am that which came from the Nun.
I am the light that forever shines in the darkness;
I am the Ever Becoming One.

Guide:
We call thee Atum Ra. We who are the sons and daughters of
the first cause. We seek the light that forever shines in the
darkness.

Voice of Atum Ra:
You who are the children of Atum, know thy origin.
I am the light that shines within and without.
Above and below.
I am thy soul, thy spirit, thy beloved.
I am the that which you seek,
Forever the sacrifice that you might live.
In the beginning were you created from mine own hand.
Henceforth shall you know the joy of knowing the Oneness.
Your destiny is also Atum Ra who is all.
Hear the words of Atum Ra who is both creator and created.

Guide:
Hail be to Atum Ra, who is both Father and Son. Born of the
first Mother, who is the Nun.

Voice of Atum Ra:
To the Light of the New Dawn,
The right hand of Atum shall stretch forth

From the starry heavens.
And the left hand of Atum shall rise
From the swirling depths of the mighty oceans
To lift the hearts and minds of his children.

Guide:
Hail to Atum who is the light in our darkness. Hail to Atum who is beloved of his children. Hail to Atum who is the truth.

Anubis:
Let there now be light in your darkness. You have sought and found the truth. *[Guide lights candles for each person.]* Thus was it known by my kind before you, that we are all one. Threaded together like pearls by the light of Atum. May your paths be now lightened by knowledge, truth, wisdom, and beauty. Prepare yourselves to depart from this place and go with my blessings.

Guide:
Hail be to Anubis.
Blessed son of thy father Osiris.
Beloved of thy mother Nephthys.
Guardian of the bright Isis, Mistress of Magic.
You who hath roamed the deserts and the heavens.
Who walketh in the darkness and the light without fear.
Weigher of Hearts, Guardian of Souls, Great Embalmer.
You have opened the way and illuminated our path.
We thank thee for thy presence and with our whole blessings
   do you depart now unto your own plane, as we do to
   ours.

Having departed from the secret chamber we walk back along the corridors, now brightly lit from our own candles. We are joyful and our hearts lightened. We see clearly the paintings and the hieroglyphs on the walls. There is a surprise, for, clearly, we see our very selves, our very journey painted on the white plaster, from the time of our arrival in the cornfield to our meeting with Atum Ra. Above each head is painted a small, yellow, winged Sun disc.

We arrive blinking into the early morning sun. We have been in the chamber a whole night. The air is cool and a soft breeze blows upon our faces. We are greeted warmly by the young Pharaoh and our bearded friend in the blue robe. We thank Pharaoh for his hospitality and prepare to board the boat that will take us back along the Nile. Before we set sail, the man who is so strangely familiar smiles at us, as if to say. "Do you not know me?" With his own hands he gives the boat a push and we are on our way. The square sail is hoisted above us to catch the early morning winds

As we journey along the canal and turn into the river, we look back and gaze upon the painted face of the mighty Sphinx and the sharp white pyramids. Between them shines the Sun—Kephra, Atum Ra in his scarab form rolling the Sun disc into the morning sky. Now we know, we understand that we have always been part of the whole. There has always been a Great Plan and we all belong within it.

There are signs of life along the banks of the River Nile, animals and birds. They too take on a new significance for us. All comes from Atum and everything carries the divine spark of He who split himself apart that we might live.

We journey in silence for a while and, all too soon, we arrive back at our starting point and clamber, tired but happy, onto the shore. We thank and bless the oarsmen and take our pathway back through the cornfield, where the tall figures of Isis and Osiris await us. Before we depart, back through the Gateway of Malkuth, we are each given a gift from the Land of Khem, given by the hand of Isis herself. She says: "Because you have remembered us, we shall live in the hearts and minds of men and women. May the blessing of Atum be with you."

Before us is the great doorway upon which is painted a picture of the tarot card, "The World." It opens. We walk through and find ourselves in this time and in this place. Companions, in your own time, awake.

Sekhmet, Goddess of Fire and Vengeance

When I was 7, I had a dream that I related to my mother. A lovely golden lady with a lion's face had come to me and given me two lion cubs as a present. I was told they would look after me as I was growing up, and that their names were Pashat and Seshat. At the time, I knew nothing about ancient Egyptians or their animal-headed deities, but my mother bought me a book of Egyptian mythology and sat back to see what would happen.

My world suddenly opened up. I became engrossed in the lives of the Pharaohs and their gods. My parents patiently translated the complicated texts into language a 7-year old could understand, and answered interminable questions. They gave me reams of drawing paper on which I drew gods and goddesses for hours on end and made up stories for them, seeing them as personal friends.

When I was older, I was taken on a trip to the British Museum where, despite their efforts, my parents were virtually unable to drag me out of the Egyptian galleries. When I first saw the beautiful statue of Sekhmet, I became quite agitated, for *this* was my golden lady, *this* was my goddess.

At 13, I went through my first initiation and decided to dedicate myself to Sekhmet. Most women identify with lunar goddesses, but this was not for me! I needed the solar gods, the deserts and the heat of an equatorial Sun. I needed Sekhmet, daughter of Amun Ra, fearsome and powerful.

My story, I have since found, is not unusual. Many women find this goddess fascinating and are drawn to her. To this day she remains as powerful an influence in my life as when I was a child. In times of crisis, I have stood before her statue and become completely absorbed by the energy and power that still emanates from that wondrously carved basalt.

Since early times, Sekhmet has inspired passionate loyalty and love in her devotees—surprising since she was a goddess of war and destruction. The legend says that Ra, the Sun God, decided the human race had deviated too far from the path of righteousness. He consulted with the other gods and it was decided to annihilate them and begin again. Sekhmet, the Mighty One, Daughter of Ra, was despatched to Earth to carry out the destruction. Once there, she was overcome by a bloodlust so powerful that even the gods were appalled and took pity on humankind.

Unable to stop her, they tricked the goddess with drugged beer, causing her to sleep deeply. When she awakened she was no longer driven by the desire to kill. So, the question remains. Why does Sekhmet draw so many to her worship?

I believe she is far older than many of the contemporary Egyptian deities and has her roots in Nubia and Libya. She represents total feminine power, for her father, Atum Ra, placed her above himself, calling her his eye. So she became greater than the other gods by being set above the heart-center of the Creator-God himself.

The name Sekhmet has its roots in the Egyptian Sek-hem, meaning powerful or mighty. She is often called Sekhmet-Ra, "the power or might of Ra." Yet she also has a benign side, for her priests were healers and surgeons. Only they could set broken bones or perform the delicate brain operation known as trepanning. One of her many names was "The Bone Setter."

Sekhmet was the consort of Ptah, the God of Life. With their son, Nefertum (later indentified with Aesculapius), they formed the Triad of the city of Memphis. Gazing at a statue of Sekhmet, one is immediately aware of the sheer power of this goddess. She seems remote, almost alien, yet also touchable— so feline you can almost hear her purr.

I believe today many feel the loss of personal power. We are drained by the demands of jobs and lifestyles, and by the need to compete. For us, Sekhmet is like an oasis in the desert, representing a return to that which matters, self-realization, the awakening and knowledge of our inner divinity.

This pathworking is the result of many months of hard work and meditation. Sekhmet is not an easy deity to access, for she is dual in nature, so a degree of caution is advised. Approach her with care. The lady suffers no fools, and she will be watching. The nature of the working is a journey to the inner temple of Sekhmet. (Don't worry if it takes you several tries. It took me months.) Once there, if you have understood the signs along the way, you will realize the true nature of the goddess. You will also have learned a great deal about yourself. Read on and enter the world of the powerful, the awesome, the beautiful goddess, Sekhmet-Ra.

—Tamara Ashcroft-Nowicki

INVOCATION
Far have I traveled in my search for you,
For love of you have I dared to cross the burning deserts,
and felt the midday Sun strike upon my neck.
For you have I braved the mighty oceans
whose thunderous waves dashed the boat of my life
upon the unforgiving rocks.
And only now has my search brought me to
an understanding of your truth.
Golden daughter of Ra.

Only now do I know that each beat of my heart,
Each drawing of breath,

Each conscious thought, started with you.
For you were there before my first infant cry,
You are the Awakener from the slumber of death.
You are the rage and the roar of Life.
And, like the lion, you come once again to seize me.

Prepare yourself as for all pathworkings. You may have a single candle to aid concentration. Relax and regulate your breathing. Close your eyes and visualize the room in which you sit, then allow the image to ripple and fade gently.

Imagine yourself in space. Around you, set in a midnight sky, are thousands of stars, gateways to other places, times, and worlds. Before you, still burning in space, is your candle—a focus for your meditation. Your feet are in contact with what appears to be the smooth black marble of a temple floor. You are aware of another presence, warm and

benign, and you are not afraid. Your senses become attuned
to the faint scent of incense. Opening your inner eyes slowly,
you see before you the figure of the jackal-headed god,
Anubis.

He is very tall and the black-and-gold-and-lapis mask
makes him appear to tower over your seated astral form. He
wears a simple kilt of pleated linen and, on both upper arms,
two heavy gold bracelets that gleam against his copper skin.

Anubis is the Way Shower and the protector of all who
travel, be it on the physical level or the inner dimensions. No
harm will come to your physical body or astral form while he
is your guardian. This is his temple, a place between the worlds,
dusted with starlight and alive with the cosmic hum of space.

He beckons you to follow him. Rising from your seat, you
walk across the temple floor, cool and smooth beneath your
feet, toward two mighty pillars, one black and one white. They
stretch up into infinity and act as a doorway.

There are no stars between them, just intense light. Anubis
takes your hand and leads you forward and through the opening. For a moment, you feel disoriented, but when you open
your eyes again, you are dazzled by brilliant sunshine and become aware of an intense heat on your skin.

You look about you, surveying the landscape, but there is
nothing for miles in every direction but the burning red-gold
sands of a vast desert. Strangely shaped dunes shift and shiver
in the wind and undulate toward the horizon like living things.
Above, the sky is deep cobalt blue and the noonday Sun
watches you like a huge yellow eye. It is a fitting place for the
daughter of Ra to dwell.

Anubis points to the south and you realize with a sinking
heart that, although he is your guide, this part of the journey
you must do alone. So, bravely, and mustering all your courage, you begin to walk. You seek the Temple of Sekhmet, but
you have no map, no water, and you are utterly alone.

And so, Seeker, as you walk through the desert, perhaps
you should think about what it is that you seek? Why are you
here? What do you want from the goddess, Sekhmet? And if
you find her, what will you say?

You scan the horizon with eyes already blinded by a relentless Sun, looking for a sign of a temple or dwelling, but you see nothing. How often have we searched for something— a truth, a love, a place, an object—but never find it?

The sun beats down on your head and neck. You walk the steep slopes of dune after dune, forever hoping that over the next slope you will see . . . something, something other than sand. How many times, Seeker, have you climbed in your own life with hope in your heart, only to have that hope dashed and your heart crushed with disappointment and longing?

You thirst. You thirst in the desert and you are alone. Exhausted with the heat, your tongue swelling against the roof of your mouth, longing for water, you are unable even to call out the name of she whom you seek. How many times have you burned in a desert of your own making? Burned with longing, with lust, with desire? For something that never comes, but that forever shifts, like the sands, out of your reach.

So dehydrated that you have no tears with which to cry, your search seems futile. In despair and frustration, in a rage of longing, you stand still. How many times, Seeker, have you cried in secret? Shedding tears of loneliness in places where you thought no one would see or hear?

"But I see you Seeker, I hear you. I know who you are. I see you with my lioness eyes. I hear your silent footsteps on the desert sands with my lioness ears. I smell your despair with my lioness nose. I am watching you and biding my time."

And so, still thinking yourself alone, you make one last effort. It is so hard to put one foot in front of the other. And . . . your feet touch not sand, but bone. Looking down, you see a field of bones about you—animal and human alike. Stepping carefully, you attempt to cross them, but their sharpness cuts your feet and they bleed. Your blood on the whiteness of bones and sand, the grinning skulls—this is a place of battle and death. Have you battles, Seeker? Have you faced death? And so, longing for life, are you willing to survive against the greatest of odds? Is life not like a battle? In life, are there not many little deaths to which you have succumbed and from which you have been reborn? What sustained you through those moments? Was it faith? The will to carry on? Where is that will, that faith, now?

And she watches you, with gleaming golden eyes. Ready to seize you. Coming from behind like all predators. Did you think you were the Seeker, after all? How arrogant of you. For all this time *she* has sought *you*. She has brought you to this moment of moments. She is the one who will never let an opportunity escape, here and now . . . you know it.

You turn. She is there. In huge lioness form, crouched, every muscle taut, ready to spring. The focus of all her attention is upon you. In your mind, you already feel the teeth, the claws, the snapping of bone, and the tearing of flesh and the flowing of blood. Yet strangely, you are not afraid. You are elated and . . . at last . . . so alive. Fully conscious, fully aware, you give yourself utterly to this moment of moments. To the bliss and the ecstasy of total surrender to the love of the goddess. You close your eyes, smiling. You feel no fear and you hear her roar of triumph.

"Ah, but it is not what you expected, is it? Thus have I seized you, but not destroyed you. For you have given yourself to me and, in doing so, I have awakened you to life and realization. For am I not the "I" of Ra, the Ever Becoming One? You are a child of Ra and beloved by him. You shall become again and again at my hand, for it is my hand that raises the Sun each dawn with the promise of a new day and a new life. To understand my mystery, you must understand that. Many before you have walked through the desert of illusion created by themselves, thinking themselves alone and in despair. Walking upon the bones of the past that make them bleed again and again inside. Thinking that my temple is but a mirage, they despair and give up. But in giving yourself up to death, you are always reborn, for mine is the house of life. Open your eyes and rejoice, for you live. You have survived and this is your coming forth by day!"

The words of the goddess ring in your ears and you open your eyes to the light of the Temple of the Sun. Around are shining pillars of gold, so tall that they seem to hold up the sky itself. The air is filled with spiced incense and there is a vibrancy and energy in the atmosphere that fills every cell of your body with the urgency of *life*.

Before you, seated on a throne of gold, flanked by two columns upon which burn gigantic flames, is Sekhmet herself. She is clothed in scarlet and gold and wears the mask of the lioness. In her right hand, she holds an ankh, the symbol of life, that she extends to you in blessing.

"I am Sekhmet-Ra and I existed before all time. I was when all life was but a dream of Atum, and it was I who made the dream real. I am the Awakener from Sleep, the Awakener from Death. Remember this, child of Ra, remember this when you struggle or are afraid or are in need of me. I shall come, always, with the promise of a new beginning. Go now to your own place and time."

You become aware of the presence of your jackal-headed guide who gently leads you from the Sun temple. You have no need now to cross the desert, for it holds no power over you. As you leave, you look back at the Temple of the Sun, radiating and shining forever in the desert, there for all who have the eyes to really see and the courage to seek.

Swiftly, Anubis leads you through the pillars of Force and Form that form the gateway home. You find yourself once more in the halfway temple of Anubis, the Gateway of Stars. Seat yourself once more before the candle, that has remained burning steadily throughout your journey. Remember to thank Anubis for his presence and guidance.

Now, looking deeply into your candle, close your eyes on the astral plane. Feel yourself connect with your physical body. Feel the weight, feel your hands on your knees, your feet on the floor. When you feel totally connected, open your eyes and re-orient yourself.

Because this is such a lengthy working, it is advisable to shower or bathe afterward and have something to eat and drink to ground your physical being completely.

Now that you have made the journey to the Temple of Sekhmet, you may go again as you please, without having to go through the initiatory desert-crossing.

Note: This is more than a simple pathworking. It is, in point of fact, a *solo ritual* that employs the method of pathworking to achieve a very high level of communication with the god-form. It is not to be undertaken lightly, but with due reverence and thought. It can have a remarkable effect on those who undertake this inner journey, and may indeed bring about something close to an initiatory experience.

—Dolores Ashcroft-Nowicki

Aphrodite, Goddess of Love and Beauty

When we think of Aphrodite, we are tempted to see her simply as the Goddess of Love and Beauty. Many invoke solely along those lines, to attract love or to make themselves more alluring to the opposite sex. This is all right on one level. These are attributes of the deity that should not be overlooked. But Aphrodite has a far more universal role. And a deeper understanding of her nature needs to be recognized before the pathworking is attempted.

In Greek legend, Aphrodite was shown as the archetypal, beautiful blond, married to Hephasteus, the crippled blacksmith of the gods (and son of Zeus and Hera). Though there is little doubt that he adored her, she was continually unfaithful, namely with Adonis, a beautiful but stupid young man who left her only to get himself killed. Her next love was the more rugged and manly Ares, the God of War and yet another son of Zeus! Aphrodite was caught with Ares in several compromising positions. This displeased Zeus, who would have struck the amorous pair with a thunderbolt (made for him, incidentally, by Hephasteus). However, Hermes intervened on their behalf and convinced Zeus to see the funny side of it.

The Greeks saw their gods as having all the lusts and passions they themselves experienced. Quite a contrast to the Egyptians, whose masked gods set the blueprint for the lives of their worshipers as respected teachers and helpers.

When I visited Greece several years ago, I was overwhelmed by the warmth and generosity of the people. It is truly a land of the vine, and love and family unity are of the utmost importance. One can easily see how the ancient gods of various countries took on a national identity. The pantheon of Greek gods is like the people of Greece themselves: warm, passionate, vibrant, and alive.

There are many legends concerning the birth of Aphrodite. Some say she was the daughter of Poseidon and a sea nymph, others say that Zeus himself was her father. A third legend claims that, when the young Zeus castrated his father, Chronos, the severed genitals fell into the ocean, which became pregnant with the Love Goddess. She was born fully formed from the foam of the sea and was carried in a seashell to the shores of Cyprus, which became her adopted home. Alighting at the bay of Paphos, she was so dazzling and so beautiful that even the gods held their breath.

That Aphrodite was originally connected with the sea is most interesting, for the sea itself is an ancient feminine deity, the Mother from which all life sprang. This could mean that the cult of Aphrodite is much older than was first thought. When considering this goddess, therefore, we should think of the ocean with its vast depths, teeming with life, some parts so deep it has yet to be fully explored. Through the sea, Aphrodite has connections with the Great Mother. She herself gave birth to love in the form of Eros. (Erotic love was born of her passionate mating with Ares.)

Like the sea, Aphrodite has her wild and darker side. She was certainly not very loving to her daughter-in-law, Psyche, whom she made suffer in her long search for her love, Eros. But Psyche's tale has a message for us, if we heed it. It says much about the true nature of the goddess and the nature of love.

Psyche's journey is the sacred journey of the soul. For the love of Eros, she is willing to accept any trial that Aphrodite presents to her as an obstacle to her goal. Eventually, Psyche realizes that earthly lust is not necessarily true love and she becomes transformed and lifted up into the heavens to become one with her beloved Eros.

The soul and love in its highest form are surely synonymous. When you listen to a piece of music that makes your heart soar. When you see a beautiful sunset that takes your breath away, or feel the emotion when you look into the eyes of your newborn child for the first time—this is Aphrodite. But she is also the passion of the sexual embrace, the desire for union, the thrill of doing something wild and dangerous. It is her energy that causes sperm to join with ovum to create new life—for this is *love* and it is beautiful.

▼ ▼ ▼

When you prepare for this pathworking, make yourself comfortable in your chair with feet firmly on the ground. Light a candle to the goddess to help you in the pathworking. Green is a color particularly associated with Aphrodite. To prepare yourself for the meditation, be conscious of the room where you are, breathe deeply, and close your eyes.

The room gently ripples and fades and you find yourself on a sandy beach. It is early evening. The Sun has set and just above the horizon is the thin crescent of a New Moon. A little higher in the sky shines a brilliant light. It is Venus, the Evening Star. You are aware of the place where you find yourself. The air is still warm from the day and, on the night breeze, you can smell the distant pine forests intermingled with the scent of the sea and sand.

The waves lap playfully about your feet; the water is warm and inviting. The sound of them gently breaking against the shore in an undulating rhythm lulls your senses and the stresses and tensions of your own life melt away. You feel happy and relaxed. Allow yourself to enjoy this for a few moments. Listen to the sounds of the ocean and let yourself become one with its rhythm.

Presently, from behind you, you hear the sound of singing. Women's voices high and lilting. You turn slowly. Behind you, where the sand meets the sea, you can dimly make out the sweep of forested hills. Beyond that are the dark looming shapes of snow-capped mountains. Through the trees, you see the flicker of torchlight and the barely discernible white-robed figures descending to the shore. The singing becomes louder. Although there are no words, from somewhere deep within yourself, you recognize it. Your heartbeat adjusts to its rhythm and you find yourself raising your own voice to join the melody.

The forms become clearer. A group of women dressed in white robes and bearing torches are now appearing through the trees. Flowers are woven into their hair and they carry more flowers in their arms. Some carry flagons of wine, fruits, bread, and other delicious foods. They sing and laugh and dance as they approach. There is an air of celebration and expectancy. You feel that something wonderful is about to happen. You catch the mood and become part of it, and part of the group. Flowers are pressed upon you and some of the women decorate your hair with them.

You follow the women, still singing, into the water. It feels deliciously cool against your skin. As you go, flowers are thrown into the water and there is much splashing and laughter, as with children at a party.

Suddenly, the noise stops. One of the women raises her hands in salute to the Moon and the Evening Star. All laughter and singing stops. The women left standing on the shore also raise their arms in salute. The priestess of Aphrodite speaks the salute to the goddess.

Aphrodite
Foam-born Daughter of Zeus
Goddess of all that is love.
All that is beautiful.
Eagerly do we await your presence here.

> **To celebrate with you**
> **All that is life,**
> **All that is good.**

You and the women are silent and there is anticipation in the very air you breathe. Something will happen, something will become real.

The water, now waist-high, becomes almost a living thing, sensuously caressing your skin, warm as a lover's touch. The sandy bottom of the sea beneath your feet shifts and moves. The very night breeze ruffles and tousles your hair, as if unseen fingers were gently teasing you. It is as if life has become more real, more delicious, more vibrant. Or it may be because a part of you has opened up fully to it.

The women start a slow chant. Again without words, but on a deeper note. It pulsates with the rhythm of the ocean that now begins to swirl and eddy about you, frothing and foaming and dashing itself against you and the rocks.

Before you, the foam and spray rises from the water, first as a water spout, then in the form of a human shape. All at once, laughing and beautiful, Aphrodite herself rises from the waters. Tall and shapely, with her golden hair streaming about her, each curl entwined with tiny shells and pearls.

The goddess, you, and the priestesses walk together from the sea toward the shore. Others have now joined the throng, young, old, both men and women, for the celebration of love and beauty has no boundaries. All are welcome to celebrate the return of the Goddess of Love.

As Aphrodite walks from the water, she is clothed in white robes by her priestesses. A fire has been lit on the shore and there is singing and dancing, feasting and merriment. The atmosphere is joyful and you feel happy and warm in the love of this group of people.

The High Priestess presents to the goddess an emerald belt encrusted with pearls, tiny shells, and aquamarines. This she clasps about her waist. It is the Girdle of Aphrodite, said to be so powerful that it will turn aside even the thunderbolts of Zeus himself.

The Priestess comes to you and takes your hand. "You have come far to seek our goddess. Come and speak with her, ask her what you wish to know, tell her what you seek, for she is all that is love, all that is beauty."

Slowly, you are led to the feet of the goddess and you find yourself almost overcome with her radiance and beauty. You understand now why the gods themselves held their breath at the first sight of her. Why mortal men and women strive so hard to capture love and beauty for themselves.

"But love can never be captured," she tells you, "nor can it be chained, imprisoned, or coerced, for love is free and has wings." Her green eyes look deeply into your own. She takes your hands in hers.

"So, speak to me of love, tell me of all that you hold dear, what are the things that you find beautiful? Has love been kind? Or unkind? Speak to me and I will hear and I will tell you what only your ears will hear and what your heart has always known."

Slowly and hesitantly, at first, you speak to her. This is your time with the goddess and all that you say to her is private, between yourselves. Spend as long as you wish in this conversation.

What do you love?
What or whom do you hold dear?
What are the things that you find beautiful?
Has love been kind? Or unkind?
What have you learned about the nature of love?

Aphrodite bends close and whispers her responses to you. Finally, she raises your face with both hands and kisses both eyes, as a mother would her child.

"Remember this and, with open eyes, see that all begins and ends within your own heart. Love can never be pursued or won with tricks. Love simply *is*. Love is within you and all around you. You were born from love. All life is born from love. Life *is* love. All that exists comes from love. *You are love.* There is no need to pursue that which you already are."

From her jewel-encrusted belt she takes a single bright stone and places it in your hand as a gift. During this time, it has been as if the two of you were alone. Now, you become aware of the music, the voices, and singing around you. The warm sea breeze once again ruffles your hair. It is time to go. Thanking Aphrodite and the priestesses, you silently take your leave, as the celebrations continue.

You walk a little way down the beach, your feet sinking into the sand. You turn and look back at the happy crowd of people joyfully celebrating life and love. Love of each other, love of their children, of togetherness and belonging, love of being alive. Though you are now alone, you do not feel lonely. You are part of all this and you know you belong. You look at the shining jewel in your hand, as a testimony to reality and awareness.

Gently now, feel yourself back in your seated form. Feel your body heavy and relaxed, your feet connected to the floor. Allow a little time to re-orientate yourself. When you come to full consciousness, you feel happy, relaxed, and filled with joy.

"For I am already that which I seek, and the truth of this is beauty."

Hecate, Goddess of the Dark Moon

The worship of Hecate is said to have originated in ancient Thessaly. Although primarily thought to be members of a witch-cult, the devotees of this goddess really worshiped the dark cronelike aspect of the Great Mother.

Hecate has often suffered from a bad reputation. She is associated with all aspects of death, transformation, and change. She can thus be likened to both the Morrigan and Cerridwen of the ancient Celts. But Hecate has every right to take her place within these pages. Indeed, not to acknowledge the dark aspect of the goddess would be a mistake.

The darkness of Hecate is that of the cave, of winter, and of earth. She is a primal goddess and presides over birth and the laying out of the dead. In this way, she is also associated with Kore, or Persephone. Hecate, being an earth goddess, also has dominion over potions, herbs, and spells. Not surprisingly, it is mainly women who have been attracted to her worship. Not only can the goddess whip up a pretty infallible love potion, but her initiation rites (usually associated with the dark of the Moon) included that of the first menstruation and the menopause.

For all women nearing midlife, Hecate is a powerful force that, if approached in the right way, can help maintain vitality and vibrancy, for she is the Goddess of the Roots of the Powers of Earth.

For both men and women, Hecate holds the link to the ancestors. This link is a source of power and knowledge, for just as the dead were laid to rest in the womb of Earth, so did Hecate preside over the death rites.

It is natural to feel a little apprehensive about meeting this deity. She is not nice; she is not even particularly inviting or approachable. She is as wild and as fierce and as old as Earth itself. But making contact with the darker aspect of the goddess goes a long way toward satisfying some deep longing within ourselves. It is a contact with the very Earth from which we come, and thereby with all the elements that make up our physical bodies, flesh, blood, and bones. It is also a contact with those we have loved, but who have now passed over— yet still live within us. Above all, it is a contact with that which acknowledges that life will survive.

Despite the ravages of modern life and all that humans have done to this planet, Earth is still our mother, and still loves us with ferocity. In whatever way, in whatever form, Earth will continue to give birth to life and, in the same way, she holds the power, the force, and, the will to destroy it.

▼   ▼   ▼

Prepare yourself for this meditation in the usual way. Ensure that you will not be disturbed for at least one hour. Get into a comfortable position, wearing comfortable clothes that do not restrict you. You may light a single candle (dark blue) to aid your concentration.

Breathe deeply in and out to a count of four. Do this at least three times before relaxing into a normal rhythm. Breath is our connection to life and this plane of reality and existence. Keep connected to your breathing on this journey. For, though you are quite safe, you will be traveling deep within your own subconscious and could fall asleep.

Let the breath take you down into your own inner depths. Relax and allow your eyes to close gently. Remain in quiet meditation, allowing yourself to do nothing but be still for the next few minutes.

As you open your inner eyes, you find yourself in almost total darkness, aware only that you are somewhere outdoors, on a windswept plain. Above your head, the sky is filled with stars, but no Moon. Beneath your feet, you can feel tough shrubs and grass. A cold wind chills you, as it blows from distant mountains looming blackly against the horizon.

As your eyes become accustomed to the dark, you see a mound directly in front of you, not unlike a neolithic tomb. Concentrate on this mound, for you see it now with the eyes of a psychic. The mound appears to shimmer with a silvery blue light that undulates and writhes like a snake. The mound itself seems to swell, shift, and change in the astral light, opening up to you as you stand patiently before it.

Gently, as the mound opens, you become aware of figures, men, women, and children, who step from the opening—shadowy at first, but becoming clearer as they come toward you. Some you may recognize as members of your own dear family who have passed on. Others you will not know, but you feel a deep connection to them.

See them come toward you now, dressed in garments of different times, different generations, different countries. Feel the love, the warmth, and the pride they feel toward you now, for they are your ancestors and you are their sum total. You are their promise of ongoing life. As you live, so do they, for they are your own flesh and blood.

Do not be afraid of them, but greet them lovingly. See your line, your generations going back through time, as they step from the mound. Some lived until they were very old; some died young, some in war and battle, some peacefully in their sleep. See them all coming to you and surrounding you with love and pride. Some reach out with wonder to touch you to feel that loving connection. Look into their eyes and their faces. See part of yourself in them.

At last, the First One steps from the mound and the others make way. If you are a man, the First One will be female; if you are female, he will be a man. The First One steps toward you. Do not be afraid of its appearance—the roughness, the low brow and coarse hair, the nakedness. The First One knows who you are and has been waiting for you, for this moment.

The First One is close now, touches you—your face, your hair, your eyes and body—and is pleased. Gently, you are guided to the mound, to the opening from whence the ancestors have come. You look at it with some apprehension, especially when you realize that you are expected to go headfirst down that narrow gap.

You disrobe, taking off everything until you are naked, for any clothing would be a hindrance now. The First One rubs into your skin a mixture of pig's blood and fat. Slowly, you step to the opening of the mound and look into it. It is dark and forbidding. Take a deep breath and dive in headfirst.

You feel a rush of sensation as you hurtle through earthy, but smooth, tunnels. Down and down you go. As you travel, images of your own past rush to meet you. From childhood and early adulthood, faces of people you have known and half remember. They speak to you, but you cannot hear what they say. Eventually, you land with a bump at the bottom. Naked and covered with sticky mud . . . how like the First One you are now!

You find yourself in a round, rocky cave. A dim redness is cast by the light of a simple peat fire. Over it hangs a large black, iron cauldron. Stirring the cauldron with a thigh bone is a woman. She seems to be neither young nor old, her black hair is streaked with gray and her eyes are fierce and wild. She wears coarse, dark woolen robes and heavy copper bangles. About her neck, she wears a necklace of small bones strung on human hair. Her skin is dark and creased with lines, but she is, nevertheless, handsome and powerful. This is Hecate.

She does not look at you, but continues to stir the cauldron, muttering into it and throwing in handsful of seeds and herbs. Occasionally, she shrieks and laughs.

Shivering, feeling chilled and damp, and with something close to fear, you eventually pluck up the courage to draw closer to the peat fire to warm yourself. She raises her dark eyes and looks at you. The maniacal fire has now gone from her glance and, when she speaks, her voice is low and powerful.

"I am the one who guards and tends the cauldron of your life. Come closer and look at your life, feel the power and presence of all those who have gone before you. Those who have fed the sacred water that you might live *now*. You, in turn, shall both feast and drink from this so that your line can go on and your life be filled with meaning and vitality. Come closer and see your life in the cauldron."

You move closer and peer into the churning liquid, surprised to see how crystal clear it has become. You see yourself reflected back with startling clarity. Everything you have been, everything that has happened to you, both good and bad, happy and sad, is here, for life is both bitter and sweet.

"Now do you stand at the crossroads of your life, for why else would you have made this journey? Roads that cross are my domain. Places where an old woman sits and waits for the traveler to come and ask the way. Speak, and tell me of your path; which way do you want to go? What do you seek to help you make this journey?"

Now you speak to her of your hopes and dreams, your wishes and needs. Whatever you have lacked in the past, tell her everything. As you speak, she continues to stir the cauldron and it churns and froths and bubbles with life . . . your life. When you finish, she stops.

"Then, child of Earth, you must understand who I really am. Every man, woman, and child, every living being, is a cauldron, a sacred vessel that holds the wondrous spirit of life. The Great Mother tends the cauldron, stirring it into life and adding the herbs and spices that are the many experiences of that life. Some are foul and some are sweet; some burn like fire; some soothe and heal. Some give pleasure and ecstasy, others pain and sorrow. Life teaches many things and, in the course of one lifetime, there are many little births and deaths. But I, who am the guardian, see the lines of power and spirit pass from generation to generation, filling this sacred vessel. Few make the journey here to the source of their power. Fewer still drink from the cauldron filled with the blood, flesh, bones, and spirit of their ancestors. What choice will you make now?

"In drinking from this cauldron, you will take into yourself the power of your ancestors. It will strengthen and aid you to make the right decisions in your life. It has the power to give renewed life and vitality, and it is your right to take it, if you so wish. For the ancestors have much wisdom to offer, if you but listen to their voices."

Hecate takes a rough wooden bowl and fills it from the cauldron and passes it to you. If you accept and drink from it, you may taste wine or water, milk or herbs, sweet or bitter, for all lives are different. Whatever you drink is the sum total of what you are and what is right for you at this moment. As you drink, think of your life. What do you want? What do you need? Which way do you want to go? For you are now at the crossroads.

If you have drunk, then you will experience a sense of deep satisfaction and peace of mind, as if some great need has been filled, and it is time to leave. You thank the goddess for her help. She no longer speaks, but remains bent over the cauldron, tending it with ferocious devotion.

You begin the slow ascent up through the tunnel. It takes all of your strength and will. At last, exhausted and hot from your exertions, you emerge as a newborn from the mound. Only the First One remains waiting for your return. The mound shimmers with astral light and you realize that the ancestors have returned to their own place and you must return to yours. But there is one final task for you to do. You face the First

One and look into the dark, almost animal, eyes without fear, and you say to that First One: "Give me your power and, in doing so, return to the light with my blessing and thanks for the life you have given to me."

A small glimmer of understanding appears in the eyes of the First One and a hand reaches out to yours. Something passes between you and, suddenly, you are alone on the mound. The astral light fades and the mound is nothing more than an ancient barrow on a windswept plain. In your hand is a small fragment of yellow bone, a piece of that first ancestor who lived thousands upon thousands of years before you, but who also knew of the power of Earth and of the Mother.

Now, take up your garments and robe yourself against the chill night air. It is time to reconnect with your own time and place. Take three or four deep breaths and feel, once more, the heaviness and reality of your own meditating form.

Take a few moments to adjust to the full reality of this level. On doing so, it is recommended that you bathe or shower and eat and drink in order to fully connect with Earth's plane. Record your impressions before they fade.

This is an extremely powerful pathworking and it should not be attempted if you are overtired, ill, under stress, or depressed. Neither should it be undertaken more than once in a full season. It takes that long for the results to make themselves felt on the earth level.

Those who are new to high-level pathworking or to occult practices in general should delay attempting this working until such time as they have prepared themselves for what can be a life-changing experience.

5

Celtic Pathworkings

The word "Celtic" has many meanings. It has come to mean anything concerned with the British Isles and that part of France that is, in fact, not France, but Brittany. The Celts are comparative newcomers to these islands. The ancient Cymri, the Picts, and the Iberians were here before them and have left an indelible mark on the land itself.

As with all lands over which different peoples cross and recross, the legends of invaders, conquerors, and native peoples alike have become entwined. Now it is difficult to separate them. Indeed, I do not think one should even try. Their bonding has become so perfect that it has a pattern all its own. A wondrous, mystical, magical pattern, best symbolized by the familiar, intricate Celtic knotwork.

Even a drop of Celtic blood in your ancestry can trigger the mystic in you. When it's more than a drop, you can get lost in the mist-wreathed legends that surround the Blessed Isles. People with more Viking blood than Celtic may find these too "fey" for their liking.

These four pathworkings include the unusual group-working format. The Guardians of Albion is extremely visual; the Seven Sleepers takes its theme from a legend found all over Europe in various forms. The basic theme of the Castle of the Grail was given to me by W. E. Butler, but this is an updated version. Return to Tir-nan-Og was given its first public hearing at an S.O.L. conference in the form of a dramatized working by a group of students, supervisors, and guest speakers. The Creation of Avalon is based on the legend of Atlantis.

The Guardians of Albion

First, take a blue felt pen and, with it, draw a spiral pattern in the center of your palm. Now hold your hand out, flattening the palm as much as possible. Look at the spiral pattern in your hand. Wait for it to begin to "flash," drawing the eye first forward and downward, then outward and upward. As the alternating movement intensifies, close your eyes and keep the pattern going with your inner sight. Now close your eyes and "see" the spiral within. When it is clear, change it again and "see" it as a pattern under your feet. Make it bigger and bigger, until you can stand upon it. Then walk, following the pattern, into the center. When you reach it, the spiral stands on end and the center opens like a door and pulls you in.

Around you, it begins to grow lighter, as if dawn were speeding toward you. You begin to see the outline of trees, rolling hills, rivers, small streams, and huge forests of closely packed trees, their dark greenness offsetting the lighter grasslands. It is early morning and you are over Albion the Blessed, as it once was, green, still, quiet, and, as yet, almost empty.

You, yourself, are simply an idea, a premonition of the being that will be born sometime in the future. You have no body, no substance. You exist only as a thought from the future. You move lower, to a height just above the treetops. There are no power lines, no buildings, no fences or walls, no roads or fields—just narrow tracks made by animals. The only sounds are those of birds, the wind in trees summer-heavy with leaves, and the call of animals.

On the grassland, there are wild ponies, rabbits, hares. Along the edge of the forests, you catch an occasional glimpse of wild boar, wolf, and bear. Deer, too, are plentiful—the small roebuck, the much larger elk, and other kinds that no longer exist in your own time. Though you have no physical body, your senses are still there, lifted to a much higher level. Use your sense of smell to search out the smell of grass, wildflowers, the heavier scent of trees on the verge of blossoming, the musky scent of animals as the wind changes.

Will yourself toward the sea, or rather, toward where it will be in the future. For where we will one day see the Channel, there is now a steep cliff edge that sweeps down to a wide savannah as far as the eye can see. Great herds of grazing animals cover it. Here and there, small hills and higher ranges lift upward. Many streams and rivers crisscross the plain and there is one large lake of clear water. Rise higher and you will see that Albion is much larger than it will be in the future. What you know as Land's End now juts out as a range of small mountains covered with trees.

You experience a momentary sense of vertigo and when you look down again, the vast plain has gone and a shallow sea can be seen. Lyonesse is still there, but already the hungry waters are eating away at the land. You see a small fleet of ships, similar to the Long Ships of the Vikings that are yet to come. Small groups of people move about a cluster of huts built of wood. Though they are poorly dressed, they walk with an air of those used to a better life. Already they have tamed some of the wild horses and pigs. Wolf and bear skins are drying in the sun, tightly stretched over frames of wood. Beyond the village are patches of green that may be wheat or barley.

What you see are those who escaped from the doomed islands of Atlantis. Go nearer. Three young men circle the village, on guard against wild beasts and perhaps other people. They wear padded leather jerkins over a short leather kilt. Arms and legs are also armored with leather. Close-fitting helmets cover their heads and they carry short, heavy swords of metal. Slung on their backs are longbows and quivers of metal-tipped arrows. Look well and remember them.

Rise up and follow the coastline. Here and there, small settlements have begun to appear. The growing of food and the taming of animals is evident. Inland of the mouth of a river lies a large area of marshland at the foot of a great rounded hill. The marsh is silvered with small streams and, at the edge, lays a shallow lake on which have been built huts that rest on wooden logs planted deep into the lake bottom.

The people here are shorter, darker, more stocky in build than the Atlanteans. They have developed a particular kind of pottery with a small lip at the edge. From this they take the name "The Beaker People." A short, dark, heavily built man tends a fire and watches over the village through the hours of the night. He carries a wooden staff as a weapon. There are few who could stand against him.

Pass on, until you come to the mountains of the future land of Wales. Here you encounter a small, dark people with a curious, but beautiful, lilting language. You watch a tall gray-haired man in a multicolored cloak striding over the high passes, followed by a young man who carries a strangely shaped leather bag on his back. As the Sun sinks westward, they come to a small stone building surrounded by many smaller wood and clay huts. Small children, dogs, goats, and hens scramble around the tall man, as he and his companion enter the village. The door of the stone hall is flung open and the light of a warm fire streams out, along with the smell of cooking. Another man and a woman with hair that brushes her knees welcome them in.

Most of the village crams itself into the hall and waits impatiently while the bard and his apprentice eat. Then he gestures to the younger man to bring him the leather bag. From it, he takes a harp lovingly carved with a stem of flowers growing up the frame. The wooden tuning keys are each carved as the head of a different animal and the wood gleams in the firelight with the patina of age. The bard strikes a chord and music, wild and sweet, fills the air. The clear voice of the apprentice sitting beside him lifts in song.

> *My harp, it hangs on a green willow tree,*
> *Alone, all alone.*
> *The wind through its strings all tattered and torn,*
> *Makes moan, makes moan.*

Now where is the tower,
And the radiant bower,
Love's own, love's own.

Tear-filled eyes steep'd in mournful pride,
Bereft, alone.
My love rose up at the fall of the tide,
My own, my own.
Stricken be the tower
Sadness fill the bower,
Love's flown, love's flown.

I drank of my love's rich splendor,
With her alone.
Sun, Moon, and stars, veiled were their splendor
By her alone.
Though ravishing the kiss,
And sea-deep the bliss
I am humbled and alone.

You move on through the night until, in the early morning mist, you see an island off the coast. Dark with forests of oak it is and filled with the power of the white-robed Druids. In a clearing stand twelve men and women in snowy-white robes. One carries a curved knife with a golden handle in one hand, in the other a branch of golden-leafed white-berried fruit. A young girl prepares to offer her blood to the land that it might be fruitful. She goes with pride and love, for she will become one of the Guardians. Wearing the sacred berries in her hair, she passes from life into greater life.

The forests are thinner now and fields are larger. Houses are made of stone and decorated with mosaics and courtyards where fountains play. The Romans have come and their roads cover the land. Along the borders, a rough wall punctuated by guardtowers crosses from sea to sea. In the blackness beyond the wall, figures slide through the undergrowth. The Roman soldier at his post leans on his spear and dreams of the warm south and a dark-eyed maid with soft breasts. He dies without a sound as Picts cross the wall of Hadrian. But his spirit remains at his post and becomes a Guardian.

On a heather-covered hill in the far north, a clansman wakes in the night as he is called to war. By early morning, his widow walks among the dead to find him and bring him home. She will continue to walk the highlands and call home the dead to their native hearth, for she is a Guardian.

Facing the North Sea on Holy Island, a monk prays in the Chapel of St. Aidan, oblivious to the sudden flurry of shouts and cries. The Vikings strike swiftly and without mercy. The praying soul continues its orisons, praying for both enemy and friends alike, as a Guardian should.

In the fenlands of the southeast, a man wearing the golden circlet of a king sits before a fire in a poor woman's hut. He is playing a battle over in his mind, deciding each move as in a game of chess. Outside, in the bitter northeast winds, his enemies creep closer. But he waits, for the dark, sucking lips of the quicksand protect him. Alfred dreams on. He will lose, we know. But in losing he will gain his Guardianship.

Off Beachy Head, a Spanish galleon goes down. On the shore lies a wounded man. The folk of Albion, for no good reason, will sometimes take an enemy to their hearts. This Spanish sailor will be cared for and healed. Spain will become a memory to be shared with his children, who will never speak his language or see their father's city of Cadiz. He will forget and become part of Albion's soul and take his turn as a Guardian.

On Plymouth Hoe, a young boy stands gazing out to sea where his heart lies. In years to come, his name will ring through history and the waters below him will resound with his name. Drake, Sir Francis Drake. A Guardian, like the others.

You look out to sea, as the Sun begins to sink, then turn to face the land of Albion. As twilight falls, they come to take up their places, as they do every night of every year. Celt and Saxon, Angle and Jute, Norman and Druid, Atlantean and Pict, Viking and Roman, Phoenician trader and stranded seaman. They come silently to take up their posts. A few have names that ring like bells. Most are simply people who loved the land in which they were born, or died. Raleigh and Spencer, Sir

Philip Sidney and the slight figure of Richard Plantagenet, the second of that name.

William Rufus, the Witch King, stands by Thomas à Becket and Thomas Moore, all religious enmity forgotten in the greater cause. Effingham and Cecil, Hadrian and Hereward the Wake, the slight figure of Kipling and the stout cigar-smoking Churchill, Douglas Bader and Montgomery. A platoon of the Gurka Rifles and a band of fierce Sikhs stand side by side with a Cavalier and a Roundhead. Charles Stuart and Cromwell, no longer kings or usurpers, but Guardians. There are others too, those who have left their natural home in other countries and made Albion's cause their cause. Polish airmen and soldiers, Dutch and French, and young Americans whose forefathers sailed in the Mayflower. Asian refugees, dark, smiling faces of African descent, and tall weapon-bearing Pathans and Hindus. All who have drawn from the breast of the White Goddess are accounted her children.

A silence falls, as the sun touches the sea and sends a beam of brilliant light toward the gathering. As it touches the first white cliff, the mighty throng divides and the Guardians look toward the one who comes at each turning of the season. A wondrous figure, clad in cloth-of-gold edged with myriad pearls. A collar of fine lace frames her sharp-featured face and throws into contrast the flame-red hair.

Drake and Raleigh go forward to kneel and greet the woman they call Gloriana. In the final burst of sunlight, her voice is as clear and strong as it was that day on the wharf at Tilbury Dock, with the Armada in sight of Devon.

"My loving people, we have been persuaded by some that are careful of our safety to take heed how we commit ourselves to armed multitudes for fear of treachery. But I assure you, I do not desire to distrust my faithful, loving people. Let the tyrants only fear. I have always so conducted myself that, under God, I have placed my chiefest strength and safeguard in the loyal hearts and goodwill of my subjects.

"Therefore I come among you at this time . . . being resolved in the midst of battle to live and die among you all, and to lay down for my God, my kingdom, and for my people, my honor and my blood. I know I have the body of a weak and feeble woman, but I have the heart and stomach of a king, aye, and of a King of England, too. I heap foul scorn on Spain or any prince of Europe who dares invade the borders of my realm. Rather than allowing any dishonor to grow by me, I myself will take up arms and will be your general, the judge and rewarder of your virtues in the field. Come the four quarters of the world in arms and we shall shock them.

"I know of your forwardness. You have deserved crowns and we do assure you, on the word of a prince, that they shall be duly paid. In the meantime, no prince commands more noble and worthy subjects. I doubt not that, by your valor in the field, we shall shortly have a famous victory over these enemies of my God, my kingdom, and my people."

Her voice falls silent and the darkness grows around us. We are the children of Alba, the White Goddess, so named for the great Chalk Downs on which so much of our history has come about. We are now, as always, a land of many nations. The mixture has made us strong in the past, and will continue to add to our strength in the future. At our feet is the center of a spiral path. We follow it, feeling it slope downward toward the physical plane, feeling the added weight of matter come upon us as we do so. As we reach the final step, we take a deep breath, hold it . . . and let it out, coming into full consciousness as we do so.

The Seven Sleepers

When you are comfortable and relaxed, close your eyes and wait. After a while, you build up the feeling of a wind in your face. It is clean and fresh and smells of autumn and wood fires. You feel cool and add the feeling of a warm woolen cloak about your shoulders. Now, bring in the feeling of walking along a road. You can feel the uneven surface under your feet, so it must be a track or a path rather than a road. The wind suggests that you are probably on a hillside. Certainly the place has the sense of open countryside. Now open your inner eyes.

You are walking along a footpath that will take you toward an ancient hill fort. On one side is the sea. On the other, the land slopes down to a wooded valley. Once it was a guard against the Vikings from the sea and, earlier, from the invading Normans. Now it is overgrown and all that can be seen are grassy mounds arranged in a rough rectangle. There are several levels, rising to where there once stood a hall and a tower within a protecting wall.

It is very quiet and only the call of seabirds as they wheel overhead breaks the stillness. You wonder what kind of people they were, and how they lived their lives. There is a legend about this strange and haunted place. They say that, beneath it, seven knights lie sleeping. At the entrance to their underground hall is a great horn slung on a baldric of gold. If this horn is blown, it will awaken the sleepers. Then they will mount the horses that await them and ride forth to do battle. So goes the old tale.

You begin to climb to the top of the hill fort. It is steeper than it looks and, toward the top, you have to scramble on hands and knees. Once there, however, you have a wonderful view. Immediately before you is the sea. Today it is a greenish-gray color and the waves are white-tipped and slow-moving. Far out to sea is a ship making its way to harbor. Moving clockwise, you can make out a distant headland wearing a fluffy hat of mist and cloud as it huddles over the bay beneath it. From there on, your view moves inland to rolling hills, some of which are topped with circles of ancient beeches now turning red and gold. Small villages hide in the valleys, leaving only the tops of the church spires to spy out the land. You feel heady with the view and the air.

As you turn, you notice a much taller "hump" at one end of the fort. It is grass-covered and ground ivy has wound around it, totally covering whatever it once was. You walk over and pull away some of the growth. Beneath there are stone blocks that look as if they had once been a part of the tower.

Pull away some more ivy and you discover an archway and the top of a flight of steps. Testing each step as you go, you follow them down. At first, you mean to go only as far as the light will allow you to see. But you find yourself going down and down. By your calculations, you must be under the fort by now. Then the steps come to an end and you are in an underground passage made from stone, with a rounded ceiling and archways every ten yards. You begin to walk forward.

A faint light filters along the passage. It comes from a place some way ahead. You walk on. Before you is an open door of weather-beaten wood. Its panels are warped in some places and have shrunk away from the frame. You can see how thick it is and how strong it would once have been. It has bronze studs running down each beam from top to bottom and, in the center, there is a small grille through which it is possible to see into the room beyond. The huge hinges are of iron, as is the lock. The key lies on the ground, as if it had fallen, or been dropped in a hurry.

Hanging from an iron hook by the door is a great hunting horn. Its mouthpiece is banded with silver; wider bands of the precious metal decorate it further down. Each band has been engraved with intricate knotwork. It hangs from a faded, threadbare baldric that was once scarlet, but has now faded to a deep rose, its delicate gold-thread embroidery torn and discolored. For a moment, you are tempted to take it down and try to blow it, but then you remember the legend. If you do that, the knights will awaken. Cautiously, you step inside the door and look around.

It looks like the crypt of a large church. The floor is flagged and the ceiling vaulted. At the far end is an altar on which a light burns steadily. You do not wonder how this can be; you accept it, for you have been overcome with a sense of wonder and awe. The fragrant smell of incense fills the cold air.

Arranged in a half circle before the altar are seven couches covered with deep-blue silk. On each couch, fully armored lies a man, his head resting on a blue silk cushion. Each knight clasps a naked sword along his body, the hilt resting on his breast. The scabbard and belt lie at the side. Leaning against each couch is a war shield bearing the coat of arms of the knight. His helm, with its decorated crest and plume, is placed at his feet. Along one wall stand seven pure-white horses. All are saddled and ready. The bridles are of velvet and leather and are jeweled. Each stands tethered, ready to be mounted.

You touch the cheek of the nearest knight. It is cool, but soft and pliable. The same is true of the horses. You see on the altar a chalice covered with a veil, and a platter containing wafers. Communion is ready for them to take before they ride out.

Beside the altar is a chest filled with gold and silver and precious things. Among them is a small box of carved wood. It is locked, but the key is in the lock. There is also a mirror, a dagger, and a lantern with an unlit candle inside. As you stare, you hear a footstep. Heart pounding, you turn. An old woman stands before you wrapped in a cloak. Her face is lined and wrinkled, but gentle and full of wisdom. She speaks:

"Do not fear, I am not here to harm you. Only those who are meant to see this sight are permitted to find the way. But you cannot stay long or else the spell that binds these warriors to their long sleep will engulf you also. You may partake of the wine and the bread, and then you may choose one thing from the treasures you see beside the altar. Choose carefully. Some things are not what they might appear to be."

You go to the altar and uncover the chalice and the platter. You sip of the wine; it tastes sweet and heady. The wafer is slightly salty and melts upon the tongue. Then you turn to the treasure and make your choice. The old woman smiles when you come to her. She shows you the great door behind the tapestry, through which the knights will ride when they wake. Now you, too, must leave. As you do, you accidentally knock the horn and its makes a hollow sound. One of the knights stirs, opens his eyes, and asks; "Is it time?"

"No my son," says the old woman. "Go back to sleep." The knight sighs, lies back, and closes his eyes. She looks up and motions you to leave. You pass through the door and into your own time.

The Castle of the Grail

Relax and close your eyes. Create in your inner world a mist like the kind you see on autumn mornings at sunrise. Feel the coolness and the dampness as you walk into it. Sound is deadened in the mist, as if you walked far above Earth. It thins out and you step into a sunset world with a green valley below you, and a small town. You can hear the distant sounds of people going about their business, cows lowing as they wait to be milked, the clatter of carts drawn homeward by weary horses, the voices of women gossiping.

On the other side of the valley, a road winds up to a castle overlooking the valley, town, and hills beyond to the sea in the distance. The battlements show a gleam of fire from the braziers lit to warm the guards in the cool of the night. Windows glow with candles. Pennants blow in the wind, and horses hooves clatter on cobbles. The sound of hammer on iron comes from the forge.

The topmost pennant displays the head of a red dragon on a white-and-gold background. This is Camelot, the castle of Arthur, the High King. We descend into the valley, noting that we are dressed as pilgrims in gray robes, warm cloaks, stout leather shoes, and staves.

The way is fairly easy and we are soon on the road. By the time we reach the town, most houses are closed against the coming night. But some people are abroad and the ale house is doing good business. We enter it to ask the way. Inside, there is a cheerful fire to warm us. The floor is made of packed earth covered with straw and along each wall are trestle tables and benches. A cauldron, filled with a stew that smells delicious, bubbles over the fire. It is early yet, but the maids are bustling about preparing for later.

We are invited to sit at one of the tables. The landlady comes and asks from where we have come. We answer truthfully—from a place very far away. She accepts this and offers us mugs of cider or ale. We take off the heavy cloaks and there is a sudden silence. Over our left breasts, embroidered in red and gold, is the symbol of the Grail.

The landlady curtseys low and offers us the hospitality of her inn. Grail seekers are always guests here. She puts before us thick slices of bread spread with a strong-smelling cheese, and a bowl of sliced onions. This is followed by wooden bowls of the stew. We have coins in a leather-lined pocket so we can pay for our food, but our hostess will hear none of it.

She sits and talks to us about others that have passed this way and, when we tell her we are bound for the castle where we have business with the king, she offers to send her son to show us the way. When we have finished, we rise and bless the lady and her inn and take up our cloaks once more. The son comes with a lantern and we follow him into the night.

The road to the castle is steeper than we thought and it is good that we have a guide. We come at last to the drawbridge and the lad hails the guard. The bridge is let down and we thank the boy and give him some coins. Inside the castle walls, we see a large courtyard with stables and kennels for the hounds. The bright forge fire of the farrier lights up everything. One of the guards asks our business and we answer that it is with the king. He takes us through into the inner ward of the castle, where there is a lawn and fruit trees and a place for the ladies of the castle to sit and talk. Here is the entrance to the castle proper.

We enter . . . Camelot. From the high vaulted ceiling of the great hall hang three circular candelabra, each carrying thirty or more tallow candles the thickness of a man's wrist. More light comes from torches in iron sconces along each side. Rich tapestries glowing with color adorn the walls and, beneath our feet, sweet grasses and hay cover the stone-flagged floor. On each side, wooden tables are set, leaving the central area, with its fire pit, clear for the servants. For two-thirds of their length, the tables are covered with linen and have chairs set at intervals. The other third is bare and has wooden benches.

At the top of the hall, raised above the rest, is the king's table. It faces the length of the hall and its chairs are high-backed and richly decorated, with those of Arthur and Guenevere being the most elaborate. The table is set with fine linen and the plate is of gold and silver. In the center of the table is a large, elaborate silver saltcellar.

We have arrived in the middle of the evening meal and the hall is filled with knights, ladies, and servants. Cei, Arthur's foster brother, sees us. He calls out.

"My Lord, strangers in the hall!"

All chatter stops immediately. Several knights rise to their feet, hands ready on the hilts of their swords. We come forward into the light and throw back the cloaks so that the Grail symbol is clearly seen. A buzz of surprise runs around the assembled company. From the shadows behind the king comes a slight figure dressed in soft grays and deep purple. It is Nimue, the Enchantress. Her voice is clear and carries through the hall like a bell.

"Those who carry the sign of the Cup of Cups are welcome in Arthur's hall. How are you named, strangers, and for what purpose do you come here?"

One of our company steps forward and bows to the king and queen, and to the one who speaks for them.

"We are seekers who have been called to the Castle of the Grail. We are bidden to ask the king for horses, and for knights to ride with us as protectors." Arthur rises—not a tall man, but strongly built and with a noble face.

"If you have heard the call of the Grail, then I will do all in my power to aid you. Will you dine with us?"

Our spokesman thanks him, but explains that we have already eaten. The king turns to his assembled knights.

"Who will ride with the seekers? Three are needed."

"I will ride." The speaker is a tall dark-haired man with a proud face. His tunic is of black velvet edged with gold, its sleeves dipping almost to the floor. The king nods, smiling.

"I would have laid my life on your offer, Lancelot. Who else?"

"I will go."

"I also."

Two knights rise to their feet—young Gareth of Orkney and Sir Dinadan, the joker, whose laughing face belies his strength as a knight. All three summon their squires and leave the hall to prepare for the journey. We are taken to the high table and, having greeted the queen, we are seated and given wine. Arthur tells us that horses are being prepared and questions us eagerly about our summons to the Grail. We explain that we are of the priesthood of Atlantis, and that the Moon Bowl, once the sacred vessel of Naradek, is now part of the Grail, the newest symbol of a power older than time itself.

A servant comes to tell us all is ready for our leaving. Arthur rises and toasts our journey in wine, joined by everyone in the hall. We thank him and his company and leave with the servant. In the outer courtyard, the three knights, armored and horsed, await us. There is also another rider, cloaked and hooded.

The grooms help us to mount our horses and arrange the thick cloaks comfortably. The guards run to lower the drawbridge and we ride, in double file, under the stone arch and take the high road that leads over the rolling downs.

We can see the town below us, as the Moon rises into a clear, starry night, turning everything to silver. The horses carry us swiftly over the ground and soon town, castle, and hills are left behind. The wind is in our faces and we hold the cloaks tightly around us to keep warm. As we crest the top of a tree-crowned hill, the extra rider reins in the horse and turns to face us. The hood is thrown back to reveal the face of Nimue.

Arthur has asked her to open the Second Road, the Faery Road, so we can make the journey more quickly. She bids Lancelot set his dagger into the earth to keep the road open until we return. He drives the metal deep into the ground. Then Nimue opens the Second Road with a ringing shout, in a language older than the sea. The air shimmers, cracks, and peels back to show a landscape that seems to fit over the one we know. An older scene, the trees are thicker, the earth itself shimmers with light, everything is tipped with magic. We see figures that flit among the trees, and winged creatures, long-vanished from Earth, fly overhead. Unicorns step delicately from the trees to watch us pass and white figures dance in and out of ancient stone rings.

The ground flies beneath the horses, who seem fearful of this place. On and on we ride. Sometimes it seems we ride high above Earth. At other times, we gallop through the shapes of trees that exist on the Earth we know, but not in this strange place. Ahead there is another gate, a rippling cut in the fabric of time. We pass through and find ourselves before a castle with tall slender turrets, built of delicate pink-veined stone. The drawbridge stands open, ready for us. High over the tallest tower flies a white banner emblazoned with the device of a silver chalice. It is the Castle of the Grail.

The knights ride ahead and we follow, all but Nimue. She stays behind, explaining that, as one of the Faery Folk far older than the Grail, she cannot enter Christian ground. We ride into the courtyard and dismount. It seems deserted, but not neglected. We pass into the inner ward. We hear the horses being taken away and turn to see them led by invisible hands to water and feed that await them. We come to the door of the great hall and it opens silently. The knights cross themselves and enter before us, their hands on the hilts of their swords. Inside, all is richness and beauty. A table stands ready with mulled wine to warm us.

From the hall, a stairway leads up to another floor. There are many corridors, all with doors leading off them. Some rooms are richly furnished, others are bare. We see other stairs, but leave them unexplored. Then Lancelot calls to us. He has found a door marked with the symbol of the Grail. He opens it. The room inside has been simply furnished as a chapel.

An altar with a half circle of high-backed chairs before it occupies the far end. Three arched windows of exquisite stained glass fill the wall behind the altar. A pierced screen stands in front of a door on one side of the chapel. Before each chair is a velvet hassock. We feel the power and the sanctity of this place and silently take our places in the circle of chairs and wait. We hear the sweet voices of a choir approaching, but, although the voices grow louder and seem to enter the chapel, we see no one. As the processional reaches its climax, the door behind the screen opens and a priest enters. There is an air of serenity about him that calms us. He is tall and fine-boned, with a small beard and snow-white hair. He wears a simple white robe. In his hands, he carries a veiled cup that he sets down on the altar. He turns to us.

"Long ago, I was known as Joseph of Arimathea. When he was young, I brought my nephew, Jesus, to this sacred isle and we walked its green hills together. After his death, when it was necessary to hide the Sacred Cup, I remembered this place. I brought it across the sea and placed it in the keeping of one I could trust. Once in each hundred years, I return to celebrate the Mass with the Grail. This time, I have lingered so that you might come and be served at the Table of the Grail.

Those who come with you may be present, but you, Lancelot, may not yet partake of the Grail, though you may stand in its veiled presence. You know the reason for this. Gareth, you may also stay in its presence and will see it unveiled. Dinadan, you alone of these knights may drink from the Grail for you are the Divine Fool. The seekers may come now and partake of the Sacred Cup.

We go forward one by one and take the merest sip of wine. It flows through our veins like fire. The pain, as it cleanses body and soul, is almost unbearable. Dinadan comes to take his share, then pauses and humbly offers his place, if it be allowed, to "the best knight in all the world." Joseph smiles but shakes his head. The knight drinks, then turns and kisses his two comrades on the lips, thus sharing with them the little he can. Joseph smiles.

"For this, be thou blessed, dear Fool."

One of our number steps forward and asks why Nimue cannot enter the castle and take from the Grail. The priest answers.

"The Faery Folk may take from the Cup, all that prevents them is their fear of being refused. All things that live may come to the Cup, though sometimes it will be withheld, but only for a reason and for a while. It will be given when the time is right. Now you must go, but I will come with you to the gate."

We leave the chapel and make our way back to the gate where our horses stand ready. Just outside stands Nimue, holding her horse's bridle. Joseph calls to her.

"Nimue, Lady of the Fair Folk, if you wish, you may drink from the Cup of Cups. It is your right and the right of all your kind. This you may tell them. When next I come, they are welcome to enter the Castle of the Grail."

For a moment, she stands, eyes wide. Then slowly, she approaches and takes a sip from the Cup. Her face lights up and she closes her eyes in ecstasy. We mount once more and take our leave of the Guardian of the Grail. The doorway to the Second Road opens up and we pass through into the world of Faery. No longer is it empty. Our way is lined with the Sidhe, the Fair Ones, waiting to see us pass and to look upon the first of their kind to take of the Grail. And so we come to the gate leading into this world and here Nimue bids us farewell. She must go and spread the news to her people. We pass through to find ourselves at the drawbridge of Camelot.

In the darkness of the Moon's setting, Arthur waits for us, alone and unattended. We thank him and the knights for their kindness and help. Arthur asks wistfully if our time still remembers him. We tell him, "Yes, and all those who made up the Table Round." They look at each other with smiles, well-pleased at this. We turn and go down the hill. The mist closes about us and we walk through into our own time and place.

The Creation of Avalon

I am the Keeper of Records for that place of many names, but ofttimes called the Blessed Isles. So you will understand more fully why they are thus named, I will take you upon a journey through time and space. I will show you the wonders of Merlin's Enclosure and you will speak with those who have guarded its secrets since the beginning of its history.

We stand wrapped in the mantle of space lit only by the light of the stars as it travels through the universe recording all that transpires. As the light passes us, we are gathered into it, held like a mote of dust. Faint echoes of past events in every corner of the universe surround us as we travel, and it seems to us that long aeons pass.

Below us is your solar system, its brilliant Sun surrounded by circles of planets. Each sings its own song of existence as it treads out its ordained path. The third planet is a beautiful thing of blue and white and silver set against the black velvet of space. We drop down to it, following its dawn as it rouses life to a new day. We speed over a range of newborn mountains and down into the valleys, pass over forests, and halt before a shining ribbon of water. We see before us the gleam of chalk cliffs as white as a swan's breast, impregnable as ancient Caer Sidi, beautiful as the White Goddess whose living body makes up this land of magic and mystery.

Waiting for us is the first and greatest of its priest-guardians. Through the ages, he has guarded, served, and cherished this land. No warrior-king has arisen but he, Merlin, has trained him, aye and her too, for there have been warrior-maids whose blood has watered the grass and flowers of Britain. Listen as he tells us how it all came to be.

"Before the lands of the West were drowned and went down into a darkness of their own making, Narada, the Manu of that Age, walked in the land of Albion. The place he loved most he named Ynys Afal-Llon, the Happy Isle of Apples, for it grew the sweetest of that fruit. Here, he sought peace from his task of bringing to the human race an understanding of its divine destiny. So great was his love for this place that he climbed the tall hill that stood in its midst and summoned to him the lords of Flame, Form, and Mind. He called also the Cherubim and the Beni Elohim, the bright Chasmalim and the fiery Seraphim. The lordly Aralim and the golden-crowned Malachim came at his bidding, for he was the Beloved of the One.

"From each of the company he asked a gift that would enhance the power of Ynys Afal-Llon. As each one passed before Narada, a small part of the essence of their power went forth from them and became part of Ynys Afal-Llon forever, spilling over into Albion itself. With each gift, the isles grew in beauty and power. Look and see it come about."

We watch the story unfold. There, upon the tor, we see the shining form of Narada and about him, in a circle, stand the Great Ones. They are like columns of flame in every color the mind can imagine. From the Ashim comes the power to endure, the Cherubim give strength in adversity. The gift of the Beni Elohim is that of clear speech and the power of the written word. Beauty in all its forms comes from the fair Elohim.

"Blessed be the land with beauty," they sing, "Fair its women, its shores, mountains, and valleys. Let it be covered with gentle mists and a cloak of green. It shall be the dwelling place of the Elven Folk"

The regal Malachim offer a line of kings and queens that will never fail, a royal line to rule with the grace of the Creator until the land of Albion shall be no more. Courage, loyalty, and love of justice are given by the Seraphim, the warrior-angels who serve under Michael. Never shall the men of Albion flee before an enemy, but their mercy shall be as great as their courage. The shining Chasmalim give the gift of clear sight. The seers of this land shall be renowned through the ages and will speak with clarity and vision.

The Aralim give the gift of magic in all its forms and fix its source at sacred points in the land itself. This, above all others, is the gift that will make the name of Albion ring through the centuries to come. The Auphanim offer their gift of wisdom to enrich the wise ones of this land and make them like unto the gods themselves. But the most blessed gift is still to come.

From the very throne of the one Creator come the Four Holy Creatures. They lift the physical vale of Ynys Afal-Llon away from Earth and place it between the worlds and dimensions. There it will remain forever as it was. No part of it shall decay or die, but will stay as it was on this day. Those that find their way to it, or who are brought to it by magical means, shall be gifted with youth and eternity. Here, the Holy Four promise, all heroes, wise men and women, the great ones of the land shall come in their time to be ready for the last battle.

All this is decreed, but, because all things have their price, these gifts may only come to pass if a sacrifice of love is made. Narada offers himself gladly, but the Holy Ones say, "Your time is not yet come; it must be another." Narada weeps, for whom could he ask to make such a sacrifice. As he weeps, there comes walking up the winding serpent path to the summit the one whom Narada loves beyond life itself. She comes, walking in beauty and grace, with flowers in her long dark hair and the early morning dew on her lily-white feet. She bows low before the Great Ones and speaks.

"Narada, servant of the Most High, Priest of the Sun, my love, and my joy. You have asked the Great Ones for their magical gifts that Afal-Llon may be set apart forever—that Albion may be blessed with magic and mystery beyond all other lands. They have agreed to do so if a matching sacrifice is made with love. So it shall be. With this knife, I give my blood willingly and with love so that all shall be as you have asked, my love."

Before Narada can stop her, Epona sinks the knife into her breast and her bright blood spills on to the earth and blesses it. The Four Great Ones gather around her body and build above it a web of light, and as Narada watches through his tears he sees a great wonder. The body of Epona sinks into the ground and her spirit becomes one with the soul of Albion. A web of light spreads in all directions, covering the land and sanctifying it with the power of the willing sacrifice. Then the Great Ones depart and leave Narada with his sorrow.

Then comes the voice of Epona from the earth beneath his feet, from wind in the trees, and from the rocks, hills, rivers, and streams, from the high mountains and the deep valleys. She bids him lift his heart and speaks of what is to come in future times and the part that Albion will play in the future of the world. She will be part of it, of this land he loves so dearly, until, one day, another willingly takes on the burden of sacrifice. Then she will be free to join him.

Narada looks and sees before him a white horse. It drops at his feet a golden ring that he had given to his love. Then it turns and gallops away. Now he understands how great is the magic of woman, for it is the magic of love itself.

Many thousands of years have passed and Narada has long since returned to his own place. But Epona works her magic through the womenfolk of Albion. They have become great seeresses and guided the land to greatness. Through her power, they have ruled as queens and warrior-maids. They have given birth to heroes mightier than any seen before. But always in Albion there have been two who held the keys of Afal-Llon, a man and a woman. The priests of the mysteries of Britain take as a title the name of Merlin, and the priestesses have become the Nimue. Epona, too, is remembered and worshiped as a goddess who walked the green ways of England in the form of a white horse. Her image is cut into the hills high above the valleys so that her sacrifice will always be remembered.

Thus speaks Merlin, the magical heir of the first of his kind. We see before us a path of interwoven colors and, with the Merlin, we walk high above the ancient land. Before us are the gates of Avalon, the name by which we now know Afal-Llon. We pause as they open wide to allow a mighty throng from the Isle of Apples to emerge. Nimue speaks:

"At Midsummer each year, these gates open wide and the mighty ones of Albion's past come forth to walk once more in the green land of their birth. For seven days, they have the freedom of Albion. When the Midsummer fires are on the hills, that is the time to watch for them. There is Boudicca with her daughters, and Caractacus, a Celtic chief of great renown. Beside him walks Hereward, surnamed The Wake. Behind is Alfred of the Saxons and Llewellyn of Welsh blood royal. The beautiful woman clothed only in her hair is Godiva, who gave her modesty that her people might go free from taxes. There is Harald Godwinson, who lost to the dark Norman, William. Yonder is Robin i' the Hood and with him the Foresters of Nottingham and Maid Marian, whom he loved.

Now come Drake and Raleigh, Philip Sidney and Henry, the victor of Agincourt. A brave band of men. Robert the Bruce and Rob Roy, aye and Wallace, too. Old quarrels forgotten at this blessed time. We see many we do not recognize and Merlin tells us that there were, and are, many heroes unsung. Unknown men and women both, they have earned their right to rest in Avalon. Edith Cavell passes by, accompanied by a young man scarce 20 years old. His body lies in Albion's greatest cathedral, Westminster Abbey. We know him simply as the Unknown Soldier.

Young men in leather flying jackets from the Battle of Britain and women in uniform, and an elderly man walking more slowly. He smokes a large cigar. Churchill always returns at the time of his greatest triumph. All are smiling and joyful.

The Elven Folk follow and scatter, each to that place they know best. Lastly comes Arthur and his knights. For a short time, the Blessed Isles will be filled with the power and magic of the old days. It is a time to work for the good of the land. But we know there is more to our being here than this. Merlin turns and smiles at us, and bids us remember him. Then, still smiling, he sinks down into the earth and becomes one with it. We turn to Nimue, who smiles through tears and tells us:

"It is time for Epona to be freed. He wished to reunite her with Narada, and, to this end, he has taught me all he knows, as I shall teach the next one. I will wait until another will come and release him, as he has released her."

A white form rises from the earth, tall and slender, with dark hair falling to her knees. Her eyes are filled with joy and love and she holds out her arms. From far beyond this universe comes Narada in his form of light, a man built of stars. He enfolds her in his arms and she, too, takes on a form of stars. Together they rise into the night sky and are lost to our sight.

Around us, all grows dim and we feel the pull of our physical bodies. But what we have seen, we will remember. Come next Midsummer, we will watch for them.

Awake to the world.

6

Pathworkings of the Craft and the Fairy Faith

Strictly speaking these two traditions should be separate, but they do have close ties and I hope those who follow these traditions will forgive me for linking them in this way. The Fairy Faith has a larger following in the United States than in England, where, if it is followed at all, it is done so in a closely guarded way. Few will admit to knowing much about it.

Though I am not claiming to be an expert, it appears that the Fairy tradition in England is found mostly in the western isles of Scotland, North Wales, and the Isle of Man, and in certain more remote parts of Ireland. Though I certainly know people who are steeped in this tradition and have taken part in some of their rites, the pathworkings that follow are of my own invention. The ones I have been privileged to join in are part of "withdrawn" information and cannot be given out.

The Celtic tradition is one of the richest veins of magical knowledge on this planet. True, the magic is mostly of a mystical nature, but the sheer beauty of its words, music, and rites overrides all barriers and "leavens" the whole area of magic. The books by Caitlin and John Matthews have opened up the Celtic Otherworld for everyone. No one has done more to uncover the beauty of its mythic power and the splendor of its inhabitants.

The late Colonel Seymour, Dion Fortune's Moon Priest, was another master of Celtic magic. For more information, read Alan Richardson's *Dancers to the Gods*, Gareth Knight's *New Dimensions Red Book*, and my own *The Forgotten Mage*.

Within the Hollow Hills

You stand in the darkness of an unlit room. Before you is a half-open door through which comes light. You drift backward from the light, slowly, until it is just a faint brightness in the distance. Make a quarter-turn to the left and see another light. Move toward it until you see that it is another door. It opens and you cross the threshold.

Before you is a green plain crossed by many small streams. From the center rises a great oval hill around which spirals a narrow path. On the top of the hill, looking toward the sea, stands a man wrapped in a long fur-lined cloak. His face is very old and lined with care. His eyes, however, are vitally alive and full of wisdom. He sees you and gestures for you to climb up and stand beside him. He greets you courteously.

You ask where you are and he tells you that this is the Tor of Ynyswitrin, also known as Glastonbury. You look at him closely and realize that this old man is the Merlin of Britain, the Archemage of the Blessed Isles. He again looks across the land and you ask him why, and for whom he waits. He sighs, sits down on a stone seat, and tells you to sit beside him.

He tells you it is time for the firstborn of Gaia to leave Earth and seek another place to live. The Fair Folk, the elves, the fairies, the heroes, gods, and goddesses. The Lordly Ones, the makers of magic, are coming to this place from all over the Blessed Isles and beyond. Merlin has found a way whereby they can leave a world where they are no longer welcome, where there is no room, no time, no green place, no rest or gentleness, and no belief in them or of them. Now he waits for them to come and, in one great act of magic, he will open the doors of this great hill and they will pass within, away from the world of humans, to a place they can make their very own, with no hindrance from the world of humans.

From this time, the world will be without the Fair Folk. No great heroes with magical powers and weapons will be born. Darkness, war, and injustice will rule. Humanity will believe only what they can see and touch, not what their feelings show them. The Fair Folk go, not willingly, but because they must. They will take with them those things that must pass from Earth, lest they be lost forever.

You look down and see three figures climbing the tor, all carrying harps on their backs. The Merlin goes to greet them, calling them by name: Taliesin, Amergin, Llewarch. They answer joyfully. He brings them to you and, courteously, they mask their surprise at finding a human here. Your eye is caught by a gray cloud in the otherwise clear sky. In it can be seen sparks of brilliant light. You ask the Merlin what is this gray cloud rushing toward the tor. He replies that it is the Fair Folk coming to the Great Parting.

You watch the cloud draw near and see that it is made of thousands of strange beings, the smaller being held aloft by those bigger and stronger. The small folk scramble up the tor to greet the Merlin; the others settle down at the foot. The black Kelpies and the gray Silkies are carrying their magical skins. Brownies and Boggles, Pookas and Palugs, and green-skinned Dryads. Tiny winged nature spirits and spectral hags. Along with them are the heroes who never die and the ancient gods and all their kind. From the cold lands of the north comes one-eyed Odin, riding his eight-legged horse, Sleipnir. Thor comes and golden-haired Sif. Frey brings his sister, Freya. Frigga, Loki, and Baldur are here and the Valkyries in the flying ship named Skidbaldnir. Heimdall on his three-headed horse leads the dwarves who carry the tools of the trades as miners and smiths. Fenris, the ancient Wolf God, prowls behind.

The Merlin turns to the east and points and, there in the distance, we can see the Elven Folk, tall men and beauteous women dressed in green and gold and riding elven steeds, the like of which no human rider can control. The Trolls from the icy mountains of the northeast, the Villies and Dukobours, the Banaceks and Domovoi of the high Tatra Mountains. After them come the archetypal figures of children's stories. From now on, they will come only in dreams. Never again will they be met on the highway or in the deep forests or in the quietness of the woods at eventide.

Now, from the west come the giant warriors of the Tuatha and their womenfolk, as tall and as fierce as the men; Nuada and Deirdre of the Sorrows; Cuchulain and Maeve; Lugh, with his great spear of light; Dagda, with his cauldron; Danu the Goddess of the Boyne; Fohla, the Keeper of the Apples of Youth; and Aengus Og, with Etain the Beautiful. Great horses follow them and giant hounds, dainty maidens lead snowy unicorns by their golden horns and feed them choice grass roots. Swan-maids sweep in and land to change into human form on the green lands below the tor. From the northwest comes Mannanan and his court, Gwydion, an archmage to rival Merlin, but one who nevertheless bows to him in deference. Rhiannon and her birds, dark-browed Pwyll, Arianrhod, Llyr and Llew Llaw Gyffes, and, far behind, sad-faced Blodeuddew follow and find their places.

Across the sea, far to the south, come the many gods of ancient Egypt. Atum Ra leads his children, Shu and Tefnut, Geb and star-born Nuit. Isis and Osiris with Horus and, just behind, Set and Nephthys, and Anubis with Thoth, recording all that is going on. Behind them come the Titans, no longer chained, Prometheus and Atlas, maimed Chronus and sweet-faced Rhea. The rowdy Olympians, Zeus and Hera still quarreling, Ares hand-in-hand with Aphrodite, and Hephasteus limping behind them. Hermes flies overhead with Iris, while Artemis and Apollo drive their bright chariots. Pluto brings his beauteous Persephone, while Demeter walks behind with Hebe. Poseidon and Thetis rise from the distant sea and travel via the rivers and streams to the foot of the tor. Pan comes last of all, surrounded by his satyrs, fauns, nymphs, and nixies.

From farther east come the many gods of India. Tara and Brahma, Shiva and Kali, Rama, Indra, Laxshmi and Vishnu, and elephant-headed Ganesh. Izanami and Izanagi, hand-in-hand, follow the Sun Goddess of Japan and a whole retinue of gods.

Now come the Melusines and Lamias, the ancient gods of the earliest days, so strange in form and shape that even Merlin is curious. Ogun, the African war lord, and Eurzulie-Freda, Yemana, and Papa Legba, Le Baron Cimitére and Damballah.

From the depths of the sea, from the ancient drowned lands, come the earliest gods of all, led by the snowy-winged Pegasus. Finally, from Albion itself, come Wayland and Epona, Brigantia and Mona, Herne and the Wild Hunt, Aradia and Celemon, and the small Fairy Folk. They can no longer live with humankind, but must pass from Earth in order to keep their reality against a time when belief in them will open the door again. From now on, only in the mind's eye and the heart's temple, may they be met. But Merlin has decreed that, if the heart be true and the belief is there, the doors will open and those who are young in heart may go through and meet with those who have passed.

Still they come filling the vale of Avalon until it seems that there is no more room and no more gods or Fair Folk left in the world. The last to come is Arthur with his court, Igraine, Morgan le Fay, Lancelot, Guenevere, Gawain, and all the Table Round and the court of Camelot.

You look out over the gathered company and see that even the mythical beasts have come; the griffin and the basilisk, the lion and the white hart, the roc and the dragons, the genies and the jinn, and all the beasts of legend. As the Sun begins to set, Merlin starts to form the gate that will lead under the hill and far away.

All is silent, as the mighty throng loans him their strength and their powers. For many hours, he concentrates upon the base of the tor. He delves deeply into the memory of Gaia and seeks out the gods that were before the earliest gods. The lightning strikes the tor time after time, and, time after time, Merlin reels back exhausted. Then Gaia herself cries out from her depths and with a terrible rending sound, there opens at the base of the hill the mouth of a great cave. It is dark and deep and, for a moment, it seems that there is nothing more. Then, from this open heart of Mother Earth, there comes light and music and the sound of bells ringing deep under the earth.

Sweet scents pour from the cave and the voice of Gaia herself is heard calling to them.

"Come my children, come my beloved Firstborn. Rest in me and have your beingness in my heart."

The mighty gathering rises, and under the guidance of the Merlin, they begin to pass into the Hollow Hills of Earth, each finding a place according to their needs and desires. With them go the birds and animals, the beasts of the field, forest, mountain, and plain. Yes, even those who have passed from Earth, decimated and exterminated by humanity. The fruits of Earth will go with them and take root in the places of the Fair Folk.

With music and song, they pass from the world of men into the heart of Earth. Some look back and sigh, others pass straight on. For three days and three nights they pass, until the plain around the tor is empty. The last to enter are the Court of Camelot and the Knights of the Round Table. Arthur Pendragon pauses before you and unbuckles his sword, Excalibur, and its scabbard and gives them into your keeping. His voice is sad, but gentle and forgiving.

"This must remain on Earth. When danger threatens these Blessed Isles, use it to defend those weaker than yourself." Then he rides through the opening. Merlin also comes to you and gives you a horn bound with gold on a baldric of red silk.

"When danger threatens, blow this horn and I will open these gates again and the old gods will return. This I promise. Do not think we leave you entirely. We shall be in your dreams and in the hearts of those for whom we are truly real. But we will not walk Earth again excepting on one night in all the year, All Hallows Eve. Then, with the dead we will return to bless this land with our presence. Farewell."

He walks through the opening and it closes behind him. You are left in the silent moonlight of an autumn night. You look up at the tor and see it ringed with light that comes from the powers that now have passed within. In your hand is the Sword from the Stone; around your neck hangs the Horn of Nuada of the Silver Hand. You have been a human witness to the passing of the gods. From this time, the story will grow and the hills of Albion will be seen as the doorways into the lands of the Faerie Folk, the gods, and the heroes of old. Keep all this in your heart and know that you have been blessed.

Walk toward the small hill and you will see the door through which you came. Enter the space between the worlds. Then make a quarter-turn to the right and see a light in the gloom. Go toward it. It will grow larger, until you see the doorway into your conscious world. Cross over into the physical. Take a breath, let it out slowly, and wake refreshed, with the knowledge that, within, you hold a sword and a horn placed in your keeping for the future. Guard them well.

The Riding of the Sidhe

Use any of the doorways given to pass into the space between the worlds, or any method you prefer to alter your consciousness. Enter a soft warm darkness that reminds you of the star-filled body of the Goddess of the Night Sky. For a while, you float in this star-filled void, enjoying the feeling of warmth and comfort. Then you look to your right and see, far away, the image of another door that opens onto another world. You drift toward it, until you can see the door quite plainly.

The light that comes through it has a different quality than the light your world offers. You step through and find yourself in a city you know well. It may be any city in the world. Yet, as you stand in the street filled with traffic and people, you know you are in it, but not of it. You know that this world is parallel to yours, because it is filled with silence, despite the crowds. You are totally invisible to the people milling around you. The traffic rushes through your insubstantial form with a feeling like a draft of air.

Then you hear, on the evening air, the sound of a horn. At first, it is far away and you strain to hear it. Then it sounds again, louder and more insistent. Finally, like a silver clarion-call, it rings through the night air, shattering the silence and sending a shiver of apprehension and anticipation rushing through your veins. The streets dim and shift out of focus. Everything begins to move in slow motion and you sense that something is coming toward you. You turn around and see, in the far distance, a light that moves and shifts this way and that. It changes color, from brilliant white through many shades of green, then changing to blue and gold and deep rose and other colors you can feel, but not really see.

As it comes closer, you begin to see shapes within the light, and to understand that the shapes *are* the light. Nearer still and the shapes become figures of people, men and women varying from very young, almost children, to a seeming age of mid-twenties. All are beautiful beyond belief, with eyes alive with life and vitality. You notice that, mixed among the humanlike forms, are some that are less than human. Fauns, centaurs, small winged beings and shambling dwarves, tall, thin almost-transparent creatures, and others whose forms constantly fluctuate between humanoid and . . . other.

You are watching the Riding of the Sidhe. Every Full Moon, they ride to collect luck, power, and grace from the Moon Mother. Long ago, they rode in the human world. But when humanity turned to the use of iron and science, they lost their belief in these things. Then it was that the Fair Folk decided to leave our level of perception and moved sideways into a world that was the same, but of a higher vibration. By their magic they did this, leaving us to live among our own shadows. Some humans can adjust to this parallel world. They can see and hear it. But the Fair Ones are cautious and no longer befriend us easily.

The Shining Ones approach, closer and closer, and now you can see them quite clearly. They appear to be in an orderly procession. First come the smaller folk, dwarves, fauns, pixies, and young Fairy children. All are playing some kind of instrument: trumpets, pipes, flutes and panpipes, drums, tambourines, and flageolets. Others have circles of sweet-sounding bells and small harps. Your spirit throbs to the music and your feet move restlessly to the beat. They pass you, smiling and laughing, their slightly slanted eyes and pointed faces giving them a sly look. Behind them come the larger Fairy Folk. Girls dressed in filmy silks of delicate colors, with flowers in their hair and carrying garlands of flowers that are no longer seen in our world. The scent is overpowering, heavy and sensual. A gentle breeze coming from woods and forests unknown to humans lifts their long hair until it floats about them in a silken web. Dryads and Nereids, nixies and wood nymphs pass us by. Some are winged, like butterflies, and dance in the air hand-in-hand or in long lines like a trail of blossoms. A few of them are Bacchantes, clad in doe skins, beating small drums, and clashing brass cymbals. There is a wild look about them that makes us wary.

Behind them come the young men, some dressed in silks and velvet, others in moleskins and garments of leaves. Some are green-skinned, some nut-brown, others fair-skinned. All are beardless. Older fauns and satyrs dance among them, their goat legs cavorting wildly to the tune of their pipes. Now come those who walk more sedately, wrapped in long glimmering cloaks. Their eyes are watchful, their movements catlike. They are the Shape Changers and they act as both warriors and guardians for the Fair Folk. Some pause as they pass us and regard us with curiosity, then move on to be followed by the Weres, the loping wolf and the massive bear, the wildcat and the Kelpie horse.

Now come the hobgoblins and the brownies, the folk of the cottage and hearth fire. They love humans and work with them as they care for the land. The tall Bean Sidhe walk by, wringing their pale hands and sobbing. At their heels the white-coated, red-eared Gabriel Hounds quest from side to side. Will O' the Wisps float after them and marsh sprites flit in and out of the throng.

The centaurs clatter past, laughing and drinking from wine skins. Some of them have riders, pale-skinned Fairy women who are dressed only in their own long hair. The walkers who follow are those who serve the nobles of the Fair Folk. Dressed in colorful liveries, they carry jugs of rare wines and baskets of fruit and sweetmeats of all kinds. It is their delight to serve all who would eat or drink. They pause to offer cups of gold and silver and finely engraved glasses filled to overflowing with the heady wines of the Fairy world. Do not taste, do not be tempted, *not until the ultimate cup is offered.* Do not touch the fruit, the ripe cherries and darkly sweet strawberries, or the red, red apples of Avalon. Let them pass. The greater prize is to come.

Finally, there comes into sight the Fairy court. The horses are of two colors, black as night and white as milk, with manes and tails that sweep the ground. Shod with starlight, saddled with moonbeams, bridled with jeweled green leather, yet they are not half as wondrous as the beings who ride them. It is given to few to look upon the faces of the high-born Sidhe.

Fohla of the Raven Hair is the first. Like black stars are her eyes and her smile rivals the dawn over the green hill of Tara for beauty. She wears white velvet belted with rubies and scarlet slippers. On her hand, she wears a ring centered with a star's light trapped in a pearl. By her side, pacing on a coal-black steed, is her consort Euan Dubh. Tall as a tree, with long curls as black as his horse, he is clad all in cloth-of-silver, his cloak lined with scarlet and edged with beads of jasper. A single star shines on his brow. He carries a spear with a shaft of blackthorn, its head a flame from the tail of a meteor.

Etain the Beautiful comes riding and pauses to look down upon us. Her hair is the color of fire newly lit, caught into a net of gold thread. A crown of gold and emeralds sits on her royal brow. Her eyes are as green as her jewels and her mouth is a ripe berry-red. Clad all in green velvet, with a cloak of russet and gold, she is a queen indeed. She smiles and looks back at her lord who follows.

Few mortals have seen Aengus Og of the Bright Face. He was born when the world was young and untouched. Gaia herself was his mother, the Sun's first ray of light his father. Undying and eternal is Aengus and early he withdrew from the company of mortals. His armor is of sunlight, frozen in space as it raced to touch Earth. The helmet that hangs from his saddlehorn is made of flames drawn from the heart of the oldest Sun in the cosmos. The sword by his side was cast from the echo of the first word of Creation and the belt that holds it from the silence that followed. He wears no crown, for his beauty crowns him. He carries no emblem of power, for he is power in himself. He stops before us and looks down, then gestures with a hand. A servant comes running with a silver chalice filled with wine. Aengus takes it and bids you place the point of the knife you find hanging by your side into the liquid. It seethes and boils for a moment, then clears, cleansed of all Fairy guile and deceit. You may drink and be safe. Aengus will not harm you, but he wishes you to see something and to remember.

It tastes as you wish it to taste—sweet or dry, red or white, strong or mild, ale or mead. About you, the city fades, and you are standing in a land of peaceful beauty. Overhead, a Full Moon bathes all in silver light. A servant brings you a horse and helps you to mount. Then, with a laugh, Aengus and his court ride on, gathering speed now and flying over the land. From the left comes another group, this time of wild, hard, leather-clad riders, horn-crowned and trailed by black-and-tan hounds. Their leader is all in black and wears twelve tines upon his brow. Herne comes with the Wild Hunt to join us.

From the right come the shining forms of the Tuatha de Danaan and the mighty sons and daughters of Mannanan Mac Llyr. We are surrounded by the Lordly Ones and feel the joy of life that fills them. It also fills us while we are their guests. We ride, we ride, and the wondrous horses beneath us leave Earth entirely and rise up, over the night-bound forest and across silver seas bathed in moonlight. As part of the Fairy court, we gallop across the Moon, appearing like shadows in a magic lantern to those who might be gifted with the inner sight. We circle the heavens and ride around the far side of the Moon itself. Below, Earth looks peaceful and beautiful, so beautiful we pause to look, realizing that this lovely planet is our home. Etain rides past.

"Don't stop," she calls and is gone.

Her warning comes too late. The Fairy horse beneath us crumbles into moondust and we are falling down, down, and down, toward Earth. Tumbling slowly, spinning like a sycamore seed, drifting and dreaming like a slowly falling cloud. We are not afraid, but seem to be caught in a dream from which we are reluctant to wake. Far below, we see the lights of a city and, as we fall nearer to Earth, the lights of a room in which sit the bodies we left so long ago. Gently, softly, like gossamer threads from a spider's web, we fall into them and slowly, with no ill effects, we wake to our own time.

Return to Tir-nan-Og

A dramatized pathworking for ten voices.

Characters: Puck, Titania, Oberon, Rhiannon, Gywdion, Llyr, Arianrhod, Aengus Og, the Lady, the Lord

Music: "The Hollow Hills," from *The Immortal Hour*, by R. Broughton

Puck:
The luck of the day to you gentlefolk. Allow me to introduce myself. I am named Puck, or sometimes, Robin Goodfellow. I have many names, but those are the best known to you. I am as old as the Chalk Downs of England and as young as the first lamb of next year's spring. I will be your guide across the shifting web of time that spans my world and yours like a gossamer veil. How say you? What am I? I am a sprite, as English as an apple, as Welsh as a song, as Scottish as a lament, as Irish as an argument, and I hail from Tir-nan-Og.

Did you think my world was like yours, divided into tiny pieces? Each one held to the one race? Not so. My world exists in layers, like an onion, and is as sweet and as sharp to the tongue. In my world, you may walk in an instant from one level to the next, though you scarce seem to have moved an inch. To us it is all the Land of the Ever Young, and you are invited to set your foot beyond the fields you know. Then you will be in the country of the Lordly Ones who dwell within the Hollow Hills that contain a universe within themselves.

Come, the birds are singing their evensong and we must be back ere morning yawns. Follow, follow. See here is the ancient track with a thousand, thousand years of footprints for a carpet. Here is an oak tree planted before Alfred was born. Sing, little wren, go tell them we are on our way.

Oh, can you not feel the old ways and the old places springing up about your heels? See yonder ring of stones, the Dancing Maidens they are called. Who put them there I do not know, for they were standing when I was young. Come with me, dance with me, take hands and weave in and out of the stones as the Sun curtseys low in the sky. Round and round and in and out, up and down and all about. Leaping high and bowing low, all together, *here, we, go-o-o-o-o.*

Oh, it is cold here between the worlds. There is no air or breath of life, no warmth, no light. Step on, step on, 'tis only a heartbeat away from my world we are. Yes. Here's the light, the Sun, the fragrance of my world. Continue the dance up to the end. Up and down and round about, skipping, crowing, mopping, mowing, and here, here is a lady you must see. Merrily met, Titania, I have brought you new companions from the dull world outside.

Titania:
Ah, Robin Goodfellow, as mischievous as ever. I hope you have not frightened our guests too much? Did he bring you by way of the ring of stones? For fie, Puck, it is the worst of the journeys to this world. On this ill-mannered sprite's behalf, I ask your pardon. I will take care you have a more considerate guide on your journey back. Follow me and I will bring you to the Hall of Oberon. Here, beneath this ancient hill, lies the palace wherein you will see all those Fair Folk you count as legend. You will find in your belt a blade of iron. No, do not put it near me. Fairy blood cannot bear the touch of metal. Drive it deeply into the lintel above the door. Now you may leave when you will. Till then, drink deep and be merry. Hail, my Lord Oberon, King of the Fair Folk, greet you our guests.

Oberon:
I greet you all right well, come sit and feast with us. It is far too long since those of your world came a-visiting. Though

once, there was a time when it was more common. See there, the tall man with the dark curls and a winning smile? We took him from his bride on their wedding night. As the wedding party rode back from the church, they crossed our path. In that moment, he was touched with the gift of Fairy sight and saw us clear and bright. When all our people had passed, he was there among us and has remained. His new-made wife wept many a tear, but fickle she then proved and wed another scarce a season on. He dwells with us content and, though his birth year saw also that of bluff King Hal, yet still he wears the glow of youth and will until that day when all shall return to the Source.

You have a question? Ah, yes, always the same one. Is it true that we Fair Folk have no souls and will be damned at the ending of the world's time? Think you the One who created us both, who gave us youth and beauty everlasting, would at the last desert us, his first children? Man was ever vain and proud and thought himself the only one with the spark of God within. Oh, child of Earth, you of the bloodline of the fallen stars, your pride still blinds you to the glory and sacredness of all life. Come drink with us and let old hurts grow dim. I tell you truly, when all time ceases, mayhap your kind and mine will go on together hand in hand. If not, then to our separate destinies we will go.

Puck:
Good Lord Oberon, I am bid to take these earthlings farther. The song birds of Rhiannon call them on. Come, skip lightly and, in the timing of a cat's jump . . . we are here, in a glade of sunlit trees. 'Tis here the Lady Rhiannon likes to teach her songbirds all their notes. My Lady, they are here.

Rhiannon:
Come close to me and listen to my children sing. Are they not beautiful? They listen to every word uttered on Earth and bring them to me. From lover's tears and smiles, I weave melodies for the wind to sing at night in the high branches of hilltop trees. From the murmurs of mothers bending over the cots of

their sleeping children, I fashion cadences for the spring harebells to practice. Listen well and you will hear the voice of the one you love the best. I will make a song from that and you shall hear it when next you come a-visiting. Come Puck, let us take them back to the hall and watch the delights fashioned for the entertaining of these guests by my kinsman, Gwydion the Mage.

Puck:
[*aside*] I find it tiresome to be at the beck and call of all these fingers. [*mimics*] Puck, come here. Puck, go there. Sweet Puck, fetch my cloak, my horse, my harp. Oh, for a world to myself and no one to fret my senses. Come then, here's the hall. Gwydion is the Master Mage and delights to make fantasies for the ladies. See there, out of a bowl of crystal water, he brings a swan with feathers of silver. So sweetly it sings that each note becomes a flower, or a jewel. Now the swan becomes a cloud and, from its fleecy nest, come nine maidens dancing, carrying garlands with which they drape the company. Ho, hum. I find it dull. It is the same old tricks. How's this . . . a new one? A mermaid swimming through the air playing a harp of gold. Now that's a laugh! Plop she goes like a soap bubble. I can sing as well as that. Oh. Oh, Oh, good Gwydion, I meant no harm. Do you take these asses ears from my poor head! Poor Puck, to tease him so.

Gwydion:
Ill-tempered sprite. Titania dotes on you, but I would banish you, an it were possible. Feel no sorrow for this ass-eared fellow, he is always deep in mischief of some kind. See, for your delight, fair guests, I will make these daisies into pearls. Take one, each of you, and think of me when you hold it. Come, walk with me through the hall and out into the sweet air of Tir-nan-Og. It is night now and the Moon rises from the sea yonder. Look closely and you see a silver form rising with it from the waves. My kinsman, Llyr, comes to welcome you. Well-met, cousin of the running wave. Does the Lady of the Silver Wheel come with you?

Llyr:

She does. Her chariot comes close behind me, but I raced ahead to greet these children of Earth. How strange to see such folk. You must forgive me my words. We see so few of your kind in the Land of the Ever Young. Will you stay with us? If so, I offer my kingdom for your pleasure. I will teach you to ride the wild white horses of the sea, and how to tease the mermaids into song. Yes, stay with us and we will search the deeps and plunder them of treasure. When you tire of that, I will steal Arianrhod's chariot and take you riding among the cold, bright stars.

Arainrhod:

Indeed you will not, Wave Prince. My chariot is not for those of earthly blood. It was a gift from my father, Mannanan the Mighty. What do these folk here?

Llyr:

They have come with Puck, and you should be more gracious, Lady Silver Wheel. Well you know that only *they* come who have the invitation of Aengus Og himself. As always, they are offered the choice of Earth or Fairyland. To leave their humanity behind and taste the fruit of immortality or accept death, the gift that is for humankind alone and of which the Fair Folk have no knowledge. Friends, stay with us. A few days here and you will gain back your youth and become more fair. We have many here who would join with you in the pleasures of love. Our men and maids know well how to give and receive pleasure.

Arianrhod:

What choice is that? Who would not choose our ways instead of death and darkness? They will choose to stay with us. On this I will place a bet with Goodfellow. A golden belt clasped with a star, against those pipes on which you dote.

Puck:

My pipes were a gift from Great Pan. I'll not lose them for all your honey'd words. Three-faced Goddess, I'll not bet with you.

Arianrhod:
Poor sprite, always looking for mischief and not liking it when it is found. So, children of Earth, you come to Tir-nan-Og to make your choice. You'll not have long to wait. As I drove my chariot across the midnight sky, I saw the Sidhe gathering for their Hosting. Even now, they cross the space between their level and ours and, for a space of time, will wend their way through all the worlds in turn. Even Earth will see their shining troop and many there will be tonight who never again will sleep in a mortal bed. Children will creep from their cots and wander into the woods to be lost forever to humankind. Lovers will be separated when one sees and yearns toward the fair Sidhe and the other remains blind to their glory. Aye, Aengus is abroad tonight.

Puck:
He comes, he comes.

Gwydion:
This sight never fails to make me weep. The very stuff of space itself pulls back and opens like a giant maw. Inside is blackness from which no light escapes. Then, from a point like a birthing star, the light seeps through and tears a way across the sable sky. Nothing of my magic can compare with this causeway through the worlds. See, they come, the Lordly Ones, the Hosting of the Sidhe. Here come the knights, riding row on row, their horses black as a beetle's wing. Their helmets shine like moonlight and their armor was wrought from the heart of a thunderstorm. Their tall spears hold lightning on their edge.

Arianrhod:
I love to see the musicians that follow the knights. Their drums and fifes sound so gay and lilting. They walk with such an air and cast a spell with their music. The horses step in time and their harness bells jingle in tune. So brave a sight to see. One that has dazzled many a mortal eye and led it from their world into ours. I could find it in my heart to envy the beauty of the

Danu. Aye, even I, Arianrhod, can be as green as any village girl. How say you, Rhiannon?

Rhiannon:
Their beauty is that of the Firstborn of the Creator when the pattern was fresh and bright in his mind. Now come the lords and ladies, some walking, some riding. Such horses are born of the wind and have dreams for manes, so light and fragile they appear. Their hooves have never felt the weight of Earth, but always tread above it, disdaining all, not of their own world. To ride such a beast would gladden any heart.

Titania:
Their faces are far beyond the beauty of the other Fair Folk. In their Hosting, they are terrible and powerful to behold. Of all the people who once held Earth in their domain, these were the fairest. Their womenfolk were as mighty in battle as their men, their swords as keen, their fury as dreadful. Yet their faces are as delicate as flowers and their eyes like jewels. Hear them sing. Many have followed that sound and never seen the hills of Earth again. Their hair is a net to catch the hearts of men, just as the smile of a Lord of the Sidhe has gained many a wife from the daughters of Eve. After all these centuries, the blood runs thin in our veins and few children are born to us. We must take from Earth to bolster our numbers.

Puck:
'Tis said, proud Titania once offered her love to Aengus of the Bright Face and was spurned. Were you not fair enough Lady?

Titania:
Sharp-tongued imp, you will always find a way to dig and hurt. He was gentle and kind and spoke soft, to my heart's soothing. His heart was not for me. As the God of Love and Youth, he belongs to all, the favored son of Danu, the Bright One, He of the Shining Face. I count it no disgrace to have offered my love to such a one. Unlike you, ill-tempered pixie that you are, I have a need to love and be loved in return.

Puck:
Love . . . what is that? A dream, a dance of words, a moment
of forgetfulness, a fancy for the minute. I care nothing for
love. I live only to dance and sing and tease the like of proud
fairies like Titania.

Oberon:
Hush, it is forbidden to squabble when the Hosting is near.
Would you risk a dark look from Aengus? See, after the host
has passed, there comes one rider on a silver horse. The tallest
and fairest of us all is Aengus Og. Blessed is he who fills the
worlds with love. His cloak is woven from the dreams of fair
women. His jewels are cast from the laughter of lovers. His
sword was forged from the pain of the first betrayal of love's
trust. His shield is love itself. Oh happy mortals who behold
the Lord of the Danaan, the King of Tir-nan-Og. Bow down
before such majesty. Aengus would speak with you.

Aengus:
Hail, Fair Folk, well met upon the path of the Hosting.

All:
Hail, Aengus, Lord of the Tuatha.

Aengus:
Are these that stand with you children of Earth? If so, they
are welcome to my realm of joy and beauty.

Puck:
Even so, my Lord. Plucked from Earth like feathers from a
chicken. I thought to make you laugh, to make them envious
of the Otherworld. T'was a fancy on my part.

Aengus:
Hard-hearted sprite. Your envy of humankind and of their
unknown joy at the gates of death has always set your passions against them. Yet you cling to them and mix with them
to try and learn where they go when riding on their last

breath of life. This is not the time to chastise you, but mind your ways, or you may find yourself placed on Earth for good. These earthlings now become my guests and are under my protection. Though I am bound by the laws of Tir-nan-Og to ask them if they wish to stay and be eternally young, or return to Earth and live out their appointed time. This I must ask, it is the law. How say you, lady [to a woman of the group]?

Lady:
My heart yearns to Tir-nan-Og, but I have kith and kin on Earth and I will not leave them. But I thank thee and bless thee for thy courtesy, Aengus of the Fair Folk, to the amount thou art able to receive.

Aengus:
So be it, though I would you had said yes, for you are most fair and comely. Many a knight of the Fair Folk would seek your hand and give you joy and fair babes to nurse at your breast. And you, my lord, will you stay or go [to a man of the group]?

Lord:
Bright though your realm may be, yet, my lord, I would not leave Earth. I am mortal and intend to remain so, and will receive the grace of death at my appointed time.

Aengus:
These answers I accept. But join me in the Hosting. Few mortals have such a chance. Ride with us across the many worlds into the web of time. Ho there, horses for our guests!

Puck:
And me Lord Aengus, and me . . . please.

Aengus:
Aye, even you, small imp of envy and deceit, for you do have times of goodness in you.

Puck:
To horse, to horse, we ride with the Sidhe! See the web of space peels back and we ride . . . we ride . . . we ride, across the coldness of the space between the worlds. There below us is Earth, gleaming in the light of Arianrhod's chariot.

Arianrhod:
Ho there, earthlings. I ride with you. Race with me.

Puck:
Over the black and silver sea and across the mountains tipped with white, like the snowy breasts of fair women, we dip and soar. Has your heart ever felt such freedom? Across the world we race toward the west, where the heart of the Children of Danu ever yearn. To the green velvet hills and plains of the Blessed Isles. My own place is here. We dip like swans and before us lies The Trod, the magical way that is the Second Road of the Sidhe. Such paths of power crisscross these Isles. It is here that all worlds meet and from such paths are men and women, and children too, taken from Earth to meet the gods and depart with them, never to be seen again.

Aengus:
Halt, my friends. It is here we part and take our leave. Here you may watch us pass at the fullest time of each Moon. At that time, I will again offer you a choice. Three times I may offer and, after that, never more. Perhaps, one day, you will accept and depart with us beyond the fields you know. To each I grant the power to change your life, to know its beauty and its joy. Now, I must to the Hosting. But know this—that I, Aengus, Lord of the Sidhe, envy you that unknown grace to which each one of you will pass in time. It is something I and my kind will never know, though we have our own destiny when time ends. There is a place for my people far beyond anything we can imagine, but it is nothing compared to the joy that you will know. Do not weep for us, but look to your world and make it as fair as once it was. Farewell. I shall look for you when we pass again. Of all mortals, you shall have

sight of me and not be tempted, unless that be your wish. But, you must *ask* to follow.

Puck:
I shall stay awhile and find some sleeping fairies to pinch and tease, some slovenly housewife to pull from bed, some dunce to lead astray in the mud. Hey, hey, for Puck and his delights. Farewell, farewell . . . farewell . . . Rub your eyes and waken mortals . . . you have been dreaming all . . . awake . . . awake . . .

7

Angelic Pathworkings

Angels have been depicted in so many forms that it is hard to know how to describe them in a pathworking. The Victorians were very fond of angels and painted them as beautiful androgynous figures with swanlike wings and long curling hair, swathed in voluminous white garments. "Insipid" is the word that springs to mind.

Most angels are patterns of energy created to undertake or perform one particular action and nothing else. Archangels are another thing altogether, and are ensouled in the same way that the elemental kings are ensouled. Therefore, they are capable of independent thought and action. I have found that the best way to picture them and to interact with them is to see them as geometric shapes in bright colors—not as "pretty" as the Victorian pictures, perhaps, but not so complicated to visualize. This does not detract from their efficiency or their ability to act when asked for help.

One vital point to remember when working any kind of magic is that one *must* ask before one can be helped. Angels, elementals, and gods are willing to help, but the law says they must be asked for help. Yes, they probably *can* read minds, but the act of asking is what triggers the help. If you think geometric shapes are odd, look at some of Albrecht Durer's engravings of angels. They come with legs like Greek columns, torsos like clouds or even a blazing Sun, and with arms and heads not even attached.

With angelic magic, the trick is to learn to accept other forms, and I *mean* other forms, and ways of being. The Bible often refers to "God speaking from within a cloud." If you are able to accept a cloud of gaseous material manifestly more intelligent than yourself, you are on the way to being able to work with angels.

The Seven Before the Throne

Sit comfortably and relax. Look at the door to the room in which you are sitting, then close your eyes. Imagine getting up and walking forward three paces. Open your inner eyes and look at the room from *that* vantage point. In the imagination, turn around and look at yourself sitting in the chair. Take note of how you look from that angle, then turn around and walk to the door and open it. Now turn and look back at the room from that angle. Now walk to the front door and open it. Turn and look back the way you came.

Turn again, but this time, as you step forward, the astral body remains where it is and the mental body goes forward alone. Turn and look back and see the misty form of your astral body standing there. If you look down now, you will find that you have no visible form at all. This is as it should be, for you have left the levels of form for those of the mental and do not need anything other than your consciousness of self.

Before you lies a pathway to the higher levels built of light, color, and sound. Let your consciousness drift along this path, higher and higher, experiencing its texture in all the ways it can offer you. You begin to feel an inner vibration. This increases as you approach the higher levels. A low, musical hum can be heard. It contains every note, every cadence you have ever heard. It grows and becomes more distinct, until it suddenly materializes as a glory of sound. What you are hearing is as much as the human ear can accept and convey of the harmonics that surround the One Creator. This is the sound of God still creating and sustaining the cosmos it brought into being in the first moment of self-recognition. What we have always thought of as the throne of God is a web of sound, color, vibration, and light, all of which are variations on a single theme.

This awesome chord is upheld and charged by untold millions of God-created minor energy patterns that vibrate on the same level and help to extend the chord outward. We know these energy patterns as "angels." To our limited sight, they seem to be highly condensed cores of light that spread outward, becoming less and less dense as they reach their perimeter. We are far beyond that point, but we can observe the turning, spinning, radiating light that is the point of all creation. As it spins, it absorbs, transmutes, and re-creates its own substance. Nothing is lost, nothing is forgotten. All is used and changed again and again.

Surrounding the immense central core, yet still at a distance from its absolute center we can see seven much smaller spinning centers. Each vibrates one of the seven colors our human eyes can understand. These are the Seven Before the Throne, the foremost of the archangels whose own vibrations, which are variations on that of the One, serve as a container for the infinite power source that created them and us.

Metatron, Michael, Gabriel, Raphael, Uriel, Ratziel, Tzadkiel. Their names ring out like a carillon of silver bells. Now that we have seen this inner circle, we begin to pick out others. Four intensely brilliant points of light can be seen almost touching the outer edges of the core. Understanding of their nature fills our minds. These are the Four Holy Creatures whose nature none can fully comprehend. Beyond the Seven, we see ring on ring of small spinning centers that mimic the Great Center. These are the angelic throngs: Thrones, Seraphim, Aralim, Principalities, Dominions, Ashim, Elohim, and more.

Among these, some shine far more brilliantly than others. These are the ancient ensouled god-forms and the ones we know as the Manus, or teachers. So it goes on, ring after ring of smaller and smaller patterns of energy, all of them minor but accurate versions of that which created them.

The Logoi of solar systems, devic forces, oversouls of life-forms are included in this, representing all manifested life-forms of the cosmos. Each is a facsimile of its creator, but with potential to understand and experience physicality. We are part of this immensity. We are minute copies of the One Creator. We are a living, breathing, thinking part of it. It is a part of us. That is what makes us shine so brilliantly.

Our attention is diverted, something is happening in the core. It shimmers and ripples with color and sound. Like a huge shock wave, it flows outward and is strengthened by the surrounding rings. Further and further it travels and, with it, comes a cry of pure love, a recognition of its own begetting. It is the call of the One to its manifested children. It reaches us, flows over us, caresses and loves us. We are caught up in a wave of love, to be healed and transmuted by it.

The circles of light become shining figures that turn to face us, the most fortunate of all living things throughout the cosmos. They bow, for our life is that which will one day return to the Source and become part of it. On the day of our return, we will bring a gift for our cosmic parent. The knowledge of manifestation. They understand that they will never know this completeness, this entirety of knowledge of spirit and matter. We shall one day claim our place at the center.

The glory about us dims and we are carried along, drifting in the gentle darkness. All about us, unseen, we hear the sound of beating wings and feel the softness of feathers. They carry us back to our own level.

The Angel of the Confessional

This pathworking needs some prior work. For several days before undertaking this working, spend some time in meditation on your own life. Look back and search out something you have always regretted doing, saying, or causing. In other words, look through the skeletons in your mental cupboards.

An enormous amount of psychic energy is expended on keeping such things "under cover."

When you have found what you are looking for, go over the whole thing in detail, omitting nothing. It is important that you make no attempt to explain, justify, or prevaricate. Now prepare for the working. Sit quietly and allow the silence to enfold you. Using your "inner" ear (if you prefer to use an actual tape do so), begin to hear, as if far away, the solemn notes of a Gregorian chant. Opening your inner eye, see around you a cloistered garden full of flowers, fruit trees in blossom, and, to one side, a small herb garden. Here and there among the flower beds, there are wooden benches.

There is a feeling of peace and tranquillity everywhere. One side of the walled area has a small wooden door that is open and you can see a small and very old chapel on the other side. For a while, you walk about the garden, letting its peace sink into your heart. Then, through the open door, comes a young man. He wears the robes of a Benedictine monk and his feet are bare. He smiles and wishes you "Good day."

He invites you to sit with him and asks your name. He gives his own as Michael. He asks why you have come. You must answer, truthfully, that you have come to talk with someone about something you have kept to yourself for too long.

You explain that you need to talk and relieve yourself of something, some past misdemeanor. You have a problem that has become a burden to you and you would like to talk about it. The brother invites you to walk with him through the gardens as you talk, and assures you that what you have to say will be kept completely confidential. He says that you may come here at any time, day or night, and he will be here, or in the chapel, and ready to listen to you.

Think carefully about what you want to say. Then begin to talk. If it helps, let the words be spoken physically, but you must keep your eyes closed and the image of the garden and the brother before you. Open your heart totally, knowing that you are safe in his hands. Sometimes, Michael may put a question, or ask you to repeat or clarify something. You may stop and sit, or continue walking.

[If this pathworking is being done in a group, there should be a lengthy pause of at least twenty minutes here, then a quiet intimation that the end of the working will begin in 2 to 3 minutes time. If it is solo, you may continue until you feel it is time to close.]

Now it is time to listen rather than talk. You ask for help and Michael guides you through the doorway and into the chapel. Inside, it is peaceful and quiet. Candles are burning on the altar and a covered chalice stands waiting. You sit before the altar and talk. Listen to his words, ask questions if you think you need to do so. Finally, Michael asks you if you understand what he has said. You must answer as you feel.

He now takes you to the altar and uncovers the chalice. In solemn words, he blesses you and gives you absolution. Then he offers the chalice to your lips. Drink deeply and offer up whatever it was that you feared, felt guilty about, or simply wanted to release. Let it go. Instead of a burden, let it become an experience, a lesson learned and understood.

Let a feeling of freedom, joy, and lightness of being fill your mind, body, and spirit. The wine flows through your veins, cleansing and healing you. The sound of plainsong fills the chapel. Although you cannot see them, you know the choir stalls are filled with angelic beings.

Before you, Michael changes, growing taller and brighter. Gone is the young brother. Before you stands the Archangel Michael in his glory. The red and gold of the angelic auric field stretches out on either side like wings. About his head is a brilliant golden light. His eyes, full of love and compassion, look down upon you, his mouth smiles and speaks a blessing that surrounds you and uplifts you with its power.

The music around you lifts your spirit and carries it like a sleeping child through the many levels of the archangelic world. As you go, you dream of multicolored images and the scent of flowers, of long-forgotten scenes of childhood filled with laughter. Gradually, your spirit descends through the worlds, until it reaches the physical world. Your sleeping self is gently united with its body. Slowly, you become aware of things around you. You open your eyes and, still filled with the wonder of the experience, you realize that you no longer carry the burden with which you began this pathworking. Awake.

When you have fully returned to this level, it is advisable to have something fairly solid to eat, and a hot drink of some kind. Do not do anything strenuous or demanding for at least an hour, but allow your inner self to rest and dwell on the experience it has undergone.

The Angels of the Crossroads

This pathworking was designed to help those who are facing a decision of some kind in their lives. Though it may not offer a direct solution, it can often make things a lot clearer. Like all pathworkings, if it is worked often, it becomes a call sign to the inner levels and acts as a summons to the angelic world when you are in need of help. Remember, all such beings will help if they can, but they must be asked for help. They cannot make the first move. They are not able, or permitted to interfere with your free will. To use a "Star Trek-ism," they have a prime directive of noninterference.

Relax, close your eyes, and build on the inner levels the image of the door to an elevator. Press the button and, when the door opens, enter. The doors close again and you feel the familiar sensation of going upward. A bell chimes and the elevator stops but the doors do not open. This is the astral level. The elevator rises again, much faster this time, then stops as another chime sounds. This is the lower mental level. For a third time, you are taken upward and now feel a slight sensation of dizziness as you enter the beginning of the spiritual levels. The door opens when you hear the chime.

Before you is a straight road of hard-packed earth. You step out and feel the roughness beneath your bare feet. You look to the right and see another road, leading into the distance. It is just like the first. You turn again and yet another road meets your eye. It is the same when you make the final turn. You are at a crossroads. Where you stepped from the elevator there is a signpost that simply indicates north, south, east, and west.

At the foot of the signpost is a large flat-topped stone, on which you sit down and think. You are taking this journey to sort out a problem, so this means you have at least four answers you can consider. One of these will always be *to do nothing*. To let matters take their own course is always one way of doing things. Sometimes it can be the right answer, sometimes not!

Think about the problem you are facing. Hold it clearly in your mind. Then (this is important), don't ask to be given a solution. Ask *to be helped to find the right solution for yourself*. To do this, you need to look at the problem from the four directions.

Stand up and face north. Begin to walk along that road. Notice that, on either side, there are fields of corn or barley. You can see wildflowers growing along the side of the road and in the hedges. This is a growing, fertile road. The solution therefore might well be "wait and see what will come up." Or again, it might be "you will have to sow some seeds of trust and honesty before the solution appears."

As you walk along, you see ahead a farm gate and, leaning over it, a man, somewhat middle-aged, with a pleasant weather-beaten face that has laughter wrinkles around the eyes. His old hat is pulled down over his eyes against the bright sunlight. His clothes are well worn, with an occasional tear and patch. He wears rubber boots encrusted with dried mud.

"Nice day, bit too dry for the crops, but it'll rain afore morning." The voice is deep and warm. "Care for a bite to eat?" He produces a snowy-white napkin that, when opened, reveals fresh-baked bread and a large piece of crumbly cheese. He opens the gate and comes onto the roadside. You both sit and eat.

The cheese, when you bite into it, is slightly salty, with a sharp, but not unpleasant, taste. He also has a stone jar of homemade cider. You eat and drink in silence for a few minutes. Then he asks why you have come, and you must place your problem before him. Be as brief and concise as you can. Don't embellish, just state the facts. Give him a few moments. Then listen to what he tells you. It will always concern the growth of the problem, when it began, how it has escalated, and how it can be stopped, or cut down and made into something else more productive.

Thank him for the advice and the food and retrace your steps back to the signpost. Now take the eastern road. As you step on to it you find yourself walking in the absolute stillness of predawn. About you, the sky is a soft dove-gray. Just ahead of you, a slight rise in the road shows the rosy glow of dawn. The landscape, what you can see of it, is gentle rolling hills with some trees here and there. The dawn chorus of birds sounds like a full orchestra.

Standing by a tree, you see a young woman. She is intent upon the rising Sun, her whole being concentrated on it. You stop and watch it with her. Everything seems to be waiting for a new beginning. That is what this direction is all about—a new way of looking at things, shedding new light on an old problem. The woman turns and smiles. Her hair is the color of honey, her eyes as blue as cornflowers.

Then the Sun peeps over the hill and the light of a new day floods over everything. You feel filled with joy and an inner certainty that this will be a special day. You turn to the woman and ask her if she will walk with you awhile. She smiles and agrees. Slowly, you both walk up the long hill and the Sun bathes you both with its rays.

You tell your companion about your problem and she asks you to look at it from far off, rather than observing it too closely. Imagine the problem bathed in quiet sunlight. She also asks if you could look at it from the opposite point of view, as if it were someone else's problem. How would you advise them? You stop and think about this. You imagine the problem to be twice as big, and then much smaller. You go over it piece by piece bathing it in sunlight. You look at your part in it, as well as that of other people. Then the woman tells you to return and take what you have learned with you.

You turn back and the Sun rises higher and higher, suffusing everything around you with complete clarity, including your problem, its root cause, your part in it, and the way ahead. When you reach the signpost, you sit down and weigh the lessons and advice you have received on these two roads. [Pause.] Then you stand up and look at the remaining two directions. You choose the south.

It leads you into a desert under a hot burning Sun. The sand is harsh to your feet and all around you are dried, white bones. You walk on for a while and then see, standing on the top of a dune, a man, a warrior, armored and armed. He hails you.

"This is a dangerous place, friend. What brings you here?"

You accept the waterskin he offers and the two of you sit together at the base of the dune, where there is a tiny bit of shade. Slowly, you tell the warrior about your problem and what the other two advisers have told you. You ask if he has anything to add. He is silent for a moment, then speaks.

"The advice you have been given is good on both counts. A new beginning based on experience, letting new growth blot out the old hurts. But there are times when one must fight for what one believes. There is a time to stand back and a time to advance. Ask yourself, is this such a time? Weigh the consequences. What will happen? Can you take the harshness that will be let loose? Have you the courage to defy the odds? If so, fight, and fight hard."

He pauses and then says, "There is nothing wrong in fighting, if fight you must, but fight cleanly and with honesty. If you win, be generous. If you lose, ask yourself if you have fought for the right things. If so, retreat, regroup, then advance again. If not, acknowledge defeat and learn the lesson. There is a warrior in everyone when necessary. Go back and think about this. You alone can decide."

You thank him, turn your face back the way you came, and walk out of the desert to the crossroads. There is only one direction left and you walk to the west.

Now it is nighttime, with a Full Moon riding high in the dark sky. The air is cool and filled with scents that you never notice during the day. Ahead, there is a small wood and you walk into it. The trees are clustered around a small lake with willows leaning over it. You sit down and gaze into the moon-lit depths. A face looks back at you from below the water. It rises to the surface and reveals itself as a woman with long black hair and green eyes. She swims to the bank and lifts herself from the water, pushing back her wet hair.

"I have been waiting for you. I know that you have walked the other directions and what they have told you. Now it is my turn to advise you. What you have been told is good and there is much there that can help you. But this is my advice. Rely upon your own inner selves. Make contact with your higher self and with the ancient power self. Sometimes you can blind your conscious mind with what you think is the truth, or what you wish to be the truth. The power self forgets nothing and retains all. It can help recall the truth.

"The higher self can offer strength of purpose and courage in adversity. Advice can be helpful, but there is none better than your own intuition. Make a choice and stay with it. Remember that the inner divinity of the spirit lies within you. It is never separated from the greater divinity of the One. Whatever you decide, whatever comes of that decision, it is all experience in the end. That alone is what counts."

She falls silent and then slides back into the water and sinks below the surface. You rise and walk out of the wood and back to the crossroads. Standing there, you look at the four directions and see at the beginning of each road the friend who advised you.

The farmer, now seen as Uriel in his robes of rich earth tones. His noble brow wears a garland of autumn leaves, berries, and fruit. He carries a woven basket of Earth's gifts. On his shoulder perches a squirrel holding a nut between its paws.

The young woman is Raphael. Her robe of dawn colors swirls about her feet. She holds in one hand a staff around which curls a serpent, and in the other, a lyre. Behind her glitters a rainbow, a promise of hope.

The warrior stands smiling as only Michael, the Warrior Angel of God, can smile. His sword and shield lie at his feet, to be taken up only when it is necessary. A true warrior is as gentle as he is fierce, as generous in victory as he is strong in battle.

Gabriel, from the Moon pool, is robed in white, gray, silver, and purple. His auric wings encompass the whole of that quarter.

All smile and wave. It is time for you to go back and solve your problem. The scene fades from view and is replaced by your own world.

The Cathedral of Harmony

Build a dark-blue velvet curtain in your mind's eye. As soon as the curtain is solid and as real as you can make it, rise up in your astral form and cross over to it. Take time to touch and feel it, then draw it back. A sylvan path lies before you, leading through a wood. On the step, is a robe of golden silk with leather slippers of a deeper gold. A cord of pale-green silk is provided to tie about your waist. Change now.

As you set out along the path, the birds are singing and small animals scuttle across the path in front of you. There is a light breeze, but it is not cold. The Sun seems to be close to high noon and there is a feeling of stillness about you. When you emerge from the wood, you see, in the middle distance, a hill bathed in sunlight and topped by a stone circle. It catches the light and seems to sparkle like tiny flames. You climb to the top and make your way to the space between the second and third stones. There is a feeling of joy in the air and, as you watch, an astral pathway manifests between the stones opposite you. The path is filled by a golden mist.

You walk eagerly toward the golden mist. Its touch is soft and faintly damp, like that of a fine sea mist, but not unpleas-

ant. As you walk forward slowly and carefully, you hear singing ahead. The voices are clear and sweet. Sometimes a single
voice takes up the melody, then others join in.

The mist thins and disappears and before you is a building, a cathedral built of crystal and faceted to catch the light.
A thousand colors come and go as the Sun moves across the
sky. The chant you heard while still in the mist is nearer now
and growing in majesty and power, as if it were a welcome
meant especially for you. The doors open and you pass within.

Within, all is cool and, at first, dim. Then, as you pause
and look around, you begin to notice the colors. The inside of
the building seems to be made entirely of color—every shade
you can imagine and many for which you have no name. The
colors come and go, building up to a chord of sound and color
that causes a vibration to start at the very core of your being.
Columns of light move across the vast spaces of the interior.
Sometimes they pause before you and ripples of color chase
up and down their fluted forms. Others change shape as they
move and become rainbows of sound and color that reach
across the vaulted ceiling and make living arches of melody.
The very walls are built of harmonic chords. You find yourself
vibrating to all this sound and color. Every particle of your
astral self responds to the music and, far away, your physical
body echoes, in a minor key, the sweeping chords you are hearing and experiencing in this temple of harmony.

Awestruck, you move farther into this wondrous place. You
become aware that it is full of beings made entirely of living
musical sound. They expand and diminish, soar to the upper
reaches of the human ear and beyond, and then sink to the
depths. Sounds that shake your spirit, causing small astral-
quakes in its structure. Some of the beings draw near and form
a circle around you. One sounds a silvery chord that seems
like a question, then another and another. They are trying to
communicate with you.

Sound a note, any note, in your mind. Make it as true as
you can and let it mean something, something simple like,
"Love." Find a note within you that *feels* like the meaning of
love. Let it emerge from your astral form. Do you see it? It is

a color. It may be golden, or rose, or a shimmering silver-shot blue. It will not be perfect, unless you have perfect pitch, but it *will* be understood by the angelic beings around you.

They ripple with colors showing their delight at your attempts to converse with them. Now think, think about *you*, about how and who and what you are, about your name and how it sounds. Think and, slowly, let a sound emerge, a sound that has the ultimate meaning of *you*. Offer this sound to your companions as an introduction. It may have more than one note, even several. It may be in a major or minor key, but it will have the meaning of you as a person, a living being.

The angelic beings swirl and dip, change and reform, swirling with colors, sounds, and chords of music. One by one, they offer their own names in exchange. Each one is a combination of sound and color, and, most amazing of all, you can understand what they mean. They are statements of the moment that these beings were created and emerged from the heart of the One.

"First note of birdsong on a summer's morning," "Sound of waves during a winter storm," "First star after sunset," "Last breath of a small bird in winter," "Rain on a spider's web," "Evening Mass and the sound of bells." One by one, they give you their most precious gift, their true names.

Clustering close, they escort you farther into the building and make a supporting chord of sound in which you can be at ease. Then they swoop off to join the others of their kind. You wait and, suddenly, there is a deep silence. It feels strange after the music, but, slowly, faintly, the music begins again. Fascinated, you watch, for the building itself, being made of sound, changes constantly in form and color. You notice beings in the upper reaches and farthest depths that are immense in size. They do not seem to move, but remain still, sounding deep resonant chords that seem to affect things far beyond the Temple of Harmony.

One of the smaller beings returns to your side and, with color and sounds, begins to explain things to you. This place is the creative soul of the cosmos itself. Here angels are created as needed. Here are sounded the death knells of stars, and suns, and galaxies. Here new ones are called forth from the heart of the One. Every single living creature in the cosmos, all that have lived since its beginning, no matter for how brief a period of time, were first created here as a note of life. There is, born with each cosmos, a sustaining and ever creating chord. Every creature, every point of life, has a part to play in that chord. When it passes from one level of life to another, its note changes and creates a change throughout the entire cosmic chord. This accounts for the intricate pattern of the universe.

When a Christos is born, a new note is woven into the whole. Those who leave a legacy of love behind them leave a pattern that will remain forever. Wars, hatreds, evil, and pain leave their mark, too, but so does love. Be still, watch and listen.

Great waves of sound and color roll like immense storms over and around you. You begin to understand, though very dimly, just what is meant by the music of the spheres. You watch the mighty chords clash against each other, creating momentary discords that then merge and form new vibrations, colors, and worlds, life-forms, suns, stars, and galaxies. Somewhere among all the sound and color, a repetitive refrain keeps surfacing. It sounds familiar to you. Then you recognize it as the sound you gave to the angelic beings of this awesome place, a sound that meant *you*. It is your name, your sigil, your own inner meaning that is being repeated over and over again. Your place in the cosmos is being pointed out to you. You are being told that there is a place for you amid all this symphony of sound and color. You are a part of the cosmos. Without you, it would be unbalanced.

You shout aloud for joy. You are not insignificant, you are not too little to be noticed by the Creator, you are not without influence in the pattern of creation.

At the sound of your voice, those that spoke to you earlier swoop down toward you and lift you up in their resonances. The fabric of the building opens up and you are carried far out into the cosmos, where all is alive and in the process of becoming. Then down again, until your feet are placed safely upon the pathway. Heart beating, eyes wide with a mixture of joy and pain, you watch as the beings reenter the Temple of Harmony. You turn and stumble along the path and into the mist. Faint echoes of music follow you as you go.

Coming at last to the gateway, you lean against it, still filled with your experience in the temple. Then you pass through into the circle and make your way down the hill and through the wood. Everything seems different now. You are aware that everything is ordained and set in its place. You listen inwardly to the sound of all living things, knowing that even the rocks, the rivers, the plants, and tiny lichens are a part of the great chord of creation. You know you have been given a gift beyond price. What is more, you can return at any time.

You take off the golden robe and place it, with the others things, on the step. Then, with a sigh, you pass through into your own time and place and seek the comfort of your own physical self. Return to consciousness slowly and gently.

8

Elemental Pathworkings

Elementals are intriguing beings. Because of this, they have been overglamorized. They are powerful forces, as ancient as the planet and as unpredictable—older than Christianity. When troublesome, they cannot be got rid of by waving a cross or by the usual methods of exorcism. You must approach the elemental kings. Only they are ensouled and only they can exercise control over their subjects.

Elementals consist of earth, fire, water, or air, and they are bound by the laws of those elements. A salamander burns, a sylph flies, undines flow, gnomes pass through earth as we pass through air. When dealing with elemental, you can only hold their attention for a short time, as their substance fluctuates with the elemental laws.

They have no conception of their danger to humans. Undines will play with you in the form of waves and tidal motion. They will support you in the water, but if their attention is drawn away, you will be left to sink. They may drag you down to play with them below the sea. They do not understand drowning.

Approach all elementals through the elemental kings or the regents of the elements, Raphael, Uriel, Gabriel, and Michael. Remember, the word "element" means far more than is usually meant by the word. Other elements—gold, silver, zinc, copper, etc.—also have elementals. The key word here is *caution*.

Earth Through the Seasons

Settle yourself comfortably and take in your hand a crystal. Any kind will do. Look deeply into and beyond the very center of the stone. Crystals are Earth's first children. Through them, she communicates with her sister planets. Earth's elementals, the gnomes, are the guardians of the her riches. This includes all growing things, including crystals, for they also grow, each in their own fashion and according to the form laid down for them.

As you look into the crystal, imagine that you see a valley with a river running through it. At one end, a mountain lifts a proud snow-capped head. At the other end is a thick forest. Between these two extremes, in the valley itself, lie small villages and farms with fields, and pasture lands, and woods.

We first come to this place at the very end of winter. Spring is about to set foot in the valley and the gnomes are preparing the earth. Farmers bring out their ploughs and break up the hard earth to make it ready for ploughing and sowing. Imagine the crystal growing bigger and becoming a doorway. Through this door you can step into the valley at the edge of the forest.

The crystal hangs about your neck and glows like fire. This acts as a signal and, within a few seconds, you are surrounded by small figures two to two-and-a-half feet tall. All are dressed in brown leather breeches with colorful woolen shirts and red leather sleeveless jerkins. They wear sturdy boots and carry small tools, spades, hoes, pickaxes, and rakes. Both male and female are bearded and have thick coarse hair tucked into knitted caps. They stand and look at you for a while. Then, one steps up and makes a little bow. He points to the crystal and speaks:

"You be earth-friend. The Mother sends you to learn her ways. We will show you."

The stone about your neck becomes icy cold. Between one breath and the next, you shrink down until you are as small as the gnomes and dressed as they are. One of them comes and takes your hand. You know it is a female by the voice.

"It will seem strange to you, but have no fear. Just make sure that, when we travel through the earth, you keep hold of my hand. No harm will come to you."

The earth beneath you becomes transparent and you sink down and down into the world below. The gnomes' bodies are different from those of humans. For them, the earth, and even stone, is like air and they can pass through it. Now you move forward slowly. You look around and see the life that lies under your feet in your own world. Green shoots pushing upward, tree roots thrusting downward. Rabbits scurrying along their burrows, moles digging insects and burrowing. The earth is full of activity. The group of gnomes you are with pause and you see a wriggling mass of worms. Your gnome friend explains.

"Earthworms are important for the soil. They make it soft and ready for the spring seeds. As you keep cows and sheep, we keep worms, and moles, and insects. They all have an effect on the soil. We are the gardeners of the whole planet. When a place is left derelict, it is we who see to it that the weeds and seeds grow over it and break it down. Left long enough, it will return to the wild in the end."

Now you rise to the world above and they show you the wildflowers and the tiny nature spirits that are their life-force. Where there are fallen trees, they encourage the process of decay so the goodness can return to the earth. They take care of the wildlife as best they can. With their axes, spades, and shovels, they clear areas so the wild herbs and flowers can seed. Your friend tells you:

"Spring is always a busy time, for the earth needs to wake up and feed and grow strong. We help the farmers who are good to the land. If they abuse it, we see to it that the farms fail and they go away. Maybe the next one will be better and we can work with them. Let us show you what summer is like."

A moment of darkness, then you and the gnomes are sitting under an oak tree. Their summer clothes are lighter—cotton and homespun linen. There is a white cloth on the grass and food and drink has been laid out. Summer is their resting time, for everything is growing well. This is their time to dance and sing and hold their revels.

They bring harps, flutes, and drums and, under the trees, they dance and sing for you. They show you treasures of gold and silver and precious stones. They never wear them though they may give them to those they like. They take you under the earth and show you greater treasures. Buried Roman villas with mosaic floors. Statues, coins, and jewels buried when war swept over the land and then forgotten. Here and there are skeletons, victims of battle, plague, and murder.

"We honor them and try to keep their rest undisturbed," your gnome friend tells you. "Sometimes, when we see such dark deeds done, we try to communicate the victim's resting place to those who can hear us. In this way, their loved ones can hope to find them and ease their minds. But the Mother knows where they lie and she gives them dreams of hope. Come let us show you the time of autumn."

Again there is a darkness, but your hand is held safely and, when the light comes again, you are standing on a carpet of red and gold and yellow. All the gnomes are busy collecting seeds, nuts, wild fruit, and anything that they can use for the winter. Some seeds they set aside for the wild creatures, others they save to put into the earth next spring. They look for holes in trees for squirrels to sleep, and collect sheep's wool from the fields to line the drays of rabbits and the sets of foxes. You join in and help to gather and sort and store.

You go with them out into the fields and collect nails from old horseshoes, scraps of cloth left behind, and anything that can be used. They take you to peep into the windows of farmhouses, where you see the children threading acorns and chestnuts and bright berries. They will hang them up to dry and then use them to decorate the Christmas tree.

The harvest time is here and the gnomes pick up ears of corn and barley scattered on the ground. Most is kept for the birds, to keep them in the winter. Some is ground for flour. Now they take you to the village church to see the Harvest Festival. Unseen by those who work the land, they file in, doffing their caps and taking their places where the fruits of the earth are piled high. They sing the old hymns and bow their heads at the blessing, their eyes shining with pleasure.

Now they will show you winter. Your hand held safely, the familiar darkness comes, and, when it lifts, it is winter and the snow is piled high. No longer in the valley, you are now on the mountain and looking out over the white brilliance of the valley under snow. But winter is the time when the gnomes work for themselves. They take you inside the mountain and show you the seams of gold, silver, and precious gems held fast in the rock. Clothed in leather and thick wool, they work in the mines to gather the precious things they love so much.

They show you stores piled high with lovely things. They like to sit and look at them and see the stones sparkle in the light of their lanterns. They have no greed. They just love the color and light. For them, hard work is a joy. To serve the Earth Mother is their faith. They sing as they work, and call to each other. Then there is a silence. You feel a presence behind you. All around you the gnomes are kneeling. You look up.

He looks like a gnome, but he is as tall as a man. He is dressed like a gnome, but his clothes are of fine leather, linen, and soft velvets. Around his neck is a chain of pure gold and on his hand a ring set with a ruby stone. This is Ghob, the Elemental King of Earth. You bow, giving him the respect due to him.

"So, you have spent time with my people. I hope you have learned from this experience and will now understand how precious Earth is to us. You have been shown the good things. The bad things, like pollution and strip mining and the cutting of trees, you have not been shown, because you already know about them. It is your kind who are responsible for them. Take back the message that, unless Earth is respected, Earth will be taken from them."

He vanishes and your friend takes your hand. It is time to go. You are taken to the place where you entered the valley. The crystal gate is open. Say good-bye to your friends and bless them. Step through the crystal into your own time and place.

Water Through the Seasons

Water is life to this planet. All living things came from the sea and a greater part of our physical bodies are of this element. Occultly speaking, water symbolizes creativity, psychism, spirituality, and all things connected with sleep and dreams. Undines have a playful nature, but can be dangerous to the very young. There are numerous stories concerning the ways of the water elementals—from the sirens who tempted Odysseus, to the nymphs of the forest pools who coax children to play with them, not realizing they will drown.

When working with water on the astral level, the danger is not so great. But undines can be dangerous on the physical level. Beaches with wide, level strands, and rocky areas where water can create small whirlpools that entice children to play in them should be checked. Sea kings are drawn to music of any kind and often rise in response to singing or a cassette playing near the water. A sea king is composed of many undines acting together as one symbiotic unit. This makes it is more powerful. I have had a close encounter with one such "being" that resulted in my being caught in a potentially dangerous undertow on a rocky foreshore. Be warned.

It may help to use environmental tapes with all elemental pathworkings. Sounds of running water, crackling flame, and wind blowing through trees can add to visual skills if played just within hearing range. Once seated and relaxed, begin by listening to the sound of water. Let it fill your thoughts and suggest its own images, as you prepare for your journey into the element of water.

As the sound fills your consciousness, release your astral body in the form of a fluid, flowing from the navel like a stream. Let this feeling become more defined. Feel the brush of smooth pebbles beneath you and a sense of rushing forward and downward. Open your consciousness and become aware that you are in and part of a stream that is tumbling down a steep incline toward a river on the valley floor. The water of which you are a part is cold, for it is early spring and these are the melt-waters from the snow-capped summit of the mountain far above.

Blend with this coldness. It does not numb you, but is part of you. Around you, sense the presence of other forms, sinuous and graceful. Everything about the undines is of a flowing nature. Their hair, their voices, their limbs. Where you have legs, their lower limbs blend in with the water and have the suggestion of a fish tail. Their voices are the most magical part about them—liquid, high, and sweet, with a haunting quality that fills you with indefinable longings. It is a longing for the original link with the primeval ocean from which all life emerged.

They surround you, touch you, invite you to play and sing with them. Allow your sense of being to flow, jump, tumble, and rush with your companions, but hold tight to your sense of self. Remember the old tales of sirens, mermaids, Lorelei, and nixies. Remember the power of their voices to lure unsuspecting humans to their deaths in the green deeps.

As you follow the stream, you pass rock pools full of water weeds, lumps of unmelted ice, and patches of early spring flowers pushing through the still-frozen earth. Everything sparkles and glitters, shining in the warmth of the rising Sun.

Soon you reach the lower levels and the stream slows down. Part of it flows straight on and will eventually join with the great ocean. Other parts branch out into smaller streams that feed the larger rivers. You join with one of these smaller streams and feel the slower pace as you wind from side to side. In this way, you pass through fields and meadows, under bridges and over stones. Sometimes you disappear altogether and go down into the earth, twisting and turning and seeking your own level, then hitting the gushing springs and being forced upward again to emerge onto moor land with peat bogs on either side.

The air is warmer, for summer has arrived. The undines chatter and dance and play with small fishes and water creatures. They swirl around pebbles and jump down waterfalls in a flurry of foam. Young children come to play by the river, to fish and to gather the smooth pebbles. They make paper boats and set them to sail wherever the water will take them. Lovers walk along the banks and make necklaces of wildflowers and throw them into the water.

Animals come to drink—cows and sheep and dogs, but also the wild deer, otters and badgers, water rats and wading birds. In summer, the life of a river is very busy indeed. Hikers cool overheated feet and fill their water bottles and bless the gift of the undines. Reeds and rushes grow high and are gathered by the gypsies to weave into baskets. Trees bend over to look at themselves in reflection. Willows dip long green fingers and try to catch the undines as they flow past. Yes, summer is a lovely time for the water folk.

As you continue, the wind becomes cooler and stronger. Rain adds to the flow, the river is now fierce and heavy and overflows its banks flooding the fields and hedges. Like a wild animal out of control, it rages across the country, overturning dead trees, uprooting others, washing away bridges, and making roads impassable. The undines react with excitement. They exult in this addition to their strength. They do not know that they are dangerous to other life-forms in such times. Higher and higher the flood rises. Houses, barns, cars, are all swept away. Sometimes you see the carcass of a sheep swirling past. Water in its strength can be terrible.

At last, the rain ceases and, gradually, the waters find their own level again. The agitation dies down and undines resume their normal ways. Soon they retreat back to the banks and farmers begin to count their losses. The autumn Sun emerges and begins to dry out the land. You feel yourself being lifted, drawn up. You feel the power of the Sun changing you from liquid to mist. Up and up you go, until you become part of the clouds that make their ponderous way across the land and sea. Clouds are the cattle of the sky gods, roaming across the world, changing shape as they go.

The year turns and the air grows cold. The wind turns bitter and blows its icy breath over streams, rivers, and oceans alike. Around you, the water undines in the cloud begin to change for the last time. You change with them. You become colder and colder and form into a crystalline shape of great beauty. Then, as the heavy cloud passes over the land, you see far below the same mountain where this adventure began.

Released by the cloud, you drift downward among all the others. The undines are sleepy now and will soon sleep and dream their winter dreams. Below you, the stream is sluggish with the cold. All around the fields and the side of the mountain it is white with snow. You settle on a rock just above the stream and wait. From the stream itself there emerges a figure clothed in water weeds, glistening with moisture and wearing a crown of pearl and coral. It is Nixsa.

"Human, for a while you have shared the world I rule and lived with those who serve me. When you return to your own world, remember the joy you have seen and experienced. I could have shown you the pollution your kind have caused, but instead I chose to show you the beauty of water. Take care of my element, for all the water there will ever be on this planet is here, now. There will be no more. Care for my element. Cleanse it where you can, save it, use it with care and with gratitude. In return, I will bless you and your kind. Return now to your own place and remember this journey."

The figure disappears back into the stream and, as you watch, ice begins to form on the surface and, slowly, the water ceases to flow. Below, the undines are sleeping, until the spring Sun calls them to awaken. Resume your astral form and allow yourself to be pulled gently back into your physical body. When you have completed your return, drink a glass of water and bless it as you drink. Remember the words of Nixsa, the Elemental King of Water.

Fire Through the Seasons

When you feel relaxed and ready, begin to build the image of a path leading into a forest. The trees are freshly budded and the new leaves are just beginning to show. Underfoot, the earth is still bare, but here and there you can see snowdrops, crocuses, and early violets. The air is crisp and there is a slight wind on your face.

As you enter the wood and follow the path, you can smell that woody scent of a fire. Ahead of you is a clearing where the trees have grown in a circle, leaving a clear space. There is a special feel to the wood at this point. The feeling of being on sacred ground is strong and you know that many rites and ceremonies have taken place here.

A small group of men and women are sweeping the clearing of dead leaves, broken branches, fir cones left from the autumn, and the old casings of chestnuts. All this is piled high in a fire pit lined with brick set at one end of the circle. At the very bottom of the pit, you can see two crossed thigh bones and the remains of an animal skull. When everything has been gathered up, one man comes with a handful of dry shavings, moss, and flint. In the old manner, he strikes fire, lights the dry material, and places it carefully in the center of the fire pit. It takes only a few moments for the flames to leap up.

It is obvious that these people do not see you, so you move closer to the fire. It flares up and, in its fiery heart, you see the salamanders dancing and weaving in and out of the waves of heat energy. More people are arriving, carrying baskets of food and wine, and a fiddler tunes up his instrument.

The people begin to dance around the fire and sing ancient songs that go back to the beginning of the race. They sing of the renewal of the Sun's power and the springing up of the seed. They leap high to emulate the rising of the seedlings as they circle around the fire. This fire symbolizes the Sun and they are welcoming its warmth on this first day of spring.

Messages to the ancient Goddess of the Corn are thrown on to the fire and the salamanders seize them and take them to their king. In the glowing heart of the fire, the elementals are holding their own celebrations. Loosing their energy, they send out waves of heat that help to awaken the trees and help the sap to rise. A new seed-time has begun and big baskets of seeds are brought to be blessed and sprinkled with wine. Branches of fire are passed over them to drive out any disease and, when the spring fires have died down, the ashes will be gathered and cast over the fields to sweeten the earth before the seeds are sown.

You dance with the people, unseen, but joining in their worship of the fire and of the goddess. The elementals leap and dance and hold out their hands to bring you into the heart of the flames. Your astral body cannot be burned, so you leap into the fire and grasp their hands and dance with them, calling out to the goddess to bless the land, for today is the first day of spring and, from now on, the Sun will rise higher each dawning until midsummer. The fire burns low and the people depart, as the first glimmer of dawn lights the eastern sky. But you go dancing over the hills, your astral body flaming and fiery with the borrowed heat of the salamanders. [Pause.]

There is a shimmer in the air and time runs ahead. You now stand upon the top of a high hill, where a great bonfire waits to be lit. It is Midsummer's Night, and, on every hill throughout the land, they are waiting for the first star to shine. Down in the fields, the corn is shoulder-high and ripening well. Fruit swells on the branch and the scent of hawthorn and wildflowers fills the night.

You wait impatiently, until the first star opens its bright eye and, with a shout, the master of the midsummer revels lights the fire. You watch with delight as answering fires leap from hilltop to hilltop. From one end of the country to the other, such fires will be lit to celebrate Midsummer's Night. Eagerly, you seek out the fire beings and join them as they dance and tumble and twist in the flames of the fire.

Breathe in the flame and let it fill you with energy. In doing so, you take the salamanders themselves into your astral body and, in turn, this will transmit energy to your physical body. Watch as the heat of the flames reaches out to touch each man and woman as they dance. Look with astral eyes and watch the energy levels in them rise to meet the outer flame.

From the center of the fire comes a figure all in red and gold and orange. He is tall and slim, with eyes like black coal. This is Djinn, the Elemental King of Fire. He takes your hand and you feel the power in him. It fills you and you dance with him. All through the night, the fires glow and the people dance and celebrate. In the early hours, when the fires die, they sleep near the cooling ashes and dream of the fires of love.

Djinn says it time to move on and passes his hand over your eyes. When you open them, you feel the difference in the air. It is cool and slightly damp. The smell of woodfires fills the air. There is a sharpness to the scent that tells you this is autumn and that a different kind of fire will be lit. The stubble of the fields is being burned off and smoke rises on the still air. Children are gathering dead wood to stack for the winter fires. Some have lit a small fire to roast apples in the ashes.

From a nearby church comes the sound of voices raised in praise for the gifts of the land, as Christian folk celebrate Harvest Festival. But in the deep heart of the country, those who follow the old ways are celebrating a different rite. With Djinn at your side, you watch as a long line of pagan folk carrying torches walk the winding path to the top of a high hill. There, a bonfire has been raised to celebrate the Festival of the Hunter. From top to bottom, the torches outline the hill, their voices raised in the old chant.

> Forest Lord, with twelve-tined crown,
> Now we come to bed thee down.
> Rest content when sleeping deep,
> Leave the Summer Queen to weep.
>
> Rest thee well till comes the Spring
> When harebells in the wood do ring;
> Then rouse thee up the maid to wed
> And seek the joy of the greenwood bed.
>
> Hunter, blessèd be thy sleep;
> Choose a maid thy bed to keep.
> Dreams of silver, dreams of gold
> Will guard against the winter's cold.

The fire leaps high, filling the sky with its glow. The chosen Hunter steps forward. Naked and horned, he stands proud before the folk. Djinn emerges from the fire to overshadow him and fill him with power. The Hunter turns to walk down the hill, and the people reach out to touch the erect phallus, for its power will bring fertility to land and cattle and women. Now he stops and takes the hand of a girl and lifts her into his arms. She is his chosen one this night. They melt into the darkness and the folk turn to their feasting.

Djinn reappears beside you, smiling, and passes his fiery hand over your eyes. When next you open them, you stand within an open fireplace that has been prepared to receive the yule log. This is the time of the Sun's return and all is prepared. A green tree, covered with ornaments and lit with hand-made tallow candles, stands in the corner. Beneath it are gaily wrapped gifts. Wine and food cover the tables and the musicians stand ready. In the fireplace, the remains of last year's yule log has been placed and sprinkled with sweet herbs, fir cones, spices, and apple-wood twigs.

The doors open and in come the folk. Three men drag in the new yule log and the waiting fire is lit. All gather round and wait until the old log is well alight. Then, carefully, the new log is raised and placed on top. There is a moment of silence, then the flames race to take hold of the new wood and soon the yule fire is blazing. The salamanders love this time of year best of all. They explode in sparks and flame and cast leaping shadows on the walls.

Standing behind the fire as it takes hold, you feel Djinn's hand in yours and together you leap through the flame and into the hall. He takes human form and together you join in the revels of the folk. From time to time as you dance and eat, you catch sight of Djinn as he joins in. Through him, all salamanders will know the excitement he is feeling. At one point, he comes to your side and you stand together, watching the company.

"Fire was the first magic," he tells you. "When the first man lit the first fire, humanity became part of it and a part of all the elements. We are in and of each one of you. Seek us out and allow us to know the world through you." He disappears and you pass through the door into your own world.

Air Through the Seasons

As you sit, relaxed and ready to begin, your body grows lighter and lighter, until it feels weightless. Like a leaf, you are caught up and carried away on a breath of wind. Dizzy, you open your astral eyes and find yourself on top of a mountain. Beside you is a young man. Elfin in features, he wears breeches and jerkin of soft blue leather, and a cloak of the same color swirls about his shoulders. His face is alight with laughter and mischief at your bewilderment. He leads you to the very edge of the mountaintop and shows you the panorama below.

He tells you this is one of the tallest mountains in the world. Looking down, you believe him. All around you on either side, you can see snow-capped peaks. The view is breathtaking, the more so because you can also see the sylphs of the air dancing, swooping, and leaping all around you. Paralda, their king, tells you that these are his folk and, together, he and they will share with you their joy in the element of air.

A cloud of sylphs catch hold of you, lift you off the mountain, and swoop down into the valley. Paralda is beside you, much to your relief. He laughs and takes your hand, and you find that you can ride the air currents as he does. Together, you follow the sylphs as they race across the mountains and valleys. It is spring and the snows have melted. You and the sylphs sweep down the mountainside, blowing the loose snow into thundering avalanches that tumble down, sweeping away everything in their path. For a moment, you think of those that might be in their path and look anxiously to Paralda. He smiles and shakes his head.

"As far as I may, I divert the danger. For those whose time on Earth has run, I can do nothing but call on those whose work it is to help them cross over. My subjects do not understand life and death. They know nothing of the physical level, only the joy of running free."

He takes you by the hand and shows you the great weather patterns as they develop over the oceans and the dry land. We see the beginnings of tornadoes and cyclones, and marvel at the power of the air, as we have marveled at the power of water. Paralda bids us pause and close our eyes.

When we open them again, it is summer and the sylphs are running through fields of growing corn, making it wave like a sea. They dance above the treetops and we dance with them. We race alongside birds in flight, and help to fill the sails of small ships. Here and there, we play tug o' war with children's kites and make women's washing dance on the drying lines.

Sylphs and undines mingle in the clouds and fall together for a while toward Earth. But the air elementals do not care for Earth's heaviness and depart before the rain lands on the grateful earth.

Pushing clouds into ever more fantastic shapes and blowing them along occupies much time and the summer evenings are filled with the task of making music by leaping in and out of the leaves. Sometimes, we spiral upward on the smoke of summer bonfires and blow the flags out straight from their anchoring poles. Summer is a wonderful time for the sylphs.

Now Paralda is here again. It is time to look toward the autumn. We watch the leaves turning and vie to be the first to separate a leaf from its parent tree. Soon, our world is filled with whirlpools and eddies of leaves as they dance with us, now freed from their trees. Children run through piles of leaves, scattering them far and wide, and we run with them.

Out on the oceans, we come together and show a different face. The sylphs become fierce storms and high winds that blow ships off course and tear down frail barriers. The lordly palm trees bow down low to us as we pass and spring up again behind us. We sweep the waves up into watery mountains and blow them ashore or dash them against the cliffs. Back in the little seaside towns, we blow umbrellas inside out and toss newspapers high into the air.

We rush down chimneys, making them moan and groan, and blow through the eaves of deserted houses. We play with the seagulls, riding on their wings, and perch on the masts of ships as they struggle against the gales. Only when we hear the voice of Paralda do we leave and go to his side. We close our eyes and open them on a winter landscape seen from above. We drift down through clouds and fall as snowflakes.

Across fresh snow, we race, leaving footprints that no one can see. We color noses red with our icy breath. Up in the bell towers, we set the Christmas bells ringing and listen to the choir as they sing the ancient hymns. We see the beautiful shapes that prayers make as they fly upward and, at a word from Paralda, we carry them up until we meet bright-eyed beings who take them from us to place them like bouquets before the throne. Down we sweep again to catch the laughter of children in the snow and again carry it upward. Paralda tells us:

"This is one of our happiest tasks. We carry all prayers, no matter to what form of god they are addressed, to their proper place. It is a blessing for us, and for you. Remember this when you pray, and bless those that carry your words and thoughts directly to God." We rest and sleep, to wake in our own place.

9

Shamanistic Pathworkings

The interest in shamanism has become one of the fastest-growing aspects of the New Age. As it is almost certainly the most ancient tradition known to humanity, it deserves to be treated with the respect due to an elder religion. This means keeping it as pure as possible and not confusing it with other belief systems. It is a fact that many of the Native American tribes are less than happy at the way their ancient ways have been "taken over" by the white race.

The shamanic system of the Native American is not unique, but it is certainly one of the best known and, more importantly, it is a living tradition that has changed very little. However much can be learned from the Siberian, the Finno-Ugric and the Nordic systems, as well as from the traditions of the Native peoples of South America. Like all systems, they have a darker side. But that can be said of any tradition. I would add a warning that, if you intend to make shamanism your raison d'être, you must learn it from a master of that system. It is a demanding apprenticeship and one that has its dangers as well as its rewards.

Go into it with your heart and spirit, and it will open itself to you. Use it as a conveyance for something else and you will know the wrath of the Old Ones. Following its precepts *may* incur a physical malady at some point, but the effect will always be mollified by the power it bestows. The shaman is often called "the Wounded Healer," the wound being the price paid for the power.

Bear Woman

As you relax and prepare for your inner journey, let the tension of the day seep away, allowing muscles to let go and become limp. Through your thoughts, seek a way into the inner world and listen. From far away, you can hear a faint drumbeat, steady and compelling. Your pulse begins to throb in time to the beat and you can feel a cool wind in the your face, the scent of pine in your nostrils, and the feel of pebbles under your feet.

Open your inner eyes to find yourself walking along a path just inside a forest. You are making for a camp and carrying a large and unwieldy bundle of firewood on your back. As you emerge from the trees, you can smell the cooking fires, fresh corn bread, and see the tepees of your people scattered over a fairly large area. Away to your right runs a swift river and, beyond it in the blue distance, a mountain range.

Two children are running toward you: a boy of 8 and a girl slightly younger. You feel a surge of pride at their obvious health and strength. When they reach you, the boy excitedly shows you a row of fish neatly gutted and strung on a twig.

"One for each of us, Mother," he tells you, "I caught them all by myself."

You praise his skill and promise to cook them for the evening meal. Then you pick up the bundle you had set down and, with the little girl clinging to your skirt, you make your way to the family tepee.

Swiftly and skillfully, you coax the cooking fire into a blaze with the new firewood and place the fish to cook over the flame. With your daughter following, you take up a water skin and go to the river to get water. As you bend over to fill it, you see your face. High cheekbones, bronze skin, dark eyes under straight black brows, and a thick plait of blue-black hair that falls to your waist. It is a pleasant face, with humor in the eyes and a mouth made for laughter. The body you wear is tall for a woman and slim, dressed in a soft buckskin tunic that falls to the knee and long leggings of the same material. A fur covers your shoulders against the cold wind.

With the waterskin full, you return to the fire and begin to mix the ground cornmeal into a paste. This you spread thinly over a hot stone set in the fire pit. It cooks quickly and you roll it into a tube and set it on a large leaf, then make more of the same. It is a simple meal, but, with the fish, cooked roots, and berries from the forest, it is nourishing and filling.

The early evening turns to dusk and the meal is now ready. The camp is silent as the women wait for their menfolk to arrive from the hunt. Soon there comes the sound of horses and the hunters come riding into the camp. You stand up and look eagerly for one face, aware that your mind and body are already attuned to his coming. He is among the first to dismount. His dark eyes flick toward you, but no expression or awareness passes his face. First things first. The hunt has been successful and the meat is handed over to the elders, who will decide how it will be shared out.

It is some time before your husband comes to his fire, his tepee, and his family. He carries a large haunch of meat that will feed you all for many days. He lays it down and greets you with a quiet nod and a smile. Then he scoops up the children in his arms and plays with them while you serve up the meal.

There is contentment in you as you all eat together, and yet also a restlessness that keeps you looking toward the dark forest. Your husband notices, but makes no comment until the children, fed and sleepy, are put to bed inside the tepee. Then he comes to sit by your side and there is silence for a while. Then he speaks.

"The Moon is full tonight. The forest calls."

It is not just a question, but a statement of fact. You nod in agreement and place your hand in his. He understands that this kind of night is special for you. All the tribe knows, and you are aware that many eyes are upon you. The two of you talk quietly about many things, but always you sense his support and his love. You were fortunate to have been given in marriage to someone you already loved deeply. Even so, he had to fight for you, for others were also of a mind to have a woman such as you in their tepee. You know you are special, vital to your tribe, and there is pride in this.

The night deepens and you move into the tepee. After making sure the children are sleeping, you both disrobe and crawl into the warmth of the sleeping furs. You are conscious of the heavy silver charm about your neck and reach up to take it off. It was the wedding gift of your husband and too precious to lose. Also, it will become too tight around your neck when *it* happens. You turn into the warmth and strength of your husband's arms. He holds you close, soothing the trembling that has already begun.

Slowly the camp goes quiet as, one by one, the tepees fall silent. There is only the wind and the restless snorting of the horses as they pull against their ropes. Your husband's breathing is slow and deep as he sleeps. On the other side of the tepee, the children cuddle closer together in their sleep. You feel the moment approaching and slide gently from your bed of furs, unlace the wind flap, and go outside.

The wind is chill against your naked body, but you stand straight and tall, holding out your arms to the Moon overhead. They look different, bigger, powerful, and covered with coarse reddish-brown hair. Your drop to all fours and let your body flow into the change with practiced ease. There is the feel of increased weight, the sense of being closed in, as the bear's head forms over your own. Your nails grow longer and curve over. Your hearing and sense of smell become more acute, though your sight is not as sharp as it is when you are human.

Your rear up, standing on your back legs, and sniff the air for danger. Now you begin to prowl through the camp, taking care not to disturb anything but always watchful for danger, as a guardian should be. The horses are always nervous when you come near them, so you keep at a distance, using only your keen senses to search the area. But there is nothing. You turn and see standing behind you the tribe's shaman, wrapped in his buffalo robe. He greets you silently and you respond by rubbing your massive body against his. He is your friend and mentor. He speaks quietly:

"Bear woman, is all well around us?"

You make a check, then snuffle into his outstretched hand.

"It is well. You go now to the forest?"

Again the assent.

"Go in peace and return to us at daybreak. I will wait here and stand guard. If there is danger, I will call."

You lope swiftly toward the dark belt of trees, without noticing the tall figure of a warrior standing beside his tepee. He watches you go, then silently reenters the dwelling place and goes to look at the children. The boy, so like his father, sleeps peacefully, but the girl is restless. The man soothes her dream-filled mind with a gentle hand, then seeks his own bed to lie awake and in deep thought.

You are now deep in the forest, with all your bear senses wide awake. The human side of you is buried deep, though, should danger threaten your tribe, you would be aware of it at once. At the moment, you have other things on your mind as you stalk through the trees. Hunting for food is quicker and surer when you are part of the world of the hunted. You eat sparingly and drink deep at a small stream. A sudden noise alerts you and you go still and silent.

From the shadows comes a dark shape. It hesitates, then ambles forward. A cold muzzle touches your own and a deep rumble escapes you. You rear up playfully, using your paws to push the other bear over. The two of you tumble and fight and chase each other around, through and over the stream. Finally, you move off deeper into the night-scented forest. It is a wonderful world that you inhabit at this moment, every sense vitally alert. There are so many things to do, see, find, and scent, and always there is the companionship of your animal mate. You are conscious of a closeness that reminds you of someone else. For a moment, you recall the figure and face of a tall warrior. He lies wakeful in a lonely tepee, shedding tears that he would be ashamed to admit to others. You hear a voice in your head.

"Bear Girl, come back to me. My heart is cold and lonely without you. Come back to me."

There is always this time when you are neither fully bear, nor woman, when the call of both worlds is strong, when the love of both mates demands fulfillment. You hear the first call of a bird as it wakes to the dawn. The Moon slides down behind the mountains. It is time to go. You press your muzzle to that of your bear mate and turn to the forest path. He watches you go, not fully understanding why you have to do this, but accepting it as part of life, and knowing that you will be back.

You follow the road through the forest and reach the camp before the Moon sets completely. The shaman greets you and gently places his hand upon your head in blessing. Once more you scout the camp, then, satisfied that all is well, you make your way to the tepee. You rise up and hold out your bear paws to the last ray of moonlight and the bear shape falls away. Naked and cold, you creep back into the warmth of your bed and feel your husband's strong arms enfold you, holding you close, and the pressure of his lips on your cheek. The trembling slows, then stops as you drift into sleep.

Across the tepee, your little daughter stirs in her sleep and flings off the fur coverlet. Her little hands shimmer and briefly become tiny paws, the nails long and curved. For one short breath of time, the small head that rests on the skin pillow is that of a bear cub, then it is gone.

One day, her blood will call her too deeply to resist. Then she, too, will change and seek out her own kind in the forest. For the moment, she is but a child, the daughter of Bear Woman. Loved and cared for by her mother's human husband as if she were his own. One day, she too, will guard her tribe and be honored for her power.

As Bear Woman, you drift into a dream-filled sleep, dreaming of a far-off time and a room where another you sits and waits. You obey the pull to that future body and cross the years. You feel the chair beneath you and the floor under your feet. Your present body encloses you. It is time now to waken and leave the shape-changer to sleep.

The Night of the Shaman

In the last pathworking, the main character was female; in this working, it is male. Changing gender in a pathworking is something you should get used to doing, as it enables you to see both points of view. When you are settled and ready to begin, build before you the image of a river. It is deep and fast-running. Tied to a tree branch near the bank is a canoe. Step into it and untie the rope. Then, using the paddle, push out into the middle of the river. There, the current takes control and the canoe races forward. Before you, there is a bend in the river and the sound of a waterfall comes to your ears. The boat makes the turn and there before you is a waterfall some fifty feet in depth.

Before the falls, there is a shimmering rainbow veil and, before you can react, the canoe plunges into this multicolored mist. There is no sudden drop, only a sense of being transported into a world of utter silence. You have passed through a doorway half as old as time. Then you begin to hear faint sounds, birds calling, the sound of drums beating, voices chanting softly, the crackling of fire. You can feel a gnawing hunger deep in the pit of your stomach, as if you had not eaten for many days. There is a slightly bitter taste in your mouth. Your heartbeat is rapid and there is fear and apprehension in you.

Slowly, you become aware that you occupy the body of a boy, 15 years old. Your fear is not of death, but of failure. The hunger is because you have been fasting for three days and nights. You know there are many eyes watching you for the smallest sign of fear. You must remain calm and serene.

It is nighttime and the darkness is lit by many fires. Around the fires, the drummers sit and behind them stand the women, chanting. Out there in the darkness are your parents, your brothers, and your sister. They are watching with pride in their hearts, wishing you well on this most important day of your life. Suddenly, a torch flares into life, then another and another, until, before you, there is a pathway of light and flame. Still you wait. Slowly, the Moon appears from behind the clouds and, by its light, you can see the people of your tribe lining the way before you. They wait to see you start upon your "Night of the Shaman," the night when all your training and hard work will, hopefully, bear fruit. This night, you will return with a new name as the bearer of a vision to share—or you will not return at all.

Your much-loved teacher, "Bear Who Looks," comes to stand before you. You get to your feet. You are rather unsteady because of the lack of food, but his hands hold you firmly. He bends and whispers in your ear.

"Remember, the Great Manitou will watch over you. But if you are destined to die, do not fear him. Go with him gladly and he will be as a friend."

He hangs about your neck a bag made of deerskin and decorated with shells and beads. This will be your medicine bag. Everything you find on this journey will hold a special significance for you and can be used in your future work of healing and divination. You move slowly down the line of chanting, dancing people, staring straight ahead. You long to throw your arms about your mother and sister in case you do not see them again. But this is not the way of a shaman.

Standing with the men is your father. He is a great warrior and the eldest son of the chief. One day, he will guide and rule the tribe. You will never become a chief, though you are his eldest son and his pride in you is great. Your destiny was sealed when you were a small child. Playing by the edge of the forest one day, you did not even hear the approach of the great cat until it was upon you. To you, it was merely a new playmate. You crawled over it, pulling its ears and tail, poking curious fingers into its mouth. You did not understand that the cougar could have killed you with one swipe of its paw.

A woman had run for your parents and the shaman. Terrified for your safety, they stood and watched as the chief's grandson and a fully grown cougar played together. Then, as suddenly as it had appeared, the cat was gone, leaving you tearful and lonely. The shaman said that you had been given power over the animal world by the Great Spirit and that you had been chosen to be the tribe's shaman after him. He gave you a new name, "Brother to Cougar," and, ever since, you have been called by that name. However, when you began the initiation trials three days ago, your name was taken from you. You must now earn the right to a new name.

You walk past your father, uncles, and grandfather. You look straight ahead, giving no sign of recognition, and come to the end of the line of people. Ahead is the forest and, beyond, the mountain where you must spend the last night of your test. If the Great Spirit acknowledges your potential as a shaman, he will give you a sign and grant you a vision. This vision will be the basis of a new name and a prophecy for your people. You will be a man and a shaman in the eyes of all.

You walk on into the forest without looking back. Your only clothing is a simple breechcloth and a leather headband made by your youngest brother and beaded by your mother and sister. You wear it now, as a link between you and your family. Back in the village, Bear Who Looks has entered the trance state that will enable him to follow your progress.

The hunger of your three-day fast makes it hard to walk in a straight line. You weave from side to side, but force yourself to go on. You take a well-worn path through the forest, but soon you must strike your own path. Keeping your senses alert, you move quietly, leaving the known path and forging through the undergrowth to the foot of the cliff that towers over the river. It is the beginning of a much greater mountain range far to the north. It is higher than you have climbed before and the thought of it makes your stomach turn.

The Moon is bright enough to make your way clear and you speed up the pace. Something gleams on the path and your heart jumps. It is the first omen, and the first article for your as yet empty medicine bag. Hunger forgotten, you crouch down to look at it. It is only a bone picked clean by some animal and left. But to you, it is a prize. Carefully, you stow it away in the bag and hurry on, as fast as your weakening body allows, filled with a new sense of excitement and purpose.

The night is alive with the noise of the hunters and the hunted. A coyote's howl splits the air, making your heart race. You pause for a few moments to get your bearings and then move on, feeling the branches and leaves brush against your body as you move. You have been walking for over two hours and you are near the end of your strength. The greatest task, the climbing of the cliff, is still before you. But two more things have found their way into your medicine bag. A bear's claw and a stone with a hole worn right through it. You have memorized the places where they were found, for this will be part of their magic in the future.

Soon, you stand at the foot of the cliff and look up. It is a long way to the top and you are very tired. Your hunger pangs have returned. You have had no water since dawn and will not drink again until you return to the tribe. If you return. At this moment, you do not feel like a shaman, just a boy of 15, tired, hungry, thirsty, and afraid. You begin to climb.

Slowly, inch by inch, you make your way up the cliff. You dare not look down. At one point, you miss a handhold and slide down almost half the distance you have climbed. You feel like giving up, but you grit your teeth and climb again. As you reach above your head for the next hold, you feel something round and smooth. Holding on with one hand, you look at your find. It is a stone of great beauty, so clear you can almost see right through it. You feel it is of great importance and will prize it. Fumbling it into the medicine bag, you almost lose your grip, but manage to hang on. You are more than halfway and feel as if you have been climbing forever.

Lightheadedness sets in and you hear yourself laughing and crying and singing songs your mother sang when you were a baby. You see small shapes climbing with you. They shift form and flit from rock to rock. You know they are the little spirits of the mountain come to help you. You speak to them gently, acknowledging their presence, and hear their whispery voices answering you, telling you where to find the best holds. Where there are no handholds, they make them, digging them out of the rock for you with their long nails. You thank them, and sing for them as you haul yourself painfully upward. They sing with you. Without warning, you find yourself at the top.

The cold air clears your head and you stand panting and swaying, unutterably weary and longing for sleep. Crawling on hands and knees, you come as close to the edge as you dare, painfully sit cross-legged, and gaze up into the sky. You have taken too long to reach the top. Already the Moon is dipping toward the silver ribbon of the river far below. There are only a few hours to dawn and, by then, you must have had a vision or you cannot return. Your only choice will be exile or a leap from the mountain. You dare not think of sleep. You must watch and wait and hope for the vision and the totem animal that is ordained for you.

In the growing light, you watch desperately for the least sign. You think about your tribe and the other tribes that gather at the great festivals. Your people are like the stars in numbers. One day, you would like to take the great walk and see other places and other tribes. The stars are growing pale as you look across the world lying below you. Suddenly, you can see people, hundreds of them, but no longer proud. They are cold and hungry and far from their ancestral homes. Women walk holding dead children, warriors fall from hunger, shamed in their manhood by the tragedy that has stricken them all. Behind them come strange men with faces as pale as the Moon, carrying sticks that call the lightning and death.

You see further now, and with horror. All the tribes of the Great Spirit held like prisoners and barred from the land that fed them. They are sick with many strange illnesses and reduced in numbers. Both men and women, staggering, degraded by a strange drink that robs them of their senses.

Young girls are raped, children killed, and the plains no longer black with bison. You come to your feet, screaming with the horror of what you have seen. Never will you take such a vision back to your people. Better to leap from the mountain. Your race is doomed, you cannot change what is to come. You are only a boy; this is too much to endure. You move to the edge.

"*No*," the voice is soft, but stern. You turn and see behind you a man, but such a man. Taller than a tepee, straight as a tree, his eyes dark and bright as running water. More handsome than your father's younger brother. He wears great trailing feathers and a necklace of stones of the kind you found on the mountain. A deerhide breechcloth is his only cover. He exudes strength and majesty. By his right side is a fully grown cougar, on his left a bear. On the rock above him, an eagle spreads its wings to the dawn wind.

You know without doubt that this is the great Manitou, who rules forest, plain, river, and mountain. He guards all life and holds it sacred, and *he* has come to *you*. Gently, he draws you to sit beside him, overlooking the valley, and tells you to look again. Once more, you see into the years that still lie sleeping, and see many things both good and bad. You see and understand that, in the far future, the Red Man will disappear into the bloodline of a new race that will inhabit this land. The years will be hard and bitter with fear and defeat. But it is ordained that the spirit of the Red Man will become the guardian spirit of the new race and, because of this, it will grow strong. This race will carry the blood of many different peoples, but it will be the spirit of the Manitou's people that will make it great, and, through them, he will govern the land.

The history of the new people will be full of mistakes, for they will be like children. But they will learn slowly and, always, the spirit of the tribes will light them from within. This is the destiny of this land and its people, the Manitou tells you. It will not happen in your lifetime, but you have been chosen to prepare your people for the changes that will come.

"I will speak to them through you," he tells you. "Together, you and I will prepare them for the future. Have no fear, though it may seem as if the world will end. All is part of a greater plan, greater than you can understand at this moment. Know this, I will never leave my people or you. Speak of this part only to Bear Who Looks. He will understand. Now you must leave."

You protest. As yet, you have no totem on which to build your new name. Manitou laughs and tells you to wait and see. The Sun leaps over the horizon and you turn to see it. When you turn back again, the Manitou has gone. You begin the long climb down. Your hunger seems to have gone and, although tired, you no longer feel weak. On the way, you find an eagle's feather and a strange golden stone with an insect in its heart. In a small cave, where there are many strange paintings on the walls, you find a small flint knife and an arrowhead, great prizes for your medicine bag. You still worry about the lack of a name and try to remember all that you have seen and been told. As you take the path to the village, you hear in your head the voice of Manitou instructing you. Ahead you see the smoke of the cooking fires.

The tribe waits for you. The chief, your grandfather who made your first bow; your father, tall and strong; and your brothers. Among the women, your mother and sister, and, standing alone, Bear Who Looks. All are silent. Perhaps you have failed and are to be thrown out of the tribe to wander Earth alone.

As you go forward, the Sun rises over the mountain behind you. The people throw themselves to the ground. Frightened, you turn. Behind you in the sky is the face of Manitou; around you are the animals of the forest, mountain, and plains. Bear and coyote, wolf, deer and elk, a huge bison, rabbit, squirrel, cougar, and raccoon. In the trees are the birds. A rattler slides from the grass, twining itself about your body. You feel no fear, only a great peace and a deep heartbreaking wisdom.

The people stand up. You feel a lot older than 15, tired and hungry, but there are things to do before you eat and rest. You stand tall and straight. Your voice, yesterday a boy's treble, now rings out strong and deep, like that of the Manitou.

"These," you indicate the animals, "These are my totems. For them, and for the Manitou, I will speak. My name is Speaks with Many Voices and I have things to tell you . . ."

Rise up from the body of the young boy and pass to the top of the mountain, where you will find that door to your own time and place. Your journey is over.

The Singing Crystals

The shamans of many traditions have always known of the power held in crystals, those delicate beings who are the first children of Gaia. Select a crystal of your choice, any color or shape, as long as it is real and not synthetic. Use a drumming tape, to begin the session, but play it very, very softly. You should only just be able to hear it. If it is too loud, you will not hear the voice of the crystal.

Place the crystal at eye level and look into its heart. Every crystal begins with a seed of its kind, around which the new one will grow. This "seed" is the doorway into the crystal world. Fix your eyes on the center and allow the light from it to grow until it is all you can see. At this point, close your physical eyes and open the eyes of your astral self.

Over the drumming, you now begin to hear a single musical note. It is the voice of your guiding crystal, guiding you toward it. You are drawn into the light at its heart. Everything swings and tilts. There is a jolt, and then you are floating free in a vast space filled with light. The sensation is pleasant and relaxing, making you want to stay just as you are. As you float and dream, you begin to see small multicolored lights darting about your head. They become clearer and larger, and now you see they are crystals of every color, shape, size, and form. Some are single, others form groups of two, three, or more. All are beautiful and seem to be alive and conscious, not only of you, but of themselves as living things.

Now they arrange themselves into bands of colors with each one shading from its palest to its deepest hue. They form a ring, encircling you with a rainbow ring of brightness. They begin to move, not in circles, but undulating like waves of pure light. You turn as you watch them dancing for you, delighting in their beauty, their movement, and their color. You feel part of them and begin to dance with them, twisting and turning and tumbling as if in water, only this water is pure light. The crystals now break their circle and form patterns instead, some multicolored, others of just one shade. Their movement creates energy waves that feed your spirit.

They begin to sing, and their voices are like the chiming of silver bells giving off an infinite variety of sound. It swells and blends in harmony upon harmony that both soothes and hurts with its utter purity. As they change form yet again, so too the harmony changes, and you begin to hear a "story" hidden within the sound and color. They sing of their birth out of the fires of the incandescent Earth, newborn and spinning like a fireball. They are born of her own birth pains, of pressure and the forces of time, obeying the urge to exist that is within all things in this cosmos.

The song changes and they tell you of "earths" far beyond our solar system, but still a part of the wholeness of the Creator. They sing of others of their kind made from elements we shall never know and displaying colors we cannot see or even comprehend. The sound opens up a gateway into a place of such beauty that you cannot comprehend it fully, but the crystals form an avenue and you are drawn down to and through the gateway, and so pass through into another dimension of being.

At first, it seems dark, but that is only because you cannot "see" the colors before you, or understand the extra-dimensional forms. But you can feel the movements of these new crystals around you. They press against you and give you of their own substance. Then, as if from far away, you begin to hear the new song. It is a song of time, of long aeons when suns and planets and beings lived their lives long, before this cosmos was formed. They are now so changed by experience that they have passed through into a multidimensional world as different from this one as your world is from the first crystals. Your head begins to throb. You feel you must leave this place soon, for it is too alien, as yet, for you to deal with it.

You are drawn toward a point of light, drawn into its very heart and you become part of a crystalline web of light, color, and sound. The touch of it is cool and slightly electric. Forms twine about you and flow over you, as if they were partly liquid. Then, with a sudden movement, the unseen crystals cover you from head to toe, leaving only your eyes and mouth free. You have been turned into a living jewel.

You feel a vital essence flowing into you, into your bloodstream, filling you with the liquid light and color every crystal holds at its center. Now their song is louder, like a song of triumph and praise. You feel a sudden sharp pain between your eyes and a single white crystal sinks down into your head and comes to rest within your pineal gland. Slowly, it dissolves, yielding its light and color to the gland. Another shaft of pain and a second crystal penetrates your throat. A blazing amethyst buries itself at the point of communication and dissolves, leaving only its color.

A glowing ruby burns its way into the heart center filling it with sacred fire, followed by a topaz that flares and dissolves within your solar plexus. You are now beginning to feel the power with which you have been gifted. The colors are glowing with life. An emerald nestles into your genital center like cold green fire, and the throb of its creative power surges through your whole system. Finally, into the sole of each foot an agate penetrates deeply, leaving its psychic imprint there for the rest of your life. Last of all, a clear aquamarine settles into the crown center and, as it becomes a part of you, your own body note, multiplied by the crystals in your living self, sounds out across the cosmos. An awakening has occurred.

You know you will never be the same person. You have stepped outside the human race and, though of it, you are no longer in it, the better to serve it. The crystals are silent now, waiting. They watch and wait. You feel you must give them something in return for their sacrifice. Each center in quick succession lights up and you realize that, with these inner crystalline centers, you can now communicate with them. You understand what they are saying.

"Humankind was given lordship over Earth," they sing. "One day you will enter your kingdom and rule wisely and well. Until then, listen to our voices for we can link you with all life. Bless us, Lord of the Earth, and sing us your song."

You bless them with a full heart for their love and their gift, and promise to use it as wisely as you can. Then you stop making words and let your body sing your blessing. Let the inner crystals teach you to make harmony through the sound and movement of your own particles. Each one spinning in its place gives out a note; each group sounds an overtone. Every organ, atom, cell, fiber, and part of your body is aware of and knows its own note. You are singing your "being" song. You are a chord of harmony and, as you sound it, it takes its place in the great pattern of harmony throughout the cosmos.

The crystals join you, adding their harmony to yours and together you go singing through a world of light, sound, and color, until you reach the gateway. You pass through and make your way to your own place of beingness. Sing of your love and gratitude; sing in praise of life. Let your harmony join with and become one with all. The everyday world forms slowly about you, your weight increases, and the first faint sounds of Earth can be heard. Awaken slowly and with love.

10

Miscellaneous Pathworkings

The pathworkings in this section have no tie to one particular tradition, but belong simply to an area in which you can find pleasure, knowledge, and teaching, no matter what path you are following. There have been many times in the past years when the theme for a working has suddenly presented itself complete in every detail. The first one in this part of the book is of this kind.

There is a longing in human beings to live longer than the usual span allotted them. Throughout history, stories of "immortals" have been told around campfires, in the cosy warmth of kitchens, and the drafty halls of great kings. There is something about the idea of living forever that fascinates people. But is immortality worth the heartbreak and the emotional pain it brings with it?

Our Lady under the Earth is a dramatized working for several voices and was written to bring together many loose threads concerning the history of the ancient line of Merovingian kings. It is not meant to be a true account, but simply a theory offered in the form of a visualization. For those with a leaning toward esoteric Christianity, which may sound like a contradiction in terms but is a valid path, stories from the Old and New Testaments can offer great rewards. It is close to the training found in Jesuit seminaries. Look for a small book titled *The Spiritual Exercises of St. Ignatius Loyola.*

The Deserted Castle is a pathworking that can be expanded by those using it for as far and as long as they have need. These "serial" workings will grow with you as you explore them, and can bring about many strange events, both in your astral life and in your physical existence. They are more potent than they seem, so take them slowly.

The Fire of Immortality

The light on the altar grows brighter and brighter. It begins to elongate and, finally, it changes into a ring of fire. Through this enchanted circle we must pass to seek our destination. One by one we approach the glowing entrance and, gathering our robes tightly about us, step over the flickering flames into a corridor carved out of solid rock. When all have come through the fire door we proceed along a corridor lit by flaring torches.

The walls are covered with beautiful paintings and we can see that they are of great antiquity, far older than anything we have ever known. They show forms that are not exactly human. They are much taller and with features that, while beautiful in their way, are totally alien. The pictures show them working with humans to build pyramids and ziggurats and other strangely shaped buildings. The paintings, although incredibly old, are also strangely modern in their subjects. Here we can see a schoolroom with children, both human and alien races being taught; there, something that looks amazingly like an operating theater close to those of our own time. Other paintings show scenes of strange animals that we have never seen except in drawings of those long extinct; some show scenes that might have come from an Egyptian tomb. One even shows a solar system that is surely not ours, for it has two suns, one large and one small.

Abruptly, the pictures come to an end and we emerge from the mouth of a cave into a hot, sandy desert. Looking about us we see we have come right through a small mountain range that looks as if it encloses a valley. The peaks above us seem impenetrable and it is likely that the narrow corridor is the only way into it. Before us is a pathway of smooth stone leading down into the valley itself. It looks almost modern, it is so well made. From where we are standing, we can see the shimmer of a small lake. The remains of ancient buildings long since ruined are scattered around, and one, larger than all the rest, appears to be some kind of temple. As we walk down the road, we look inside some of the ruined houses, hoping to find some clue as to their long-dead inhabitants, but they are all empty. However the walls of some of them, the largest, are covered with paintings similar to those we saw in the corridor coming through the mountain.

Now we turn our attention to the larger building and climb the broken steps toward a door. It appears to be made of bronze and carries strangely formed and unknown symbols. The metal handles have long since corroded and it takes several of us, working together, to turn them. Finally, they give way and it is done. The door swings back protestingly on huge iron hinges to reveal the interior of the temple.

To our surprise, the inside is well lit with what is clearly an arrangement of mirrors that carry the sunlight from a place somewhere on the roof down to the inside of the building. There are many rooms to explore. Some were obviously built for teaching, with stone benches set before a raised chair of beautifully inlaid wood. But one touch sends the chair crumbling into dust. Other rooms have long shelves that must once have held papyrus scrolls, scattered remnants of which lie around in profusion. In several of the smaller rooms, we find small shrines with a raised statue of a strange god or goddess set on a plinth. The gods seem to be somewhat Egyptian in character, but they have an alien look about them, as if two different species have mingled to bring them into being. It gives us a slightly uneasy feeling to be in their presence.

We work our way slowly through the vast empty space of the temple, until we find the innermost hall. It is very large and has a high ceiling that seems to be made of colored glass.

The ceiling casts patterns upon the floor beneath and illuminates the fine paintings and carvings on the walls around us. They tell a story of the meeting and blending of two lifewaves and how, from that blending, came a race of great intelligence and skill. They lived first on an archipelago of islands that stretched across a great sea. Here, they built a civilization that was great and powerful, with many artifacts that we would have recognized in our own time, artificial lighting, surgical tools, engraved glass, fine china, and tempered steel being just a few of them. But the earth beneath the islands was unstable and, eventually, it erupted with great violence and destroyed all that had been built. Down into the ocean it went, taking all with it, obliterating everything.

The pictures show how many of the people escaped and were scattered over the whole planet. Their one desire was to try to preserve at least a fraction of their knowledge. This place we are in was such a remnant. Here, the blending that had first begun in Atlantis was set in motion once more. From this meeting of mind and bodies came the first gods.

The pictures end abruptly and we are left wondering what happened to these gods. A large altar dominates the farthest and darkest end of the temple. On it stands what is left of a statue. It shows a being apparently being consumed by flames, but the face is serene and calm. It holds in its upraised hand a symbol, a bird rising from a nest of flames.

Behind the altar is a bronze circle set into the wall. Words in a strange and unknown writing are etched into it, along with the same symbol of a bird on a nest of flames. One of us touches it, trying to brush away some of the sand in order to see more clearly. Worn with untold aeons of wind and sand, the great disk falls forward and leaves us staring at a hidden opening in the wall behind, so cleverly hidden it has remained untouched.

From this strange doorway there comes a dull roaring sound and an intermittent flicker of light. Drawn by a strange fascination we cannot overcome, we venture into the hidden passage. The roar becomes louder and then, suddenly, begins to decrease, until all is silent. We follow the twists and turns of the passage, noting that it is sloping downward all the time. Then a turn in the passage leads us to a chasm through which rushes an underground river. Over the chasm is a natural arch of sandstone. It is quite wide and has obviously been much used, since there are deep grooves in it, worn by the treading of countless feet over thousands of years.

We cross the bridge carefully, one by one, and come safely to the other side. The passage continues, but now we see small cones jutting up from the floor from which issue jets of steam and, from some, small bursts of flame. It is getting very hot and we begin to think of turning back when, all at once, we hear that same roaring sound we heard before. The passage ends in a large chamber, roughly circular in shape. Around the edge is a wide paved area; in the center, nothing. But, far below, we can hear that same roar we heard earlier, now approaching fast. Out of the hole there erupts a vast flame, fiery red, its heat driving us back toward the passage. The sound fills our ears almost beyond bearing. Just as suddenly, it dies away and the flame turns from red to blue-white and burns with a different kind of energy. It is this fire we have come so far to seek. This is the Flame of Life itself.

To obtain a renewal of our life-energies, we must enter the fire and let it fill us with its power. We can remain in this state for as long as it is silent. As soon as we hear the first faint sound, we must leave the flame or we will die. The sound returns and, with it, the heat of the true fire, and we back fearfully away into the cooler passage to wait until the next phase of the cycle begins.

While we wait, we think over what we have seen and how it came to be. The alien lifewave that came to Earth has left its mark in the genetic make-up of our lifewave. Maybe this life-giving flame is also a gift hidden away for thousands of years, until such time as its location was found once more.

Listen, the sound is dying away. The flame is changing color again. We must hurry. Let those who wish to bathe in its power step into it, *now*.

Take off your robe and throw it to the side. Stand naked and barefooted in the flame and let it play over the whole of your body. Open your mouth and draw it down into your lungs, like air. Feed it into your veins and feel it run like the fire it truly is, right through your body. It reaches the tips of your fingers and toes and lights up your brain, filling it with thoughts and ideas you have never known before. You become aware of knowledge hidden in the very core of your genetic make-up, unfolding after thousands of years of lying quiescent, letting you know of your heritage from the stars.

The rush of the flame supports your body and makes it feel weightless. It is intoxicating, like rare wine on your tongue. You can see the others glowing like stars, incandescent, radiant. You can see their very bones through the skin. They look like gods, and you know you must appear like this to them, also. A faint sound is heard. The true fire is returning. Be quick, leave the fire, step onto the smooth stone surround and get back quickly into the passage.

As the last one reaches safety, the flame bursts into life and the sound of it fills the whole chamber. Hastily, we put on our robes again and stumble back down the passage. As we go, the sound gets fainter and soon dies away. As we return the way we came, we see that our bodies are still glowing and radiating light and energy. We follow the twisting path of the tunnel and emerge once more into the silent, deserted temple. We return the copper disk to its place, hiding the entrance.

As we pass the statue, we smile, knowing now the meaning of the phoenix bird. We are filled with new strength, far beyond anything we have known before. There is a light in the eyes and a sharpness to the mind that is new. Or rather, newly awakened, for it was always there. Silently, still filled with awe at what has happened to us, we make our way out of the temple and back through the ruins of the city. The Sun is now descending over the mountains, as we follow the path back to the rock corridor through the mountains.

We know the way now, and may come again. But we also know, because the fire told us, that we can bathe in its power only three times in our life span. By taking this path, we have become Guardians of the Flame of Life. When we feel that someone needs or deserves to bathe in the fire, we may bring them here. *But we must select them with great care.* We must choose with our knowledge, not with our emotions.

From now on, as we live our lives on the physical level, many thoughts will arise unbidden to our minds. This will be the ancient knowledge gradually unfolding within us. But we must remember that knowledge without understanding can be dangerous and we must prove ourselves to be worthy Guardians. What knowledge we receive in this manner we must guard well and pass on only to those who can prove themselves worthy of it.

Only twice more may we bathe in the fire of life and, each time, there must be a good reason for it. Although its life span is immensely long by our standards, the flame we have passed through and from which we have drawn strength will one day die and lose its potency. Each person that bathes in it takes a little of that potency into themselves and away from the flame. We must not be greedy, but allow the future its share in this miracle. Now, it is time that we leave this place, for it is difficult to sustain our life-force at this level without incurring spiritual fatigue.

We turn away and prepare ourselves for the return, though our hearts' desire is to remain. Before us is a flickering circle of fire and, beyond it, as if in a distant dream, we can see the temple where we left our physical bodies. It is as if we are looking through the wrong end of a powerful telescope. How small and frail those bodies seem from this level. We pass through and find ourselves back in the Temple of Anubis.

We slide into our bodies, bringing with us all the fire, the energy, the power, and the radiance of the flame of life as a gift from our ancestors. It fills the physical self slowly and fully, healing, calming, nurturing. This will be so for the rest of our lives, unless we allow ourselves to forget this experience. All too often, we live in the moment and, when the ecstasy passes, we forget it and let ourselves fall back into apathy. That is not the way of potential initiates. Do not let this happen to you. Slowly and gently, we become fully aware of our surroundings and of the new power within us. Awaken slowly to this level.

Our Lady Under the Earth: A Dramatized Pathworking

Narrator:
Welcome, my Companions in Light, welcome. Who I am is of no importance, but, if you must name me, call me Sara. It is an ancient name and has been borne by many women of courage and dedication. The first Sara came out of Ur of the Chaldees with her husband Abram and journeyed with him toward the land that had been promised them. Though mourning her lack of children, Abram kept Sara as his wife and loved her. The Blessed One decreed that, though Sara was past the age of childbearing, yet should she still give birth to a son. And this came to pass. But there was another Sara—a servant, a bondmaid. From the hot lands of Africa she came, and her skin was black. This Sara had the gift of prophesy and, when it came to pass that she was bought in the marketplace by a young woman whose skin was almost as dark as hers, she lifted up her eyes and prophesied, saying:

Sara:
The cloud is removed from my eyes and I see across the years that are to come. Mary of Magdala, you will become the Bride of Love and the Mother of Light. He whom you love will become the Great Sacrifice, but you will bear the bloodline of the ancient Kings of Light. You and I, mistress, will journey far from this land, taking with us the child born of the Great Rite of Nuit, as all those destined to wear the Crown of the Savior are born. In a strange land, he will grow and his line will never cease. Some will wear a royal crown; others will live unknown; all will carry the bloodline of the Child of Light. These were my words, and she laughed saying, "I am a woman

of pleasure. How so should this happen to me?" Yet my words were from the Blessed One, as many years before a holy one had given a like message to Mary of Nazareth.

Mary of Nazareth:

I am that Mary, born of the royal line of Israel and given in marriage to Joseph, the carpenter. I listened and I heard the message given to me and pondered it in my heart. I knew it was true and prayed for the strength to offer my child up to his destiny. Listen to my words, Companions of Light. Never is the Savior made to stand alone without comfort. The mother, the wife, and the half brother are always there. This was so, even in the days of Osiris, when I and my sister and my sister's son stood by his body and breathed life back into it, that the Child of Light might be born. So it will always be. John it was who lowered him into my arms and prayed with me throughout that long night. It was he who spoke the Kadesh over him, he who loved him so, even in that far-distant time when the two sons of Osiris played together. He was the oldest brother then; now it is reversed.

John:

I am the half brother. John, they called me. But long ago, I was the firstborn son of the divine king and my half brother was a child that I taught to throw a spear and drive a chariot. It was fitting that I followed him through the Gate of Ages into the Age of the Double Fish. Have you never seen the inner meaning of that symbolism, the two fish tied together? We have always been part of the same great drama. We will be so again, but only once more for when the Age of the Sea Goat rises, it will be a true lord of humanity that takes on the role of Savior. I took him, my beloved brother, and buried him, not where they say, but far away in the land where we once lived. In Egypt, I buried him, and none will find him. Then I took the two Marys and, with them, Sara, the black handmaiden, and guided them to Askelon. And there, Mary of Magdala and her maid set sail for a distant land, taking with them the heritage of the Osirian bloodline. Mary of

Nazareth, my foster mother, I took to Ephesus and placed with friends. Only then did I return to carry on my task.

Sara:

That journey was long and hard for us, especially for my mistress burdened with the Child. Imagine, if you will, the scene. We left before the dawn, the town of Askelon still sleeping, stars paling overhead as the night ended. John stood watching as the distance between us grew. He was weeping silently, knowing that he would not see us again, would never see the child that would be born in a far-off land. It was for him the most bitter exile and one that would endure for all of this age. My mistress kept her eyes on him for as long as we could, then the Sun came up from the sea and filled the world with light and, in that light, he disappeared. Still, we watched as the land we loved and where so much had happened sank into the east. Only then could I persuade her to rest.

Mary of Magdala:

For days, the land upon our left side slipped past—Egypt, then the desert lands. Day after day, the same thin white line of sun-scorched sands. I stayed mostly in the cabin, out of the sun. But at night, I needed to see the stars and look up at the Moon and remember the distant past. I longed for my love. Had I not been temple trained, I might have joined him in the sleep of death, lying myself upon the waves and seeking oblivion in their depths. But that is not our way. Life must be lived and suffered, that the plan might be made manifest.

It was on a soft misty morning that I first saw the Pillars of Hercules. They were vast and narrow, much narrower then than now. The Inland Sea raced between them and dragged the ship along like a child's boat caught in a whirlpool. It took all the skill of the sailors and the captain to keep us from turning over. Then, finally, we were through and into the comparative calm of the sea beyond the sea. I had never seen anything so big, so terrifying. I felt lost, alone, and very small. That night, for the first time, I dreamed of my love.

He stood beside me and spoke softly. He bade me be of good cheer, that we would indeed come safely to shore and that there would be those who would come to us and take us to safety. Then he stood aside and I saw, behind him, the child I carried, but grown to the age of some ten years. Not very tall and slender like his sire, his hair was dark, with a little of my own lighter color mixed in. His eyes too were dark, his skin the color of pressed olives. He looked at me and smiled, and I wept and held out my arms to hold them both. But then I woke, still weeping, and Sara came to comfort me.

John:
I watched them go and my heart went with them. But I had to stay, for the Mother needed me and that had to be my first concern. He had laid this charge upon me, bidding me take her for my own mother. She waited now at a small inn on the road that would lead us to Ephesus. There, where once she had been worshiped under another name, I would leave her. For me, this life has been a succession of leave-takings, with those I loved being wrenched from me. When I feel my time coming closer, I shall go back to my beloved Egypt and lay down beside my brother. He will be waiting for me to join him.

Sara:
Our small boat crept like a field mouse around the coastline of this new ocean. Day after day, we sailed, and my mistress grew paler and thinner. Then, on a morning filled with coolness and rain, we saw other ships fishing. They came closer and words were exchanged, then one of them sailed beside us toward the land. A small harbor became visible and, for the first time in many weeks, we felt firm land beneath our feet and stood upon the soil that was to become our home.

Mary of Magdala:
Two women and a man were waiting for us, I did not need to ask how they knew we were coming. The taller of the

women had the look of a temple-trained seer. With few words, they greeted us and took us to a small house that had been prepared. There we rested for many weeks before taking the final journey. We left the sea and journeyed inland, walking a little, sometimes riding the asses that had been provided. The child had grown almost to term and I could not walk far. The land was hilly at first, then it became flatter, and there were rich lands around us full of growing crops. Never had I seen such greenery, or such bountiful growth. We passed fields of fruit trees and slaked our thirst with fruits that lay upon the ground.

After many days, we saw rising before us a long stretch of ground dotted with just a few scattered farms. This, our guides told us, was the place that had been decreed for us, the place where the Child would be born, and where I would live and die. The people came out to meet us, simple folk who marveled at our darker skin and who knelt upon the ground as we passed. I asked why and was told that our coming had been foretold and that, here, we and the child would be kept safe against our enemies. Their homes were simple, with low walls and roofed with squares cut from the living grassy earth. From afar, they looked like small hills and I, who had been used to living in the fierce sunlight, wondered how I would ever get used to living under the earth. But when the need is great, then the strength is always found within.

Sara:
The place where we would live was higher than the others, built upon a mound that looked much older. A fire had been lit, for I could see the smoke rising from the central hole. We entered by a low door and followed a twisting circular way that led into the very center of the mound. There was a large room with earth-packed walls and floor. Sheepskins had been placed on the floor and rough woolen hangings on the walls. Two smaller rooms had been cut out of the walls to make sleeping places. It was warm, and the oil lamps gave a welcoming glow. Then, as I looked around, I saw it.

Mary of Magdala:
It was carved from a single piece of black oak. Looking at it, I knew that it was of great age. The carver had struggled with the hardness of the wood, but had succeeded in giving a wondrous calm and strength to the mother's face. She sat unmoved and unmoving upon a simple seat that reminded me of the Throne of Isis back in the ancient past. The child was also dark of skin, yet such was the maker's skill that one saw only the power and the radiance that came from its face. Strangely, its hair was long, like a woman's. She was, so they told us, The Dark Mother of Life and Death, black like the earth of this region. She held the power of fertility and growth. How old she was no one knew, only that she had been here from the beginning. And one other thing they told us: it had been foretold that she would come to them from a far land, bringing the child, and, here in this place that they called Merovingia, the child would raise up a line of great kings.

Sara:
It all came to pass as had been foretold. The child, D'agobert, was born, a fine strong boy with much hair. He grew in wisdom with every year and his mother allowed his hair to grow and would not cut it, saying that it was a symbol of the kingship that had been foretold and would come about through him. My mistress became the priestess and the healer here, and, though many would have given her a home better fitting for her state, she kept to the ancient mound. In time, she gave up her life and we buried her where she had lived and sealed up the entrance, as once we had sealed the Egyptian tomb. The child, now a man, became a wise leader of men. From him was to come the line of the Merovingian kings, beginning with D'agobert the First. I left and returned to the little town by the sea and, there, I ministered to the traveling people. In your time, I will be called Sara the Gypsy and they will remember me. On the mound will be raised a mighty temple though you will name it a church. The old way will be forgotten and this place will be given a new name, Chartres. But still far beneath the earth, in the quiet darkness, she will be there,

the Black Lady of Life and Death, under-standing the church above her. There will be others of her kind, miracle workers all. In a far off land, Isis/Nephthys is still worshiped. Be at peace now, and let the Dark Mother rock you to sleep.

Narrator:
We rise from beneath the earth where the image of the Black Isis sleeps and see the cathedral of Chartres in all its glory. The empowering Window of the West shimmering with its vivid colors, the sculptures encompassing the whole, as if to act as guardians for the secret held within. We go south and east, crossing the snow-capped Pyrenees and on to the Sierra de Montserrat. We stand before its Black Madonna, who holds the world globe in her hand. Then north and east again to Czestochowa and stand before the Black Mother there, with her cheek scarred by the blade of a Turkish soldier. She weeps continually for the world. Far east now, across the great Pacific Ocean, to warmer lands that speak the Spanish tongue and the Shrine of the Black Virgin of Guadeloupe, with her sad gentle face. Finally, we return to our own time and space and find her waiting for us, arms outstretched and welcoming. Her voice is low and sweet.

"You do not need to seek me in far-off places. Look only into your own heart and there, in the warm darkness, I await you. I am the Dark Fertile Mother, as I am also the Bright Sterile Mother. I am both Isis and Nephthys, and all life is born of me. Call to me in your need and I will come to you. This is my promise. Now rest and sleep and awake in your own time."

The Deserted Castle

Prepare yourself for the pathworking by relaxing and stilling your mind. See the image of your body within the room and watch the separation of your astral form from your physical. Build the image with a gray robe, with leather belt on which a key hangs from a chain, and sandals. Turn your attention to a door in the opposite wall and see it come into sharp focus.

Push your mental consciousness into your astral form and feel it take root there. Then open your eyes and look at the door. Get yourself used to being in the astral, then cross to the door and turn the key. Open it and go through.

You find yourself walking along a woodland track just after a shower of rain. The trees have been freshly washed and their scent fills the air. The grass and wildflowers add their own perfume. Everything seems new and fragrant. Feel the dampness as your robe gathers the excess rain from leaves and bushes, and your feet become wet as you walk through the long grass. It is not cold, but damp and misty, and you are not sorry when you come to the end of the woodland and see before you, rising up from the rocky landscape, a castle.

It is everything a castle should be, with turrets and crenelated walls, a great stone gate served by a drawbridge over a moat filled with water in which fish are swimming. You walk closer and closer, until the walls are towering above you and you can see the gray stones and tiny narrow windows. The drawbridge is up, but, as you come to the edge of the moat, it begins to lower, the wheels being turned as if by invisible hands. It settles onto the bank just at your feet with a thud. You can see no one, but your curiosity is aroused and you cross over into the outer courtyard of the castle.

As soon as you enter, the drawbridge is pulled up again, startling you and making you wonder if you have been wise to enter this strange place. You walk across the deserted space, past a tilting yard where the knights train for the jousting tourneys, past a water trough for the horses. You can see a row of dog kennels with straw in them and, on the other side, some small doors. Ahead is an archway leading into the inner castle green, a stretch of grass bordered by flowers, with small fruit trees here and there. A graveled path leads right around it and up to a huge door of paneled wood carved with hunting scenes. You think this must lead into the castle itself, and step up to knock on the door.

The sound echoes round and round, and emphasizes the emptiness and deserted quality of the whole place. Gathering your courage, you push against the door and it opens slowly. Before you is a vast hallway, with stairs that climb up to a midpoint then branch out into two stairways that go up on either side. All around the hall are doors leading into various rooms. The one straight ahead and behind the stairway leads into the great hall. This is vast and has a high ceiling, with tall pointed windows running down either side. In the center is a fire pit with a spit for roasting fixed above it. On either side are long wooden tables, elaborately carved at each end. Wooden benches have been placed on either side of each one.

At the top of the hall on a raised step is another table, smaller but, again, beautifully carved. This has chairs to match. They face the hall, two much larger and higher than the rest, and are all covered with crimson velvet and provided with soft cushions. The floor has been covered with fresh straw in which are mixed flowers and herbs. From the ceiling hang circular wooden candle racks that carry about fifty candles each. All is clean and swept, as if waiting for someone to come at any minute.

You decide to explore further. To one side of the great hall are the kitchens. They are well stocked with utensils of every kind, all neat and clean. Beyond the kitchen are storerooms, empty but ready. You go from room to room, searching for anyone who might be there. But there is no one. Upstairs, the rooms are richly furnished with hangings and tapestries. Some of them look out onto tiny walled gardens filled with flowers. The turrets hold little rooms filled with sunshine. In one, there are many musical instruments, in another a loom, a spindle and a tapestry frame, and, in a carved box, skeins of variously colored wools and silks. In a larger turret room, there are many books and paintings, and an old-fashioned orrery. In another, there is a loom for weaving. Each room holds a different aspect of life in the castle.

Finally, you come to a locked door. You wonder if the key on your belt will unlock it. It does. When you open the door, you are dazzled by the sight of silks and satins and velvets, clothes of every kind and for every season. Carved boxes of jewelery too, as well as swords, daggers, and everything for which a man or woman could wish.

At last, you find your way onto the castle ramparts that look out over the land, down to the wood on one side, over mountainous country on the other. To the east, there are parklands that obviously belong to the castle and beyond them, fields and just a glimpse of village houses. To the west is a river, broad and swift. In the distance, you can see the gleam of the sea. You wish there were someone you could ask about this place.

"There is. You can ask me." The voice startles you, and you turn to find a man standing behind you. He is not very clear—indeed, he appears rather misty—but he encourages you to correct this.

"Just picture me as you need me to be. I am the castle seneschal. I will look after all your needs and those of the castle itself. But you must see me as you wish me to be."

You concentrate hard and, gradually, the figure becomes more real. He is dressed as you have decided he must be. He looks as you want him to look. His name is the one you give to him. The castle is named as you decide.

The seneschal tells you that this is your castle. All that is in it is yours, as well as the lands as far as you can see. But, if you want people and other forms of life around you, you must bring them into being yourself. They will be aspects of yourself. This will take you a long time and it must be done carefully. Each new person must have a name and a reason for being there. Each dog, horse, bird, and flower must be thought about and carefully planned. What you see about you are the basics on which *you* must build.

Together, you and the seneschal go down to the great hall and, there, your new friend helps you to bring into being cooks, kitchen staff, servants, guards for the castle, messengers, and house servants, gardeners, and maids. They are still very hazy, and it will take time before they become solid. But you must have patience.

This is enough for now. There is still a lot to do, but it must wait until your next visit. Say good-bye to the seneschal at the drawbridge. He assures you that he will look after the castle while you are gone and that, when you return, you can work on further projects. He directs you to a small door in the castle wall just outside. To your delight, it is the same door by which you entered this world. Once you open it, you find yourself once more within the room that holds your physical body. You close and lock the door, then cause your astral body to stand before your physical. Withdraw your mental self and allow your astral self to melt into your physical body. Then let it pull your mental awareness into your body as well. Feel the floor beneath your feet, the chair or cushion beneath you. Allow the sounds of this world to become real and slowly awaken in your own time.

This type of pathworking helps you to begin building your own inner kingdom and learn to rule it wisely and well. It is important that you do this slowly and do not rush things. Build too much, too quickly, and it will all vanish and you will have to begin again. Besides building your inner realm, this pathworking is invaluable if you experience difficulty visualizing, as it helps you to focus on each thing separately. Read as much as you can to help you build in the right form and perspective. Look at costumes and decide what era you wish to create here. When the castle is finished, begin to explore and build the surrounding countryside. After that, there is the sea and, beyond it, other lands and adventures. This is just the beginning of a lifetime of exploring your inner reality.

11

Pathworkings for the New Millennium

As the year 2000 comes ever closer, speculation as to the future of the world gets wilder. Exactly the same kind of hysteria hit the known world in the year 1000. Rich men gave all they possessed to the poor, convinced that the Second Coming was immanent and that their wealth might exclude them from Paradise. The earth was going to open up and swallow those who failed to convince God of their piety and holiness.

We are no longer quite so naive, but the same feeling of apprehension and lack of confidence in humanity's ability to survive is gripping many at this moment. What we really fear is *change*. We like things to stay as they are. It makes us feel safe. But, in order to progress, we *must* change, so we worry about it. Change is a natural process and is going on all the time, not just at the end of centuries and ages. It is only because so much attention is being placed on it that we see it as threatening. The Four Horsemen of the Apocalypse are Death, Famine, Plague, and War. But all occultists know nothing exists without an opposite. We must, therefore, look instead for the more benign counterparts of these four; peace, prosperity, progress, and hope. The year 2000 will usher in a time of adventure, opportunity, and, yes, a lot of changes. But we will survive. Things may be very different a hundred years from now, but we have survived big changes before and will do so again.

These pathworkings were written with faith in the future, a future of which I personally will see only the very beginning. But you, reader, will see it come true.

The Cosmic Child

Prepare yourself as you would for any pathworking. Relax and allow your mind to settle into a receptive state. In your mind's eye, build the image of the room in which you sit and see yourself sitting quietly. Beyond you is a door in the wall, an old door made of wood weathered by time. It has large iron hinges and an equally large lock with a key.

For a moment, just watch your physical body. Then see your astral form rise from it, dressed in a gray robe with a hood, leather sandals, and a leather belt from which hangs a leather purse. Move your astral form across the room until it stands before the door. Now, propel your mental consciousness across the room and into the head of your astral form. For a moment, it will feel as if you have just passed through a dense mist. Then things clear and you are looking out through the eyes of your astral body. This is not the usual way to project, but it is easier than some methods.

Open the door and pass through into a place of green hills and flower-filled meadows. Lock the door behind you and place the key in the leather purse. In this dimension, it is almost sunset. Before you is a steep hill you must climb. On its summit, you can see a tall standing stone.

The road winds from side to side and you stop to stand and look at the beauty of the landscape below you. As you climb higher, you can see that the hills continue on both sides of you, but behind you lies a dark and mysterious forest. As you climb, the sunset casts a red-and-gold glow over the whole sky. Then, it sinks behind the hills and is gone and night begins to creep in. When you reach the top, you stand and look around you. The rolling hills are just shadows of purple and gray, and the forest below is a dark forbidding shape.

"Child of Earth, you must look further than this to understand the crown that awaits you and your kind."

You turn and see that, where the standing stone had been, there now stands a tall man wrapped in a gray cloak. His face and his eyes hold all the wisdom in the world.

"The time fast approaches when you will need to make a giant leap into a new way of thinking and experiencing. The year 2000 is not just a number on a calendar. It is the moment when your entire lifewave must change, cast off the outworn ideas of the past, and take up the challenge of the future. You are here to experience a small part of it. Teach it to others."

The voice dies away and the man once more becomes simply a standing stone. You stand lost in wonderment. Then, a faint glow begins to lighten the sky and the Moon rises over the horizon. It climbs slowly, growing in strength. You hold out your arms to it, feeling its beauty and mystery draw you to worship. Slowly, you begin to grow bigger and bigger.

At first, you do not notice, but then you look down and find you can see the whole of the area, and still you grow. Now you can place one foot on the top of the hill and the other on the hill beyond it. Your view is extended to take in many square miles of countryside and, even as you look, you grow again, until you can see the whole country below you and the curve of Earth begins to appear. Still you grow.

Soon you are big enough to straddle two countries, then two oceans. Look down and try to work out where the countries, rivers, and seas begin and end. But you do not stop growing. Soon, Earth is a globe beneath your feet and your head is close to the pale orb of the Moon. You can see the craters on her face and the bits of machinery left by the astronauts.

You are now so big that your body begins to curve across the solar system. Your feet touch the two largest planets, Jupiter and Saturn. The Sun lies like a crown above your head. Then it is below your head and small enough for you to hold in your hand. It feels warm, like sun-baked fruit.

You have now grown far beyond your own solar system to become a colossus bestriding entire galaxies. You touch misty nebulae with a curious finger and gently blow on white-hot suns newly born from their centers. You watch clouds of star-matter filled with a beautiful and terrible radiation, in the center of which gleam the pinpoints that will become suns a million times larger than the one you know.

Ahead is a brilliance that dazzles you. It is the very center of the cosmos. As large as you now are, this is far greater. From its center comes a voice, gentle and loving:

"Welcome, Star Child, welcome home. This is the place from where your journey began long aeons ago. This is your true birthplace and here you will return when all your learning has been accomplished. There is still a long way for you to go. Your species has made many mistakes and will make many more, but each time you will learn a little more. When you have learned all you can, I will be waiting to welcome you back. When that time comes, you will take my place to become the creator of the next cosmos. Then I will be free to move on and continue with my own spiritual growth. Until then, return to your physical body and remember the dream."

The voice ceases and you feel a sense of loss. Then you realize you must return. The stars begin to recede and you grow smaller. The star clusters shrink away from you. The suns diminish and grow smaller as you are pulled back into your own space. The galaxies rotate and swing away, as they take their place in the great dance of Creation.

Soon, you recognize your own Sun and the planetary system that surrounds it. You watch as the outer planets pass your line of vision. Far below, you see Earth going on its way and see its face growing closer and closer, until you can place a foot on its surface. Another is set down in one of the great oceans. You grow smaller still, until you can stand upon continents, then countries, and, finally, you are back on the top of the hill, looking at the Moon as she sinks to her rest. Now you know what lies before humanity. The standing stone has gone.

The Moon is setting and, in a while, the Sun will rise on this inner landscape of the mind. Look at the beauty of the world around you. Remember what you are—a Star Child. That which is the very core of you is an immortal being, the inheritor of great power. It is power you must learn to use wisely. You walk down the hill and see ahead the door through which you came. Take the key from your purse and open it. Take a last look at the Sun rising over the hills, then return to your own world. Close and lock the door behind you.

Walk to your body and look at it closely. See yourself in a way you have never done before. Now turn and stand with your back to the form. Withdraw your consciousness from your astral form and allow it to flow back into your physical one. Let your astral form sink into the physical. There is a feeling of weight, a moment of silence. Then you begin to hear the small everyday sounds you usually take for granted. Allow them to grow louder and identify them. Feel the floor beneath your feet. Silently, repeat your name to yourself to establish your identity. Then open your eyes and return to consciousness.

This is a deceptive working, it can have a profound effect on the person using it. Use it no more than once in a month.

The Changing of the Watchers

Begin your breathing as usual. Relax as you do so and allow yourself to go deep, deep, and deeper still, inward to the point of silence within. When you reach that point, let it become a circle of brilliant light through which you can see a spiral galaxy, spinning slowly.

You pass through the circle and, in your astral body approach the galaxy. As you draw nearer, you come to an invisible barrier through which you find it impossible to pass. You pause and wait, and there comes to mind the instruction to lift yourself up to the next level. You see a stairway of blue light, so intense that it is more like radiation than light. You set foot on the lowest step, moving up in a spiral.

The stairs end abruptly, and before you is another circle of the same blue radiating light. Without hesitation you pass through.

Looking back, you see, to your amazement, your astral form frozen in place within the circle. As you realize the import of this, you look down. Vertigo strikes you immediately. There is nothing below you, no stars, no Earth, no body. You have passed into the mental sphere. Wait for a moment, until you have adjusted to this level. [Pause.]

Now you are free to approach the galaxy. It is our own galaxy, but seen from a much higher level of perception. You pass among the stars, suns, and nebulae, seeing the clouds of star-matter drift by, nurturing within their centers the tiny, hot blue-white points that are gestating suns.

Finally, you come to your own solar system and pass through it, moving toward Earth. You pause, amazed at what you see before you. Surrounding Earth is a shining, brilliant band of beings that emit many different colors, sounds, scents, and harmonies. Some are hundreds of miles high, others even bigger. Some are much smaller. Some have no resemblance to human form, others are barely recognizable as humanoid. All emit a joyous paean of praise and love that seems to be a welcome.

You are drawn into their midst and welcomed. They touch you with loving tendrils of thought and caress you with sound. Gradually, you become aware that a time of great momentum is approaching. It is this that is causing the excitement around you. As you go deeper into the throng of these Chasmalim, these Shining Ones, you come to a space where only three of these wondrous ones are to be seen.

Suspended far above the beautiful jewel that is Earth are three great thrones. They appear to be carved from living flames that constantly change form. The central throne is higher than the two on either side, but all three exude a power that makes it hard to breathe when you are close to them. Behind them stands a semicircle of twenty-four forms of only slightly lesser brilliance. These are the great Seraphim and Cherubim of legend. The ones that draw our attention, however, are those who sit upon the thrones.

On each throne sits a being, breathtaking in radiance and beauty, awesome in size and dignity, mind-numbing in the sheer power that flows from them. They have no gender. Their forms have no real shape, but flow from one to another in constant motion. Sometimes, they seem human, at others, they are a complicated pattern of swirling energy. Now, they seem to be pulsations of sound, then, a vast whirlpool of star-stuff that vanishes into its own center only to re-emerge in a new form. Who and what are these beings?

Look upon them and wonder, for they are the Aeons of the Age of Pisces. The brilliantly blue form in the center is Ramasiel, the chief Aeon of Pisces, whose task for over two thousand years has been to watch over the living being of Earth. On the right is the glittering green-and-gold form of Vacabiel, Aeon and guardian of the knowledge that was given out in this passing age. On the left is Hamasah, wreathed in amber-and-rose light—Hamasah, who was the messenger, the dove that brought the seed of light and set it with love into the human Grail destined to give it life and form.

They wait with a timeless patience for the moment to arrive when the new Age of Aquarius will begin, when the three who will guide, guard, and rule that age will take over from them. It is almost time. That is what we are here to see. We are here to act as human witnesses to the ancient drama that is enacted every two-and-a-half thousand years.

The paean of praise about us takes on a new intensity. There is a feeling of something wonderful coming toward us. We turn and see, coming from the very center of the Sun, a triangle of light, radiation, and energy. At each point, there burns a light so bright that, even in our mental body, we cannot bear to look at it for more than a second or two. With the light comes sound—sound more majestic, more wondrous, more heart-wrenchingly noble than anything to be heard on Earth. It lifts and surrounds us, and pours the balm of healing and understanding into our hearts. Then it passes and goes on to stand before the thrones.

The light dims enough for us to see three beings of like majesty to those enthroned. Yet they are subtly different. One burns with a deep violet light shot through with silver. This is Sakmaquil, the Giver of Wisdom, who will guide the intelligence of Earth for the coming age. The second glows deep sea-green, outlined with vivid slashes of orange. It is Archeron, who will lift the lifewave of Earth to new heights of communication that will enable us to reach out to the stars and take our place among those who make their home there. Finally, there is Meru-azeth, golden as a topaz, rimmed with turquoise and centered with emerald, the being who will be the new messenger, whose vibrant green heart center carries the life seed of the Bringer of the New Word.

There is silence in the heavens.

With the eternal patience of their kind, the hosts of heaven wait for the moment of proclamation, destined since the beginning of this cosmos. We wait with them. There is no time, only an endlessness of space, of life, of events beginning and ending. We wait, we wait, we wait. The Seraphim surround us, reach out and touch us, sharing their angelic vision with us. And we *see* what they see—the full beauty of the six beings who will enact the rite of welcome, the changing of the angelic guard, the passing of the emblems of authority from one age to another.

What words can describe the beauty of those who have never felt the weight of the physical, who have never sinned, never existed apart from the very cause of love itself? Know this, ye who now stand witness: it is given to few of our kind to see such beauty.

The enthroned ones rise and approach their peers to welcome them with the kiss of peace. For a moment, we see them as a six-pointed star of light. Then the rite begins. From all around us comes the sound, the voice, the *word* of creation. It calls all to witness the passing of power.

Ramasiel moves forward and joins with Sakmaquil, blue and violet flame and flare. The crown that rested upon the head of Ramasiel lies now upon the head of Sakmaquil. Vacabiel's green and gold reaches out to and envelops the emerald and orange of Archeron, and the scepter passes from hand to hand. Hamasah's amber and rose flows into and becomes momentarily one with the gold and turquoise of Meru-azeth, and the Grail settles into its new place in the heart of the receiver. The crown, the scepter and the Cup of Cups have been passed from the Age of Pisces into the Age of Aquarius.

The three who will rule and guide us for the next two-and-a-half thousand years move forward and take the vacant thrones. Those who have yielded them bow low before their peers and bless them. The voice comes once more and, speaking with no words, asks for and receives the oaths of office from the throned ones. Then, the three seats of power are taken up and placed high above the solar system of our Sun, from where all can be seen. Unsleeping, ever watchful, guarding and guiding, they will keep their places until, in the far future, another age will come to its time of being.

Gentle hands and voices indicate that it time for us to leave. Wrapped in angelic auras of delicate colors, enveloped in harmony, we are transported across space toward a circle of light. Suspended in its center we see our astral forms. A kiss of benediction on our brows and we are gently pushed into the circle and become united with our astrals. The impact, though gentle, is enough to push us back across space to where a stairway spirals downward. We descend slowly, feeling the pull of our still-distant physical bodies. Through another circle of light now, and we are drawn upward from the point of inner silence, like divers surfacing.

Very gradually, we become aware of light, of weight, of sound, and the feeling of awakening after a long sleep—a sleep full of wondrous dreams that were not really dreams. Rise up, go to the window, and look out at the world. Look up. Far above Earth are three thrones and, on them, with loving patience, sit three great powers. They will be there for the whole of this age, waiting to assist if asked, loving without being asked, giving gentle instruction when it is required. Think of them sometimes and offer them a blessing. They will, in return, be willing to help you to achieve wisdom and understanding in your work with the Mysteries.

The Rainbow Body

Colin Wilson, author of *The Outsider*, *Mysteries*, and *The Occult,* and noted for his open and inquiring mind, said, at a S.O.L. conference in 1997: "In this coming Age, humanity must get ready to make a huge evolutionary leap." He is not alone in this premise. Many famous men and women have said similar things in the past fifty years. What form this shattering event will take we have no way of knowing, but that it will be physiological in nature we can be certain. But don't worry, it will not happen in our lifetime. Somewhere along the line, possibly within two or three hundred years, our brains and bodies will undergo a radical change. What this change will entail we cannot predict, but it *will* come.

The simple act of moving into a new century, or rather the first century of a New Age, may begin the whole process. Although we will not live to see this event, we can perhaps anticipate its effects through the medium of creative visualization. Though we do not know what form it will take, we can project our minds into the far future and make a guess, a wild guess, very possibly a wrong guess. But we have nothing to lose by attempting it.

One of the things an initiate learns is that every man and woman is essentially a "multi-versal" being. That is, we exist simultaneously in many dimensions and parallel universes. We have a consciousness in each one, a life in each one, a purpose and destiny in each one. But each is minutely different. With every passing moment in time, we change our future in each universe by constantly making decisions that affect the course of that future.

What will this "leap" involve? We simply do not know, but we can make an educated guess. In the past century, the emphasis has been on communication in all its forms—radio, television, computers, a new closeness between countries. The barriers of language are falling fast. Even the scientific advances made during this extraordinary century have, to a great extent, been the product of two or three minds working together, often in different countries.

The whole thrust of the past two decades has been toward space, both inner and outer. It is, therefore, reasonable to assume that this new leap will somehow enhance our ability to communicate on deeper levels than ever before. With the advent of channeling (notwithstanding the fact that this is a comparatively rare talent, at present, despite the efforts of some who would have you believe it is something anyone can do), it may be our capacity for telepathy will be increased, along with other extrasensory abilities.

A book published over twenty years ago, titled *The Morning of the Magicians*, foretold all of this. Humanity, many widely read and important men and women will tell you, is poised on the rim of the emergence of talents that at one time, would have had their possessors burned at the stake! This change is all around us, in the very air we breathe. We are coming into our "magical" inheritance at last.

The following pathworking represents my personal viewpoint only. It is how I see all this happening. Much has been made, in the past fifty years, of the Journey of the Fool as part of the training in the Mysteries. But I see us now as beginning the Journey of the Magician, the controller of personal destiny and of the elements that make up the physical body. Make that journey with me now.

Prepare for this working with care. If possible, early in the day is the best time to perform it. Make sure you are warm and that all your clothing is loose and comfortable. Prepare a thermos of hot, sweet tea—herbal or Indian, but no coffee. Have something to eat as well. Take a little longer over the breathing and relaxation exercises. Settle into position and close your eyes.

Let the silence soak into your consciousness. Then, leaving your physical body in the chair, stand up and walk forward in the astral. Look to the door and see an archway with curtains of lightwaves covering the opening. Walk toward it and, as you pass through, imagine feeling thousands of tiny pinpricks on your skin, like a low-voltage electric shock going through you.

Once through the arch, you are on the astral level, a place of soft grays and creamy whites. There is no division of up or down. You walk on something that gives slightly with every step. All this is malleable astral matter. With it, build in front of you a series of arches approximately two meters apart. Build them with attention to detail. Color them in the following order: red, orange, yellow, green, blue, indigo, and violet. The colors of the rainbow. For a moment, while you look at your handiwork, reflect on the symbolism of the rainbow. It is often misunderstood.

It is the perfect symbol of a human being in its real form as a multi-versal life-form. The name Adam, means, in its earliest context, "Red Man," or man made from red clay. Thus it stands for your physical self. Orange is a mixture of red and yellow and stands for the lower astral self, often named as the etheric. Yellow is a pure color and symbolizes the higher astral self. Green and blue are the lower and the higher mental levels. Green is the sexual creativity that brings about children, both of body and of mind (ideas).

Blue is the level of knowledge where new and exciting ideas are born. It holds the promise of new inventions and leaps of the imagination that carry the human species forward on its journey to ultimate divinity. Indigo and violet are the two levels of the spirit. The first is the highest level achievable in the physical, the latter is the primal spark, the repository of all our incarnations, experiences, and our final realization of the godhood of the self.

As you walk through the red archway, there is a slight resistance and a low musical note is heard. Now look back. Sitting in its chair is your physical body, just as you left it. Now walk on and pass through the orange arch. There is a sensation of pulling away from something that is attached to you, and a higher note can be heard from somewhere above you. Turn your head and see your lower astral form frozen in place. Stretched behind it is a misty veil running from orange to deep red where it is connected to the physical form.

Move to the next arch and pass through. This time, you feel a weight of silence settle upon you. The only sound is a deep bell-like cadence. The feeling of tearing away from something is much stronger. Look back and you can see your higher astral form stationary within the low archway and, between it and your lower astral body, a misty substance shading from yellow to orange.

You move toward the next arch and, this time, you have to struggle to push yourself through. It borders on pain and you feel the sting of tears. You can hear a silvery note ringing in your ears. You finally get through, leaving your lower mental body occupying the space beneath the arch. The veil this time is of deep emerald green that gradually becomes palest yellow when it touches the higher astral body.

By now, it feels as if you are walking against a swiftly flowing river, but you persevere to the next arch. This is worse than the others. You feel as if your very skin is being pulled away. It burns like fire, but if you are strong enough, you can do it. If you feel you cannot bear it, then return, making your way back through the arches and into the physical where you can rest. Try again another day.

If you get through, you will find that you have left behind you a sky-blue form in the archway. The sound of a high, wild, sweet note can be heard. You feel lighter, as well you may, for you are now going toward your highest mental level, trailing behind you a veil of blue.

With apprehension, you approach the last archway but one. Pause here and ask yourself if you wish to go on. There is no shame in returning to the physical. You are asked to do only what you feel you can do. Perhaps this is the time to say "enough for now." If so, return with a light heart, for there is always another time. To know when you must halt is a sign of wisdom, not weakness.

If, by chance, you are well used to such spiritual challenges and wish to go on, then approach slowly and test yourself gradually against the barrier. It is not physical pain that you feel, but an intense sorrow bordering on the unbearable. Take as much as you can and, if you can get through, it will be a great victory. The indigo mist emanating from your lower spiritual self floats out behind you. Before you looms the final arch. Go as far as you can toward it, but do not go through it. You may risk thinning the silver cord through sheer ecstasy. Look back and see the many selves you have shed. Each is held within its arch and the mist of its auric field flows back like a silken web of color to link with the form before it.

The potential of these beautiful colored forms is "held" within the magnetic field of the physical plane. You are a wondrous, beautiful, multiself of color, sound, and power. As yet, all you can really see and work with is the receptacle of all this beauty. But do not despise the physical container. It is a grail that holds the ultimate seed of light, your primal self.

Go back now and collect each form, absorbing the sound and the color as you do so. Feel it settling within you and understand that you can free any and all of them if you so wish. If you could use this spiritual sight in the physical world, you would see men and women moving about, looking like an extended rainbow-colored form, full of power and beauty. One day, when our species has evolved enough, we will be like this all the time.

You come now to stand before your physical body. Know it for what it is—the holder of life. Bless it and pour out your love upon it. See not its imperfections, but its spirituality and its potential. See it crowned with a diadem of many colors and set with the crystals of sound.

Learn to see yourself like this each day and so grow to understand the imprisoned splendor of the spirit within flesh. Understand that you chose to take this route into the lower worlds in order to make the dream of the One come true, that part of it should know all levels, from the densest to the highest. You are fulfilling that dream with every breath you take, with every moment that you live.

Take the final step now and join with your body. Feel the warmth of it and the feeling of blood running through your veins. The weight of it, the slight ache in the limbs that have been held too long in one position. Stretch out now and rejoice in your body. It may not be perfect. It may be older than you would wish, but it belongs to you and to no other. What it holds, like a precious wine within, is the gift of the One, life and spirit joined. Awake, precious soul, and go out into the world created for you.

Bibliography

Ashcroft-Nowicki, Dolores. *Inner Landscapes*. London: Aquarian Press, 1986.

———. *The Shining Paths*. Leichester, UK: Thoth Publications, 1997.

Briggs, K. *Dictionary of Fairies*. London: Allen Lane, 1976.

Cavendish, R. *Legends of the World*. London: Orbis Publishers, 1976.

Davies, E. *Celtic Researches*. Private Printing. 1804.

Diel, Paul. *Symbolism in Greek Myth*. Boston: Shambhala, 1980.

Drake-Carnell, F. J. *Old English Customs and Ceremonies*. London: Batsford, 1938.

Emery, W. B. *Archaic Egypt*. London: Penguin, 1991.

Encyclopedia of World Myth. London: Hamlyn Publishers, 1973.

Epstein, G. *Healing into Immortality*. New York: Bantam Books, 1994.

Evans-Wentz, W. Y. *Fairy Faith in Celtic Countries*. New York: Lamma Publishers, 1973.

Folklore Review, vol. 1. London: D. Nutt, 1890.

Gaskell, A. *Dictionary/Scripture of All Myth*. New York: Julian Press, 1960.

Gray, W. G. *Western Inner Workings*. York Beach, ME: Samuel Weiser, 1983.

Guadalupe, G., and A. Mangoel. *Dictionary of Images and Places*. London: Lester and Orpen Dennys, 1980.

Guest, Lady Charlotte, ed. *Mabinogion*. Cardiff, UK: John Jones, 1977.

Hodson, G. *The Coming of Angels*. London: Rider, 1932.

Hutton, Ronald. *Stations of the Sun*. Oxford, UK: Oxford Press, 1996.

Keightley, T. *The Fairy Myth*. London: Wildwood House, 1981.

Lang, A. *Myth, Ritual and Religion*. New York: Random House, 1996.

Leadbetter, C. W. *Clairvoyance*. London: Theosophical Publishing House, 1899.

Maspero, G. *New Light on Ancient Egypt*. London: Fisher Unwin, 1908.

Matthews, J. and C. *Aquarian Guide to British and Irish Myth*. London: Aquarian Press, 1988.

———. *The Western Way*. 2 vols. London: Arkana, 1987.

O'Regan, V. *The Pillars of Isis*. London: Aquarian Press, 1992.

Parisen, M., ed. *Angels and Men*. Wheaton, IL: Quest Books, 1990.

Rundle-Clark, R. T. *Myth and Ritual in Ancient Egypt*. London: Thames and Hudson, 1959.

Squires, Charles. *Celtic Myth and Legend*. London: Gresham Publishers, n.d. (around 1900).

Watkins, M. *Waking Dreams*. New York: Gordon & Breach, 1976.

Index

Dolores Ashcroft-Nowicki is one of the best known and respected of contemporary British occultists. A third generation pyschic sensitive and highly trained Cosmic Mediator, Dolores' teachers and mentors were the late C. C. Chichester, a Warden of the Society of Inner Light, and W. E. Butler, himself a student of Dion Fortune. She is the successor to W. E. Butler, and Director of Studies for Servants of the Light School of Occult Science. Dolores was a professional actress on the London stage for many years, and is an Associate of the London Academy of Music and Drama. She lent her special talents to the creation of *Shakespeare Tarot,* an exploration of the traditional tarot archetypes expressed through the plays and characters of Shakespeare's works. Dolores travels around the world and lectures on all aspects of esoteric studies and hermetic sciences. She contributes regularly to *Solomon,* the in-house publication of

S.O.L., and is the author of many successful books including *Ritual Magic Workbook* (Weiser, 1998), *The Tree of Ecstasy* (Weiser, 1999), and *New Book of the Dead.*

Tamara Ashcroft-Nowicki is Dolores' daughter. Because of her family background, it was virtually inevitable that she became interested in the esoteric study and sacred science from an early age. She was raised on the beautiful Channel Island of Jersey, Engand, and received an Honors Degree from Exeter University. Tamara is currently an English teacher; however, she is studying Traditional and Five Element Chinese Medicine and plans to become a qualified acupuncturist in the near future.